Additional Praise for
Communication Uncovered

"Anton's thoughts on reading and education, especially poignant in this time of rapidly declining literacy, are nicely complemented by the suggestions and observations on ecology of media. His characteristic wit and wisdom enliven every essay herein."
—Eric McLuhan

"Corey Anton brings a brilliantly original voice to the discipline of general semantics, the field of media ecology, and the theories associated with cybernetics and the systems view. Scholarly, passionate, and inspired, this collection of essays should be required reading for anyone interested in human communication, signification, symbolization, and mediation."
—Lance Strate, Professor of Communication and Media Studies, Fordham University; author of *On the Binding Biases of Time and Other Essays on General Semantics and Media Ecology*; past president of the Media Ecology Association and former Executive Director of the Institute of General Semantics

"This book is for the growing number of professors who are concerned about reading and traditional literacy skills in education. Aspects of communication are revealed in Anton's provocative essays which guide us to a better humanistic understanding of communication."
—Susan B. Barnes, Professor, College of Liberal Arts, RIT

Communication Uncovered:

General Semantics and Media Ecology

Corey Anton

The New Non-Aristotelian Library
Institute of General Semantics

Fort Worth, Texas

Institute of General Semantics
3000 A Landers Street, Fort Worth, Texas 76107
http://www.generalsemantics.org

Book design: Peter Darnell/Visible Works Design

Cover Painting by Valerie V. Peterson

Library of Congress Cataloging-in-Publication Data

Anton, Corey.
 Communication uncovered : general semantics and media ecology / Corey Anton.
     p. cm.
 Includes bibliographical references (p.   ) and indexes.
 ISBN 978-0-9827559-4-5 (cloth hardcover : alk. paper) -- ISBN 978-0-9827559-5-2 (pbk. : alk. paper)
1. General semantics. 2. Communication--Social aspects. 3. Mass media--Socials aspects. 4. Mass media and language. I. Title.
       B820.A58 2011

     149'.94--dc22

                        2011009710

*To the person who has made so many contributions
to this collection and to my life,
I dedicate this work to Valerie V. Peterson.*

Table of Contents

Acknowledgements

So many people need to be acknowledged and thanked for the many ways they have contributed to this collection. I first thank Grand Valley State University for the sabbatical leave enabling the production of some of this work. Such generous support and release time from teaching duties helped bring this book into existence.

I have presented many of these essays, in some form or another, over the past decade at various conferences. At the least, I need to thank the Media Ecology Association as well as the National Communication Association, specifically its Semiotics and Communication Division, Rhetorical and Communication Theory Division, Communication Ethics Division, and Kenneth Burke Society. I also want to thank and acknowledge the Institute of General Semantics and the International Communicology Institute. These venues, organizations, and institutes have given me space, time, and intellectual feedback and have helped to settle the present ideas into their existing form.

There are many of my former professors who in some way or other have impacted what is gathered here. I accordingly need to thank and recognize: Lee Thayer, Wendy Leeds-Hurwitz, Joseph Gemin, Mary Anne Moffitt, John Cragan, Sandra Metts, William K. Rawlins, Calvin O. Schrag, Lewis R. Gordon, William L. McBride, Charlene Haddock Seigfried, Edward Schiappa, Robin Clair, Mary Keehner, Charlie Stewart and Jacqueline Martinez.

I want to acknowledge friends and colleagues with whom I have discussed these ideas at length and who have helped me think about these ideas over many years, in particular Barry D. Liss, Bryan Wehr, Phil Paradowski, Abe Zakhem, Bryan Crable, Joy Cypher, Steven Mortenson, Scott Caplan, Thomas S. Wright, Lance Strate, Anthony Thompson, Alex Nesterenko, Robert Mayberry, Danielle Wiese-Leek, Robert Swieringa, Peter Zhang, and Allen Whipps. For editorial assistance and proofing in the final stages, I want to thank Jermaine Martinez, Mandy L. DeWilde, Cherilyn Denomme, and Brett Michael Lyszak. Finally, I want to thank Valerie V. Peterson for countless engaging discussions, for her extensive editorial suggestions, and for all of her love and support.

In addition, I need to thank the publishers who have granted me permission to reprint the essays that have been published elsewhere:

The Institute of General Semantics for their permission to reprint "Words to Live By: Scholarly Quotations as Proverbial Theory," *ETC: A Review of General Semantics, etcetera*, 66, (2), 167-183; "The Thing Is Not Itself: Artefactual Metonymy and the World of Antiques," *ETC: A Review of General Semantics, etcetera*, 64, (4), 365-371; "Korzybski and Bateson: Paradoxes in 'Consciousness of Abstracting,'" *ETC: A Review of General Semantics, etcetera*, 62, (4), 405-410; & "Is There a Territory Without Maps?," *Bulletin of General Semantics*, 72, 47-48.

The Semiotics Society of America for their kind permission to reprint "Playing with Bateson: Denotation, Logical Types, and Analog and Digital Communication," *The American Journal of Semiotics*, 19, (1-4), 129-154.

Hampton Press for their permission to reprint "The Practice of Reading Good Books: A Plea to Teachers and Students," *Explorations in Media Ecology: The Journal of the Media Ecology Association, 4,* (1), 65-77; "Early Western Writing, Sensory Modalities, and Modern Alphabetic Literacy: On the Origins of Representational Theorizing," *Explorations in Media Ecology: The Journal of the Media Ecology Association, 4,* (2), 99-122; "A Levels Orientation to Abstraction, Logical Typing, and Language More Generally," In Linda Elson's *Paradox Lost: A Cross-Contextual Definition of Levels of Abstraction.* Cresskill, NJ: Hampton Press, 183-201, 2010.

Peter Lang Publishing for their permission to reprint "Clocks, Synchronization, and the Fate of Leisure: A Brief Media Ecological History of Digital Technologies," from *The Culture of Efficiency.* Sharon Kleinman (Ed.). New York, NY: Peter Lang Publishing, 71-87, 2009.

The Josiah Macy Jr. Foundation for their permission to reprint the "Diagram for discussion purposes referred to as 'onionskin,'" taken from Bateson's 1955 lecture/group discussion, published in 1956.

I also want to mention that Chapter 2: "Learning about Education Metaphors: Study as a Way of Life," was first printed in-house at the *Grand Valley Review: A Journal of Grand Valley State University, 33:* Winter, 4-17, 2008, and a much smaller and more condensed version of Chapter 8, "History, Orientations, and Future Directions of Media Ecology" was printed in *Mass Media Research: International Approaches.* (Eds.). Yorgo Passadeos & Dimitra Dimitrakopoulou. Proceedings of the 4th annual ATINER Conference on Mass Media. 299-308. GREECE: ATINER Publications.

Preface

Gathering together essays written from 2003 to 2010, *Communication Uncovered* provides a broad-based multidisciplinary orientation to speech, language, symbol-use, alphabetic literacy, communication technologies, and human life more generally.

The main title, "Communication Uncovered," initially suggests that communication, or at least some of it, has not been sufficiently addressed. Areas of study not offered within a given curriculum, not taught, or basically not examined because there was too much other material to cover, may be spoken of as materials that have been left "uncovered." But in addition to identifying terrain recognized but not traversed, the title also implies the past tense of an act of "uncovering" what was previously neglected or covered-over. It, accordingly, suggests a kind of exposé whereby something that has been covered-up is now laid-bare. Here, then, the title "Communication Uncovered" is meant to suggest that relevant communication traditions and orientations have been partly neglected or outright hidden and that here and now they will be brought out from concealment for thematic and detailed consideration. And there is yet another meaning implied by the title: a final meaning that invites us to leave communication open and unbound, allowing it to be, as it were, coverless. For example, many recipes for cooking, especially those for thickening a stew or intensifying a flavor, require that the pot or pan be left without a cover. Just as many a dish or sauce can be overdone or spoiled if a lid is used, so too, many aspects of communication, as living and dynamic processes, can be ruined if not left open and uncovered.

The book itself is divided into four main parts. Part I: Pedagogical Orientations offers a pair of readings that celebrate and encourage the practice of study. These readings help to establish a context for courses with heavy reading loads and/or a reliance upon primary texts. Respect for literacy and being generally well read are significant common themes in both media ecology and general semantics. It would not take much to show that Korzybski's high doses of literacy—reading voraciously and dedicating his *Science and Sanity* to numerous prolific scholars—helped him recognize the possibility of delayed semantic reactions. Said otherwise, whereas Korzybski was highly aware of the difference between "primitive" identifications and modern mathematical languages, he seemed not as aware that literacy per se made possible the kinds of disidentification he sought to promote. McLuhan, on the other hand, suggests throughout his writings that the oral mind experiences action and reaction simultaneously whereas literacy makes possible a kind of "acting without reacting." And Ong, too, makes clear that literacy is an essential part of the process whereby words are made to sit still and become objects. In fact, whereas Ong identifies the role Learned Latin played in the development of science, Korzybski identifies how mathematical notation, with its notions of "variable" and "function," tames and organizes abstractions and basically keeps the abstracting process under constant conscious regard. In the two opening essays, then, I make a reasoned plea for people to recognize that study, and in particular the practice of depth reading, can be a vital means for becoming more conscious of the virtues and follies of linguistic abstractions.

Part II: Explorations in General Semantics angles into Korzybski's non-

Aristotelian approach by underscoring the revolutionary importance of negative principles (e.g. "the map is not the territory," "the word is not the thing"), and it admonishes that only by beginning with such negative principles can a more rigorous science of humanity be built. Much of Part II draws heavily from scholars such as Gregory Bateson and Walker Percy who, though greatly indebted to Korzybski's ideas, generated productive and useful criticisms. Some main tensions discussed in these essays regard the different kinds of abstracting that occur at both the silent object-level and within and across verbal levels. Instead of providing a tidy closed-system for handling multiple logical types and various orders of abstraction, the essays of Part II outline and identify those key concepts, terms, principles that help keep our attention directed to abstracting processes and the various consequences implied therein.

Part III: Media Ecological Studies provides historical context for the field of media ecology (including an outline of some its seminal thinkers, core concepts, and methodologies of research) and focuses upon two communication technologies that have significantly shaped and continue to impact our lives: the alphabet and the clock. By examining the different spatial and temporal orientations found within the tactile field, the auditory field, and the visual field, these essays further explicate the abstractive operations within our sensory capacities and symbolic practices. They show how communication technologies are not added on to (nor even merely incorporated into) our environments; they are the very environments in which we find ourselves. Our sense of the world, others, and ourselves is some function of our communication technologies.

Part IV: Resources and Meditations offers a pair of open-ended application pieces. Both cross the boundaries between scholarly activity and intellectual practice. Together, the collection of quotations and the collection of aphorisms suggest the value of "uncovering," or at the least not covering-over, important ideas relevant to communication.

As a whole, *Communication Uncovered* offers a composite sketch of communication and the human condition that is both synchronic and diachronic, both theoretical and practical. While some readers may engage the book in its entirety, others may prefer to read only parts. In any case, the chapters are logically related and cohere together, displaying a high degree of internal resonance and synergy. Building upon each other, the book's chapters interrelate and grow together. As final chapters try to make evident, the book intends and invites further dialogue and engagement. It offers that kind of uniquely human whole that begins to complete itself only through the active participation of readers.

Part I:

Pedagogical Orientations

"What the alphabet did was to separate thought from sensation, knowledge from experience, utterance from context, speech from speaker, and truth from presence, space, and time. Along with the idea of zero and place notation in numbering systems—themselves dependent on forms of writing for their elaboration—alphabetic reading and writing constructed a new meaning of thought and knowledge, a new epistemology, so different from the epistemology of the senses and of sense-based speech that we have only just begun to penetrate how it works. If I seem to belabor the point, it is because our habits of thinking and talking about writing have suffered so monumentally from misdirected analogy. We say that writing is merely a 'secondary code for speech,' obscuring the fact that it is a different sort of code altogether...We say that written words stand for spoken words, and that spoken words stand for things—neither of which is true, or at best, true only in such a complex and mysterious way that we haven't the least idea what 'stands for' means." (Christine Nystrom, *ETC: A Review of General Semantics, 44,* #2, pp. 112-113)

Chapter 1: The Practice of Reading Good Books: A Plea to Teachers and Students[1]

What I mean by reading is not skimming,
not being able to say as the world saith,
'Oh yes, I've read that!'
but reading again and again, in all sorts of moods,
with an increase of delight every time,
till the thing read has become a part of your system
and goes forth along with you
to meet any new experience you may have.
— C. E. Montague

On Reading Atrophy[2]

Mark Twain, in characteristic wit, once wrote, "the man who does not read good books has no advantage over the man who cannot read them."[3] What practical insight. And who can deny that today's college students have easy access to good books.[4] But we should not draw the quick conclusion that today's students take advantage by reading more good books than ever. On the contrary, increasing numbers of students do not read good books, and, perhaps just as many, at least by their own estimates, cannot read them.[5] The overall point is that the covers of countless good books stand as doors neglected and unopened, their enclosed worlds perhaps forever forgotten. The consequences of such negligence may be impossible to anticipate fully, but for now, we can identify conditions that, directly or indirectly, feed the general state of reading atrophy.

Obviously, reading is not disappearing wholesale. In fact, there appears to be as much reading as ever before. Publishing still runs high (including magazines, newspapers, tabloids, and electronic pages). People read memos and mailings, messages on product packaging and on television screens, computer texts, and e-mail. Reading remains, and some sorts of reading are even on the rise, so what is the big deal? The big deal is the atrophy and loss of a particular kind of reading.

Consider times when we engage in what could be called "easy reading" or simply "looking at information." Such activities are characterized by quick glances over familiar words and syntax. Easy reading means we access instant information, and immediate consumability--whether by the consummate reader or the semi-literate--is the measure of message clarity. This can be set in contrast with what might be called "difficult reading" or "serious study." Difficult reading takes time. Readers encounter unknown words, familiar words used in unfamiliar ways, as well as long and complex syntactical structures. "Information," if this is delivered over in difficult reading, must be ruminated upon and hence is obtained only gradually. Because students can be deeply misinformed about the demands of difficult reading (or are simply unwilling to make the needed effort), they may assume that all reading should be easy reading. Difficult reading, scorned for not being instantly consumable, is thereby defined out of the picture, and thus, many good books are avoided altogether.

A little experiment might help here: ask colleagues how comfortably they test students over assigned readings not discussed in class. Most, I suspect, feel a little uncomfortable, and many who are comfortable gain much of their comfort by assigning "user-friendly" textbooks. Now, ask students how many courses, if good notes were taken during each class session, they still could earn a "B" in without doing any of the reading. How many will suggest that this is possible in a fair number of courses? Questions along these lines reveal that some instructors, perhaps more than a few, do not rely upon students' abilities to read. Students pick-up on this and use it to their disadvantage. If only occasionally, haven't we all heard students say they didn't do the assigned reading because it was too difficult to understand? Knowing ahead of time that they later can use that explanation, some students may do just enough cursory glancing at the reading to be able to demonstrate their confusion over it. The underlying logic here is that it is more socially acceptable to be incompetent than to be lazy. There is more social utility in saying that one is unable to read than in saying that one did not, genuinely, try to read it. What could explain this? If students have bought into psychological notions of "mind," or "intelligence," or "intellectual capacities," they may believe that intelligence cannot be cultivated in the same way that industriousness can. Society holds people responsible for sloth and indolence, but ignorance and intellectual incompetence are relieved of moral weight because these are taken to be genetic and somehow beyond an individual's control. This is not to deny that some students sincerely offer the lament: "I didn't understand the reading," but not all laments are so sincere.

And, maybe teachers should be uncomfortable testing students over readings not discussed in class. Talk about what has been read is an essential part of reading. Reading is not reducible to a psychological activity. It resists such confinements, such temporal and spatial restrictions. As the works of Derrida, Ong and others point out, texts are not bound, self-contained objects. They hold crossroads, intersections of indefinite numbers of "traces," and implicitly hold eternally deferred boundaries. Moreover, what Sven Birkerts in his *Gutenberg Elegies* calls "the shadow life of reading," is more like the perennial environment where reading's progeny live. In practice this means students should read assigned readings, participate in class discussion, and then *read again*. They should not demand immediate comprehension for themselves nor immediate comprehensibility of the readings. On the contrary, they must learn to suspend their desire for immediate grasp and to read on anyway. Then, after a second or third reading and after having discussed the reading with others who also have read (and maybe after reading some other relevant texts), they can expect to be ready to begin.

Of the countless good books that could be said to be too difficult to read, consider this question. Imagine students are offered $1,000 if they can correctly answer 7 out of 10 questions over the reading. Under such conditions how many now could read a little better than before? Granted, concert pianists are not made overnight, and one cannot, even with the largest cash incentives, instantly become a great reader. Still, great readers must be willing to practice, and practice requires effort and patience. But if, as Lee Thayer would say, "Most people prefer problems they 'just can't solve' to solutions that they 'just don't like,'" then an adequate corrective isn't likely to be forthcoming any time soon.

Many if not all students could practice their reading more thoroughly. And, many if not all also could read before as well as after class discussion. But too many, maybe even most, seem to think that such rigorous reading and re-reading is not worth the effort.

Not Worth the Effort

The common-sense notion of "not being worth the effort" gets at the very heart of the growing state of reading atrophy. For starters, difficult read-ing may seem not worth the effort when compared to the little effort required by other media. The average college student has continuous instantaneous access to pre-packaged and readily grasped information through television, radio, and the Internet. The ease and availability of these other media directly feed reading atrophy. The evidence here is so abundant and overly-apparent, so widely recog-nized and frequently talked about that we need to safeguard against attending to these factors to the exclusion of others.

"We are so built," Antoine de Saint-Exupéry tells us, "that our appetites are the outcome of the foods we eat." Rather than walk around the library stacks, many students now use search-engines from home computers to access only that information which is available online. Any text recognized as not instantly con-sumable can be abandoned quickly; more readily and easily obtained information is only a click away. A steady diet of mass media (TV, Internet, and perhaps a few textbooks) means that some students rarely, if ever, come into physical contact with good books. Those who have may not have taken the needed time nor re-quired effort to encounter the great ideas available therein. If a good book never has registered deeply with students, they might not even suspect their nascent capacities to read. Given that so few of today's students seriously ruminate over challenging texts, most deeply underestimate their ability to grow in reading skill and comprehension. They fail to realize how cultivatable are their capacities for expression and comprehension.

Beliefs cannot grow where they purchase no ground and receive no nour-ishment. The context today is impatience. David Shenk well speaks to the con-temporary culture where he observes, "What if I told you that there's no such thing as a fast modem, and there never will be? That's because quickness has dis-appeared from our culture. We now only experience degrees of slowness" (1999, p. 41). Some illustrations may help to clarify this point. In class, I sometimes ask my students if they ever listen to a song or a CD more than once. Students always look at me so shocked. How could I ask such a stupid question? They all know that they listen to these things again and again. What most of them usually fail to grasp, however, is that some people read that way. I also like to ask them if, when they listen to their favorite songs, they listen to arrive at the end of them. If they don't listen to a song to get to its end, then, my question was and still is, can we learn to recover reading in that way? "Apparently not," seems to be the contem-porary response. Our world is hyper-rapid and ever changing.[6] Not surprisingly, we live, regardless of any progress, in an unprecedented state of impatience.

Student comments on reading exemplify and verify this sensibility. They say, "Why can't the authors just get to the point? Couldn't the point be made more simply?" What is this "point" which students commonly seek? If it is an adequate test question response, or worse, a sentence with sound-byte quality, then the difficulties of getting students to read good books are great indeed.

The marks of reading atrophy also appear when students read aloud in class. More than nervously rushing through, many speed along so as to have it read, to get the point said. Their hurried pace reflects a kind of scanning for information. It is obvious that they don't think of a text as a place to dwell or as a shaping stone against which to forge themselves. Most students, perhaps most people in the society at large, impatiently take information to be a thing, some kind of stuff delivered over or added to their "knowledge base." They think of reading only as a *means* to an end of information and not as an end in itself. Perhaps they assume their minds are like computers and it makes no sense to speak of a computer re-reading a text. Such faulty notions of mind and information are also a source of ready atrophy. Students too quickly assume that their minds are container-things and that information is a kind of substance that is transmitted from one person to another by way of language. They may think of ideas as transportable objects and language as a kind of "conduit" for the social distribution of personal ideas (Lakoff and Johnson, 1980). Rather than understanding themselves as creatures able to grow in abilities for expression and comprehension, they stop short and merely seek information.

Impatience also provides common sense with the notion of an "average reader." Employing such a notion for comparison, students quickly and easily take a self-defeatist position. They say, "I read slower than other people. Reading is hard for me." Whether any given person is or is not a "slow" reader is not the point. What is more interesting is the high number of people who make this claim. Going only by students' self-expressions we could conclude, logic notwithstanding, that most people read more slowly than other people. It also is interesting how we all too commonly assume that slow reading is an intellectual deficit, or at the least, not how one is supposed to read. Shouldn't we, by practical contrast, congratulate and commend those persons who have developed the competence to be slow readers?

But not all students hurry through their readings. Some can sense their unreadiness to begin yet don't understand that no one begins ready, and so, they fail to begin at all. They think they don't *have* to do the readings. Many will pass tests and courses--and some may do well without reading--from which students may infer that this demonstrates their intelligence. Some students may even skip readings altogether in a misguided attempt to produce evidence of how "smart" they are. In his essay "A Poetic For Communication," Lee Thayer (1997) addresses the subtle individualism which lends intelligibility to these actions. He writes, "And that's why people may say, 'I want to be a writer,' but not, 'I want to be a reader'...Learning how to 'be' a reader is no less demanding than learning how to 'be' a writer; it is just less romantic" (p. 79). The romantic faith in individualism is the root of many students' assumptions about reading (and perhaps of just about everything) that "everyone has their own interpretation." If this is the case, the logic goes, then there is no way to secure the *correct* interpretation. Any interpretation of the reading is just as valid as any other. Because common sense is saturated by this romantic individualism, many students wittingly or not conclude that careful study is not worth the effort.

Romantic (psychological) individualism is demonstrated also by the high number of students who claim to have their own thoughts, even though they fail to notice that they've taken that notion and expression from other people.[7] Here is further evidence: During class discussion I sometimes include quotations in response to student questions, for example a line from Nietzsche, William James, Kenneth Burke, or maybe McLuhan. In response to such citations, on more than one occasion, students have said, "O.K. Fine. But what do *you* think. I want to know what your opinion is, not what someone else thinks." I can't help but say, "This is what I think; these guys aren't thinking anything. They're dead, have been for some time! These are *my* thoughts now." My response can be explained further with an illustration: During his long scholarly career, Wittgenstein grew to disagree with his own earlier position and later offered a corrective, one which radically challenged his earlier writings. Now, if some persons only have read and still adhere to the earlier writings, whose position would they be holding? Certainly not the "late" Wittgenstein's. Additionally, student criticisms such as those just mentioned make it seem as if people aren't required to earn ideas and as if they aren't challenged to become who they need to become in order to grasp them. They make it seem as if ideas are found in books the way food is found in refrigerators. This also shows how common sense wants it both ways. On the one hand, people claim that books can be too difficult to read. On the other hand, they imply that ideas are taken from books easily, as if ideas simply lay about waiting to be adopted by less-than-original thinkers. Rather than wanting to have their own thoughts, readers ought to actively celebrate and cultivate their openness to history and to others. They thus would become willing interlocutors with the many brilliant minds who have come before them. My colleague Robert Mayberry puts it this way, "Students must learn to ask more than, 'Can I get others to understand what I mean by my words?' They more fundamentally should ask, 'Can I learn to understand what others mean by *their words?*'"

A final contributor to reading atrophy may be much larger than those so far addressed. Reading good books may seem to be less than worth the effort because we fail to imagine noble or grand purposes for learning. Without such purposes we falter, or as Thayer was wont to say to his students, "What we know is always constrained and enabled by our purposes for knowing." A practical implication is that if we sense that what we talk about has little worth outside the classroom (if we cannot imagine other reasons for knowing it) little effort may seem justified in learning it. But if we believe that what we talk about bears on what we need to know for life (if we can imagine grand purposes for knowing something), then much expended effort can seem justified and appropriate. Indeed, if course material is believed to be vital to students' futures, to their very humanity, then teachers may feel justified in requiring a great deal of effort from students. But if teachers believe that what is to be learned is of only moderate value (e.g. in course content or even in subject matter), they may feel guilt about having students work too hard on it. Some systematic avoidance of reading good books, on the part of both students and teachers, may be a kind of admission that, given the goals and purposes brought to what is to be learned from, only minimal effort is justified.

Why Read Good Books?

So why should we want to read good books? What makes reading good books worth the effort? If, as Twain suggests, "the man who does not read good books has no advantage over the man who cannot read them," then what are the advantages? Obviously, he could have meant any number of things.

Maybe Twain meant that reading good books frequently requires learning new words. One advantage of such reading, then, is that our vocabulary grows, or at least it can. Furthermore, learning new words arguably offers more advantages than merely learning new information. Let me explain. Words learned are not normally learned as facts to be recalled later. Words, qua words, are the way facts come to be known. The word "fact," in fact, comes from the Latin "factum," meaning, "to make." Words, although they are the "how" of how we are able to know what we know, are not normally known facts. When we speak we do not consciously attend to our words. The words are "focally absent" (cf. Leder, 1991) as we experience only their power to separate and merge aspects of the world (cf. Burke, 1952). Still, isn't it interesting that when you learn a new word, you can hear it when it's used around you? Isn't it also interesting that we do not experience the opposite case? We don't hear all of the different unknown words used around us. All unknown words are the same; they lack meaningful differentiation from one another. This is why any particular one can be exceedingly difficult to recall. One advantage of reading good books, therefore, is that our sense of the world grows with our growing lexicons.[8]

A second advantage comes, ironically enough, from the very effort difficult reading can and does require. Unfortunately, contemporary pedagogical focus on message clarity feeds students' assumptions that all difficult reading is a product of bad writing. "If only the writings were easier," students seem to think, "then we could solve the problem of reading." Jacques Barzun, in his *Begin Here*, identifies the larger trend of which this complaint is but a symptom:

> In the name of progress and method, innovation, and statistical research, educationalists have persuaded the world that teaching [reading?] is a set of complex problems to be solved. It is no such thing. It is a series of *difficulties*. They recur endlessly and have to be met; there is no solution--which means also that there is no mystery. (1991, p. 5)

Many good books, therefore, offer natural resistances, not problems that could have been solved by simpler writing. And more to the practical point: what are we to do with the countless good books that already have been written, many of which, perhaps most, are not models of message clarity? We should recognize this as one of their strengths. They gain part of their value because they can be so difficult, because they require patience and devotion. Is it even possible for TV to provide such difficulties? When have you heard someone on T.V. use a word you didn't know? Television, as Neil Postman observes, mainly panders to viewers and tries to keep them amused. On the whole, TV provides pleasurable leisure rather than laborious recreation and so it robs viewers of the struggle to make meaning. In his book, *The Mature Society*, the Nobel Laureate Dennis Gabor addresses how value is conferred through effort:

> ...I fall back on a simple homely psychology, based on two observations which most people will be able to check from their own experience, or from their own insight.
>
> I. *Humans are wonderful in adversity, weak in comfort, affluence and security*.
>
> II. *Humans do not appreciate what they get without an effort*.
>
> The first of these gives us a warning of the dangers, the second gives us a hint how we may perhaps be able to avoid them. (1972, p. 47)

Although students may sense the amount of effort some good books demand and also may realize the arduous struggle of becoming great readers, their quick conclusion that such labors are not worth the effort fails to recognize how effort can be a vital source of worth. In sum, an asset of many good books is that they naturally provide, as Jean Paul Sartre would say, "co-efficients of adversity." Their difficulties provide for us; they are winds or even sails.

A third advantage of reading good books is that as we work our way through them we learn how to move within particular *styles* of thought. Our own thought is thereby trained to unfold according to certain thinking styles, particular semantic choices and syntactical maneuvers. Learning how to move according to a given text's style of thought--its particular intonational contour--is not only why some good books can be so difficult, but also why they offer the advantages they do. In other words, we practice the art of reading good books not merely, nor even primarily, to access information. Perhaps the cultivation of thinking-styles remains underappreciated in contemporary life because many reading diets consist mainly of popular magazines, advertisements, textbooks, and quickly consumable Internet information. While students read such texts, the actual and implied author can fade from view. In place of a dialogue and an interlocutor they find an odd kind of thing: "information." But when they read a good book crafted by a masterful writer, the style itself can make apparent that they are engaged in a dialogue. The author's style holds a signature, an indelible mark of the book's dialogic character. When reading a textbook, in contrast, students can easily forget that reading is a practice of comprehension and expression. They may even reduce it to mechanical "information transfer." But Heinz von Foerster well reminds us that "A library may store books but it cannot store information...One might as well speak of a garage as a storage and retrieval system for transportation. In both instances a potential vehicle (for transportation or for information) is confused with the thing it does when someone makes it do it. *Someone* has to do it. *It* does not do anything" (1980, p. 19). The more education focuses on information and neglects the growth of human capacities and the direction of human aims, the less likely that difficult reading will be recognized in its advantages over other communication media.

In the first volume of his *Journals and Papers*, Søren Kierkegaard lists the entry "Communication," which includes detailed discussions of indirect communication and the distinction between the "communication of knowledge" and the "communication of capability." Communication of capability, Kierkegaard suggests, is done indirectly and remains without an "object." Although we can try to "pound knowledge *into* students," he argues, we must try to "pound capability *out* of them" (cf. pp. 269-318). This means that we must begin practicing right away regardless of our unreadiness. He writes:

> ...genuine communication and instruction is *training* or *upbringing*...Confusion arises when the upbringer instead of upbringing teaches as if he were imparting knowledge....the rule is to do it as well as one can at every moment, and then again to do it as well as one can the next moment, and so on further, in order continually to get to know it better and better. If, on the other hand, the upbringing is communicated as knowledge, one never receives an upbringing but is always getting merely something to know...The rule for the communication of capability is: begin immediately to do it. If the learner says: I can't, the teacher answers: Nonsense, do it as well as you can. With that the instruction begins. Its end result is: to be able. But it is not knowledge which is communicated. (1967, pp. 279-284)

In Kierkegaard's account, information conveyed is not as essential as the capability indirectly communicated. As organic systems of expression and comprehension, people grow in their abilities to express and to comprehend. This growth is often more vital than the imagined "thing" called information which is presumably transferred from one mind to another. The practice of reading of good books, then, helps people to experience for themselves the meaning of Allen Wheelis's suggestions that, "We have to be someone before we can know anything. And when we have become someone, the something we can know is less than the something we have become."

The advantages of reading good books are not limited to those that come from activities of reading. Some emerge later, arising from the particular subject matter read. For example, if one person reads what others have read, those common reading experiences may engender or enrich discussion on various issues or topics. Moreover, if people have read books unknown to their interlocutors, they can seem, at least initially, to be the original source of what is said. This is why plagiarism is an ever present possibility and temptation. How much mystification in everyday conversation springs from this source? Where do ideas come from? Perhaps we are deeply misinformed about the natures of both reading and persons. How can a text, a material thing to which I presumably attribute meaning, teach me something? How, exactly, can we grow familiar with any given work? Maurice Merleau-Ponty (1973) encourages us to acknowledge how our own thought is indebted to the thought of others and to notice how that indebtedness can remain covered-over. He writes,

I am Stendhal while reading him…Sedimented language is the language the reader brings with him, the stock of accepted relations between signs and familiar significations without which he could never even have begun to read…in the end a new signification is secreted. It is the effect through which Stendhal's own language comes to life in the reader's mind, henceforth for the reader's own use. Once I have acquired this language, I can easily delude myself into believing that I could have understood it by myself, because it transformed me and made me capable of understanding it…Here then, I would have to admit that I do not live just my own thought but that, in the exercise of speech, I *become* the one to whom I am listening. (p. 12-13; 118)

It is fascinating that we can understand utterances that we could not spontaneously generate on our own. It also is fascinating that we, in both listening and reading, are able to understand those who speak more articulately than ourselves. Have you ever heard someone speak so eloquently that you surprised yourself by your ability to understand and appreciate what was said? Moreover, have you noticed that what we imagine as "sayable" is shaped and formed by what we have heard and read?

William James' writing on habit and imitation is relevant here. He suggests that through imitating those we aspire to be, we come to know ourselves. He writes,

We become conscious of what we ourselves are by imitating others--the consciousness of what the others are precedes--the sense of self grows by the same pattern. The entire accumulated wealth of mankind--languages, arts, institutions, and sciences--is passed on from one generation to another by which Baldwin has called social heredity, each generation simply imitating the last. (1958, p. 49)

A phonetic text is a kind of score, a set of instructions for making sounds. Voice, including pronunciation, intonation, and articulation, is an essential component of reading and of interpretation more generally. Of course, mimetically reproducing the score of a phonetic text does not magically transmit meaning from the author's mind to the reader's (cf. Olson). In this regard, phonetic text can easily generate delusions of understanding as it allows us to accurately pronounce (i.e. to sound out) what we do not understand. Obviously then, the goal is not simply to produce sounds accurately but to carefully interpret what those sounds *mean*. In practice this means we need others to discuss readings with us.

Our talk with others about readings is an essential part of reading. But this is stated too simply. In his *A History of Reading*, Alberto Manguel tells of his reading aloud to Borges and how Borges analyzed, extrapolated, and elaborated as he followed along. Manguel's point is that sometimes, perhaps often, we need experienced readers as guides. Like a tall mountain, a good book can be difficult to climb. To scale any one, we may first need to become familiar with it, find likely spots to make purchases on its surface. For a successful climb we may need to be part of a team guided by a seasoned expert climber. Routes leading to impasses can then be headed-off, and, places where the terrain is loose and shaky can be strategically traversed.

Finally, some students may only have encountered books which address them as competent employees or well-functioning social roles. They may yet to have encounter books which explicitly address them in their humanity, as a *person*. Indeed, good books provide us with more than "facts" or "the news," and reading good books entails something more profound than keeping oneself informed. It opens us to what can be thought about and helps us learn how to think. There is a critical difference between learning how to think about what needs thinking about and keeping oneself informed. The underlying issue, the deep roots one might say, is that U.S. popular culture seems to have bought wholesale into psychological (individualistic) understandings of minds, persons, and texts. Underestimation and underappreciation of reading travels hand in hand with pop-psychological notions of intelligence and information. One of the main advantages of reading good books is that it generates incontrovertible proof, solid unmistakable evidence, of how malleable we are. Thus, resources for empirically demonstrating the shortcomings of psychological individualism are to be found within the practice of reading good books.

Closing Remarks

University mission statements often contain some definition of a "college-education." This, not surprisingly, often includes the claim that students ideally develop "life-long skills of critical thinking, articulate expression, and independent learning."[9] In practice, this means that reading good books is key. In many respects the most important thing I learned in college was how to read, that is, how to appreciate reading and book culture more generally. Perhaps reading strikes me as so essential because prior to college I read pretty little and liked books even less. I disliked comic books, read close to no fiction, and on the rare occasions when I looked at non-fiction of general human interest, my encounters were sparse, short, and lonely. I prematurely concluded that books were lame. Had I not taken college courses which required reading good books, and by this I mean NOT MERELY TEXTBOOKS, my opinion, I genuinely believe, never would have changed. If students are required to read good books they might be enticed to become great readers. People's basic attitudes about books and reading change as a result of what they do and do not read. I believe those who read good books are more likely to continue to read independently.

"In order for a dialogue to begin," Mikhail M. Bakhtin suggests, "the first voice must be heard." A book is an invitation to a dialogue, one where we are encouraged to meet authors on their terms. But because of the growing infantilization of the culture, some people may never enter into such a dialogue, for they fail to hear the first voice. Teachers must beware the temptation to meet students "at their level." Even if it is true, that "each receives according to his capacity," or even granting that, as Abraham Maslow puts it "...the world can communicate to a person only that which he is worthy, that which he deserves or is 'up to'; that to a large extent, he can receive from the world and, give to the world, only that which he himself is" (1967, p. 195) the case remains: to read a great work we may have to labor, we may have to become someone in order to understand. Reading, we must never forget, is a *practice*. If only we would take as much effort and devotion studying good books as the authors did in crafting and composing them. Then we would realize how enriched we are as we become able to engage in meaningful dialogues with the minds found within and without them. One final advantage worth mentioning is that the more books we labor over, the more we are able to read and also the more easily we, when encountering an author for the first time, accept that we always begin unready. We learn to accept that our readiness to read emerges only after we already have begun.

Practical counsel for those struggling to become great readers: Try to remember back to when you first learned how to read. When you started you were unable to read, and then, by some action, you learned how. *How did that happen?*

Endnotes to Chapter 1

1 The abstract from the original article: This paper is designed to provoke lively discussion between and among teachers and students regarding the growing state of reading atrophy. It best serves as an "inspirational" beginning piece for undergraduate humanities or social science courses which contain difficult, "primary source," readings. The paper consists of two main parts. The first addresses contemporary influences which feed reading atrophy. The second part offers arguments for why the practice of reading difficult books is worth the effort.

2 I want to acknowledge Lee Thayer and Robert Mayberry for their inspiration and assistance in my writing this essay. I also must give thanks to Barry D. Liss, Bryan Crable, and especially Valerie Peterson for their thoughtful criticism and useful suggestions.

3 Cited in Barzun (1992, p. 115).

4 I don't know what, exactly, Twain meant by "good books." I originally thought that I should offer some examples of what I mean by good books, but, after several attempts, I concluded that any such selection, no matter how extensive, becomes overly canonizing and is hopelessly complicit in too grand of omissions. Perhaps Barzun's (1992) call for the reading of "real" books, which he defines as "a book one wants to reread" (p. 115) provides enough clarity for Twain's expression.

5 How many of Twain's good books would undergraduates label "unreadable"? Or, How many of the 54 *Great Books of the Western World* which Hutchins and Adler put together would today's students find readable?

6 Notice the failure to have learned the lesson so eloquently stated by Robert Maynard Hutchins: "The more technological the society is, the more rapidly it will change and the less valuable *ad hoc* instruction will become. It now seems safe to say that the most practical education is the most theoretical one" (p. 19, 1968).

7 José Ortega Y Gasset (1958) also addresses this contrast between the veneer of individualism and the deep fact of sociality. He writes,

> With some shame we recognize that the greater part of the things we say we do not understand very well; and if we ask ourselves why we say them, why we think them, we will observe that we say them only for this reason: that we have heard them said, that other people say them. (p. 92)

Could it be that we either consciously select where we get our ideas, or that we, thinking that we are thinking for ourselves, simply take our ideas off the rack, from what anyone has said about things? Try to argue against the following: Any person who has interesting thoughts did not build them from the bottom up. No person who we find intellectually interesting is out howling in the woods. And, is it at all surprising that those who do think for themselves are those who most often explicitly acknowledge their influences and indebtedness to others? Two scholars meet. Among the earliest questions are: "Who were your major influences? and, Who are you currently reading?"

8 Well beyond the scope of the present essay, someone might document the wholesale loss of everyday terms in the English language. A vast storehouse for analyzing and understanding the most complex of interpersonal relations, English is slowly becoming more and more filled with "introductory textbookeese." Ask your students to define the words "indignation," or "venerate," or "obsequious." Most cannot. Ask them to define the difference between "envy" and "jealousy." Again, most cannot. Comparatively, ask them to define the words such as, "co-dependent," "intro-vert," "anal," "type A personality," "stressed," or, "Learning Disabled" almost all students will have some attempted definition.

9 Taken from page 2 of the Grand Valley State University Undergraduate and Graduate Catalog.

Chapter 2: Study as a Way of Life: Learning about Education Metaphors

*The best education for the best of us
is the best eduction for all of us.*
— *Robert M. Hutchins*

*…selves are not something
one can study and provide for;
they are something one struggles for.*
— *Walker Percy*

*The trouble with a cheap, specialized education
is that you never stop paying for it.*
— *Marshall McLuhan*

The Meanings of Study[1]

There was a time when study referred to concerted actions taken with regard to the written word. To study was to pore over some pieces of writing, to delve into them, to internalize them to the degree that they became part of the person reading them. For example, in his *Lives of Eminent Philosophers*, Diogenes Laertius recounts the path of learning taken by Zeno of Citium, founder of early Stoicism. Laertius writes,

> He [Zeno] consulted the oracle to know what he should do to attain
> the best life, and that the god's response was that he should take
> on the complexion of the dead. Whereupon, perceiving what this
> meant, he studied ancient authors. (1991, p. 111)

In this context the word "study" is used as a verb and it expresses a particular action or mode of being. It refers to doing something with texts, something that not only affects our complexion but vitally bears upon our ability to "attain the best life." Here, then, people undertook the task of study in order to become someone, in order to take on a complexion or be transformed. But a word's meaning never sits still, for the word "study" soon enough came to mean the room within a building named for the act of studying. "The study," a noun, now designated the physical space where persons could pore over texts or get lost in spells of concentration; people sat and studied in the study.

But then an even newer noun came to town. This was the highly modern noun, "a study," as could be heard in expressions like, "Dr. so and so conducted a study and found…". And quickly thereafter emerged the plural form, as in: "studies have shown…". Here the meaning of "study" translates into something like "research programs" or "experimental science writ large," and this latter meaning, unfortunately, may have been the beginning of the end for the original meanings of the word "study."

Many people conduct studies, read about findings and data, and people also read and write reports about studies, but the question is: do they still take the time to study? That is, people today admittedly spend a good deal of time either reading studies or reading about them, but how much time do they spend *studying readings?*

Consider for a moment the different motives behind "reading studies" and "studying readings." Immediately we can notice at least one key difference between the two: the former attempts to outwardly build a coherent base of knowledge and the latter attempts to inwardly facilitate the spiritual/existential/ethical development of character. Those who read studies often wish to find, develop, and continuously monitor the coherence of a grand trans-personal edifice call "the research;" they collectively can read the latest contributions to the "body of knowledge." This is essentially different from someone who studies the world-views of the ancients or various bodies of the world's great literature. For such study readers are neither interested in discovering what is "statistically significant" nor in accumulating coherent additions to the stock-body of knowledge.

Here is another way to come at this general issue. Now, of course, a mind is not a bucket or physical container, but we might, for illustrative purposes, imagine that minds are somehow similar to containers in some ways. Consider the diagrams below:

Diagram A   Diagram B

Diagram A represents the mind during *easy reading*, or browsing. The arrows represent information, and, in this case, people encounter familiar words and familiar syntax. They quickly access easily digestible information. During easy reading, or browsing, the container seems to be getting fuller, denser, and more compact, and so people actually *feel* like they are getting smarter. Diagram B, represents the mind during *serious study* where people encounter new words, unfamiliar syntax, and challenging or even indigestible ideas. Here, in contrast to moments of easy reading, the container itself enlarges to meet the new kinds of information. Moreover, during serious study we experience a decreased density (an increased emptiness) and may actually feel as dumb as ever. Ironically, it is at these moments, moments when we face and endure our intellectual limitations, that a different kind of intellectual growth occurs. This is so much the case that, when we deeply challenge ourselves through study and strive to cultivate ourselves, we can develop so considerably that our past, at least to those who now meet us, can be nearly absent. As other people interpret one's past mainly through the person one has become, it easily can seem as if the person one was then never even existed.

For centuries, people in all walks of life, not just scholars and academicians, have studied readings to recover resources for thinking about contemporary problems and/or to live a more personally fulfilling life. They even studied in the hopes of gaining a better sense of who they are and who they *ought to become.* Today, the contemporary scene in the U.S. seems so "pop-psychological." Many people assume that their minds or even their selves are a "done deal," something given to them at birth. Reading, they correlatively believe, does not cultivate the very fabric of mind; it merely makes information available. Many students, symptomatic of the culture more generally, seem to believe in some kind of "information stuff" that is fundamentally discontinuous with a "mind-thing" and imagine that minds remain unchanged by "information obtained." People believe they can understand something (anything at all), without being changed by way of that particular understanding.[2] All of the above, perhaps obviously, is exacerbated where information is understood as bit by bit the same, quantifiable and measurable as a substance. The basic point here is this: when all learning is equated with accessing and acquiring information, as in quickly skimming various studies or searching the web and clicking around a few convenient websites, we can mourn for the loss of study in its original and deeper sense.

To make matters worse, many people today sense the great amount of information available but they seem to presume that they personally are born atop the shoulders of previous generations, as if cultural progress is naturally given to them personally. But this belief is precisely what we need to interrogate. Søren Kierkegaard helps us begin such an interrogation where he writes,

> When a breed of sheep, for example, is improved, improved sheep are born because the specimen merely expresses the species. But surely it is different when an individual, who is qualified by spirit, relates himself to the generation....Development of spirit is self-activity; the spiritually developed individual takes his spiritual development along with him in death. If a succeeding individual is to attain it, it must occur through his self-activity. (1992, p. 345)

There seems to be no progress other than individual progress in many areas, especially in one's education. While material and technological objects may be something that the larger anonymous culture can bestow and progress in a linear way, the cultivation of self or spirit or character is not. At best, it can be exemplified by others but never bestowed by them.

And, to complicate matters, the recent proliferation of pedagogical techniques and self-driven instruction modules makes it seem that studying *should be* getting easier all the time. It is as if we, the children of the age of comforts and convenience, increasingly want a secret, a trick, some new technologies, or something that will make study easier if not more efficient. You know, something to 'streamline it' for today's active multi-tasking person. Students (and even some faculty) increasingly seem surprised that good old-fashioned study remains difficult and can't be made much easier and more convenient.

Education Metaphors

Is not all of the above, basically, how the contemporary commercialization of education came to be? It provides a backdrop in which an expression such as "students are consumers buying a degree" can seem to make sense to people. Unfortunately, growing numbers of people in contemporary Western culture do seem to think of their education as some kind of product purchased from the university. And, perhaps even more unfortunate, this too is paralleled by the steady rise of "university marketing departments" who explicitly sell "the image" of the university.[3]

Now, to be fair, we admittedly live in a consumer society and students are consumers, to some degree, in their lives more generally. And it is also hard to deny the growing tide of identity merchandising that forms the substratum of student life across campuses in the U.S. There is, moreover, so much "educational packaging" in the form of outlines, syllabi, lecture notes, study guides, hand-outs, reader-friendly textbooks with bold faced terms, grades, credit-hours, etc., that it is easy, for both students and professors, to let the "educational packaging" replace the less easily commodified habits and practices of learning. As Walker Percy writes, "To put it bluntly: A student who has the desire to get at a dogfish or a Shakespeare sonnet may have the greatest difficulty in salvaging the creature itself from the educational package in which it is presented" (1954, p. 57). Thus, the effort to provide students with some kind of consumer-package of "university-experience" unfortunately reduces what we all take education to be about.

If for argument's sake we assume that the backdrop lending intelligibility to the expression "students are consumers" is not going away soon, we might want to critically ask: Whose interests are served by it? The students? I don't think so, but, then again, maybe. Some students may take comfort in the thought that the "customer is always right." How about professors? I don't think so, but, then again, maybe. If the students are consumers and the university is a business that sells degrees, then, professors, rather than having duties to their vocation, are little more than "employees." And employees, as everyone knows, can always say, "I don't know; I just work here." Could it be that those who have the most to gain from the idea that 'students are consumers' and/or 'university is a business' are neither teachers nor students?

Xenophon, in his *Memorabilia*, suggests that Socrates refused to take money for teaching. He further suggests that this was not an act of altruism, but a refusal to get involved with someone who was willing to pay for an education but unwilling to do the necessary work. Socrates thus refrained from taking money for his instruction because he never wanted to be stuck trying to "teach" an intractable learner, someone whose only real commitment was a willingness to pay.[4] It is worth underscoring that, in this way, Socrates avoided one of the main sources of teacher burnout. Such exhaustion comes from having to deal with people who think they're buying something. Such persons may think that they have the right, or perhaps should have the right, to attend class or not, to do the readings or not, to try or not. A few might display a demeanor, a general attitude nicely summarized by postures and comportments that say: "*If I want to pay little attention, occasionally do the readings, never do additional or 'not required' reading,[5] and maybe even skip class every once and a while, that is my prerogative. I am paying for my education.*" Teacher burnout, I would suggest, emerges not directly from such behavior but because these same persons often want it both ways: they want the prerogative to care or not (to be "into" the class or not) but they also want their professors to care *all* the time, to consistently support and encourage them just in case they do happen to get into it. This is how some bad teachers became bad teachers. They got burnt out trying to remain vigilant in caring about people who want the license to either care about themselves or not.

Today, education is expensive but that's not the half of it. The real rub starts to dawn upon you only as you understand that you can't buy an education. Never could! People at best pay for exposure to the resources by which they may be able to develop habits and resources for the life-long projects of cultivating character, handling responsibilities and duties, and implementing visions.

To reveal the non-commercial nature of education, we can imagine a comic reversal where stores are transformed into universities so that "buying is learning." In such "university-stores," a customer puts a few bags of vegetables on the counter and the cashier says, "That will be $4. 25." The customer delivers over the money or at least part of it, at which point the cashier puts the vegetables into a bag and says, "O.K. You now need to read this report on food production in the U.S., this scientific report on the caloric load and mineral content of various foods, and then, you need to tell me in specific detail the amount of exercise needed to burn off the calories of these vegetables. Finally, you can give me half of the exercises now and I'll trust you to do *at least* the remaining half at home. Once we have this taken care of, you are free to take your food home." When this is what it means to buy groceries—or inversely, when personal responsibility and performance have been completely removed from education—then I will agree that one can buy an education.

But then again maybe I'm fooling myself. Perhaps the situation is exactly as described above, except the cashiers are half-asleep, half-looking the other way, and basically thinking one thought: "I get paid either way." Perhaps many "customers" walk out of the university-store without having paid the full amount for the goods. They might have cheated the store, paid less than the required amount, and /or failed to do the exercises at home. Too bad for them that it is not until they finally arrive back home that they'll realize their bag of goods has grown empty and now is nothing but a piece of paper.

It is funny that those who liken "university study" to "buying an education" seem to forget that the metaphor, "knowledge is commodity" is parasitic upon another metaphor that is just as dubious: "knowledge is a substance." We're headed in the wrong direction even courting the notion that students "receive" an education, or, for that matter, that they can buy one. Maybe we'd move closer to the truth by saying, "People build their educations." Students, that is, are given an environment which gathers others who have built up their education, and they, through collective university study, are to take advantage of the opportunity to learn with others who are also learning. One's education is co-built through co-learning and co-study. An education, to the extent that any metaphor will do, is something that can be grown or perhaps cultivated, but never merely packaged, delivered, and/or received. Part of the difficulty with the expression, "getting an education," is that education comes from what we *give to* our studies not what we *get from* them.

But this too remains limited in its own way, for an education that actually becomes 'habits of life-long learning' is never merely a building. In fact, so much on-going learning is actually a kind of unlearning: it is learning how to challenge already held beliefs and assumptions. As Kenneth Burke reminds us, there is "no construction without destruction." To build-up habits of life-long learning we may also have to tear out obstructions, to level and remove unwanted materials; we may need to weed and prune. If we are to learn how to study we must begin with the recognition that we all, each of us, have received countless erroneous facts, oversimplified accounts, and facile notions as well as pet theories that need to be expurgated, extirpated, expunged and even exorcised.

Further Challenges to Study

In his useful essay "Explanation as Motive," Lee Thayer (1997) argues that what motivates us is not the past but the future. In the classroom, for example, some students may study readings as if they want to know them for the rest of their lives, but other students may do just enough cursory glancing at them to be able to produce some kind of "evidence that they read" or at least "tried to read." These latter students read not to understand so much as to be able to say that they had read. Other students, knowing that they could say that they tried but didn't understand, don't read at all. Others still, read with ready-made critiques and look for places in the text where the critique fits. Could it be that people have created so many workable explanations for why they don't understand something that they now have difficulty taking their own study seriously?

The role that explanations play can be seen quite clearly in matter of attendance and pop-quizzes over assigned readings.[6] If professors demand attendance and have a fair percentage of the grade determined by pop-quizzes, they help provide students with socially acceptable explanations to their peers. When 'peer-pressured' to go out to party rather than do their homework, students are now better equipped to justify staying home to study. They can resort to: "There may be a quiz tomorrow."

Note that this logic applies not only to students but to people more generally, *professors included*. As Thayer suggests, "Whatever explanations or 'excuses' you accept from others are the one's you will get—from others and yourself" (1997, p. 142). I once asked students to explain what this passage meant, and one student suggested that some professors are basically lazy and like to let class out early. They may even make it seem like they are doing you a favor; they're eager to "cut you some slack" because they want you to "cut them some slack" back. Some professors, the student went on, may even openly acknowledge, though somewhat jokingly, a mutual interest in "slacking."

Then another student told of a certain professor who every night, in what was scheduled to be a once-a-week three-hour evening class, would begin with the statement, "Alright then, let's get started so we all can get home." The professor, *perhaps* trying to identify with the students, selected mutual feelings of wanting to be elsewhere as the means of identification. By setting up such a context, which was completely tangential to the class and course material, the professor helped the students find the occasion itself as unwelcoming and undesirable. He turned the class meeting into something very other than a highly desirable gathering between and among aspiring public intellectuals. All of this was accomplished in less than a dozen words. Who is surprised to hear that on average, so the student reported, the class ended more than an hour early each night and students rarely asked any questions. Apparently, how professors understand what they are doing when they study with students is just as influential as how students understand what they are doing when they study with teachers.[7] Seriously, if professors are not genuinely excited to be in class and talking about the course ideas, why should students be?

Maybe I'm being unfairly tough on such professors. Maybe such professors are so adept at pedagogical techniques that they are able to disseminate "the material" within less time. Maybe such a person has so well selected easily digestible readings that none of the students needed to study them, and, because they were so clear, no one needed to ask questions about them. Or, perhaps more hopefully, we can see more clearly the deep problems that come along with the assumptions that "knowledge is a commodity," "students are consumers," and the "university is a business."

The Value of Study in Today's Times

Anthropologist Dorothy Lee, in her challenging and brilliant essay "Symbolization and Value," (1959) discusses how symbols take on value and provides invaluable insight for professors who are interested in assuring that students' educational experiences are valuable. She begins by showing that value cannot be arbitrarily assigned or simply attributed to items or situations and further illustrates how symbols take their significance and value according to the actual situations and contexts in which they have participated. Rightly understood, her account suggests the following bit of advice about pop-quizzes, extra-readings, and other ways that rigor and difficult study can be brought into a classroom. Most professors know what happens at some point late in the semester: students begin their "meltdown" pleas for reduced workload. They might ask, "Can't we drop the lowest quiz?" or, "How about one less paper?" Such pleas and requests ask professors to loosen the reigns, basically cut the students some slack. Professors should move cautiously and think it out before implementing any changes.[8] When students are grumbling and moaning about their efforts and labors, and when they are asking for some relief, they may, in fact, be doing other than what they appear to be doing on the surface. They may very well be constructing and ritually enacting a kind of living heroism narrative. They are, as it were, dramatically setting the stage and putting themselves on it. This is why professors should rarely if ever give into such pleas, for a slackening may actually undermine the possibility of genuine student heroism. Professors who stay tough all the way through can comfort themselves by the thought that many students, when everything has settled, will be even more the heroes for having "survived" the semester.

Perhaps more context is necessary: At the young age of sixteen, U.S. citizens can attain a driver's license and then subsequently commit accidental manslaughter by way of that very dangerous piece of machinery. By age eighteen, people are able to marry and procreate legally anywhere within the country, and, at the same age, we allow people to join the military and kill enemy combatants in the name of their nation. After having thought about facing the possibility of such serious and hefty responsibilities, some students may find college, at least some classes, a bit of a let down.

Could it be that people too easily fail to understand the temporality that they are, and so, many of their everyday frustrations and difficulties arise from little more than wanting to be done? Don't people today seem deeply and thoroughly impatient? It is as if we have reduced time to space and take ourselves as wholly splayed out in some kind of spatial now. How did this come to pass?

Some response can be found in Sebastian de Grazia's *Of Time, Work, and Leisure*, (1964) which outlines the notion of "free time" as it emerged after the advent of modern clocks, mechanization, and industrialization. The early promise of automation was a life of increased leisure, but the end result turned out to be a kind of neutralized and commercialized time, a time that could be spent or wasted, a time outside the individual, a time that basically made leisure increasingly impossible. The encumbrance of this objective time, which ever becomes more available for economic calculations, makes "time wasted" sound like such a dereliction. Today, many people who sense that time is little 'their own' do as little as possible, perhaps nothing, in a pathetic attempt to prove that the time *is* theirs. Consider this in terms of practical application: In classes teachers are known for trying, at least during the first week or so, to scare students out of class or into doing the readings. Partly true, perhaps in some regards. The larger truth is that such teachers hope to appear most scary to those students who assume they can get through the course without seriously studying. These are also, perhaps not surprisingly, the students who seem to think that they are getting away with something, pulling a fast one, when they don't do them. Who, exactly, do they imagine they're sticking it to?

To recover the habit of study as a vital means for growing selves worth wanting, we need to address an important issue that could be dealt with in much great detail.[9] It concerns a mode of self-defeat, one that mostly goes unnoticed or is explained away under terms such as "average," "mediocre," or more simply, "just how things are." We might imagine a book-length treatment, the title of which would be, "How We Stick It to Ourselves: An Ecology of Intrapersonal Oppression and Self-Defeat." The work would entail a massive study of all of the ways that individuals, suffering from self-estrangement and from some adversarial relation to a felt or imagined social order and set of cultural expectations, come to believe that they are somehow "sticking it to someone" when they lay around and do little to nothing. It is as if the only kind of freedom that people increasingly understand is "freedom *from* constraint." They seem not to grasp the many ways that freedom can be liberated *by* constraint, such as the freedom to.

For further illustration of derelict freedom, let me tell a fantastical tale. There once was a boy who was born of a well-to-do family in a well-to-do town in a well-to-do culture. This boy made ample use of a devoted servant by the simple employment of finger gestures and inarticulate sounds. In time, the boy's requests grew and grew as did the range of challenging and unenjoyable obligations encumbered by the servant. By young adulthood, this pandered-to lad had grown exceptionally indolent, bored, and incompetent. He spent most days idly lying about his room, comfortably—even if rather feebly—tucked into bed, and his self-willed enfeeblement grew worse and worse. Those assigned to serve him would fetch his meals and bring him an endless assortment of new entertainments for his enjoyment. On special occasions, two additional servants would attend so that the one could fan the boy while the other would feed him decorticated grapes. At such times, the young man dreamt that an endlessly fascinating entertainment would be brought to him one day. But as might have been foreseen, frustrations deepened. The thoroughly enfeebled boy grew tired of entertainments he'd already seen, and he also disliked any entertainments that were, as he said, "not enjoyable *right now*." And so, all of the activities and crafts which might have compelled him from his nest, involvements such as: painting, basketball, playing the guitar, Latin, whittling, tennis, chess, yoga, juggling, study, etc., all were quickly dismissed because they were not entertaining on the first lesson. After years of passing time so idly, the young man's atrophy was profound. In contrast, his servant had grown strong through continuously meeting the boy's many challenging demands and he, after winning a scholarship, decided that he was *right now* ready to go off to college.

In a state of desperation, the frail young man struggled across the room, found his cell-phone and hired a new servant. And so went the story of the pathetic well-to-do young man: never able to leap and dance, he neither studies philosophy nor does he ponder mathematical paradoxes; he neither ruminates over ancient proverbs nor does he laugh and cry with the artists of the ages. Spending his time pandering to an all-too-immediate self, he failed to create a self worth wanting. He forever remained he who never became more than he already was.

Conclusion: Study as a Way of Life

As some cultural critics mourn the passing of literacy and others try to resurrect it from the dead, I, for one, join those who recognize the death sentence as prematurely declared. All hope is not lost. The larger task ahead is to recover and re-enliven the sense that living itself is an art and that serious study is one of the richest resources for continued self-growth and development in that art.

If the ends of university study are growth and development in capacities for life-long learning, then no product is ever delivered. Eric Hoffer reminds us: "...it is 'the *learners*' who will inherit the world, for 'the *learned*' inherit a world that increasingly no longer exists."[10] As the French novelist Antoine de Saint-Exupéry (1950) writes, "You sometimes hear a man flaunting his past. 'I am he who has done this or that.' I am quite willing to do honor to such a man, but on the condition that he is dead." We are never done, never completed. It's not what we've read that nourishes our soul but what we are now reading (or continue to pore over). To be a learner is to be without arrival; it is to be on a path such that the path itself is the destination.

We humanize ourselves when we study, for study is the self-activity by which we relate to others and thereby become ourselves. To study is to take seriously the promise that minds, even the minds of others who now are dead, can grow into one's own mind. To study a great mind is one of the most intimate acts in which we can engage. It is to risk becoming transformed, and this is so different than looking at tabloids or browsing the Web to inform ourselves about items and changes of the day.[11] To study, to genuinely and authentically get in the learning mode, is to celebrate a free time worth wanting. It is to develop the life-habits whereby we learn to find the time to sit in a quiet place and grow.

Endnotes to Chapter 2

1 I wish to thank, and dedicate this essay to, Valerie V. Peterson. She not only greatly assisted by way of extensive editing and proofreading, the work itself congealed out of the many discussions we have had about teaching, learning, and study. I also wish to thank Anthony Thompson for his assistance in the final stages.

2 The even more ironic posture appears in the "humanistic social sciences" where people not only assume to leave themselves unaffected by their self-understandings but they also take themselves to be the objects of inquiry.

3 Once students graduate, everything they say is, in some way, associated with their Alma Mater. I so vividly remember some of Jill Hutchins' rants. I was completing research for my Master's thesis on athletics and Hutchins was the coach for Illinois State University's Lady Redbirds. At various points through the season, she would say to them: "When you

step on another campus you stand as delegates and representatives of Illinois State University. If I see or hear anyone act other than exemplary, if you appear unsportsmanlike-like, or use foul language, you will be benched. Everything you do, how you come off, is a statement on your university. Be great out there." Graduates are henceforth delegates and ambassadors of the university. They have a responsibility to live up to the name. If, when talking to people, they say things that are bright, articulate, and useful, people will ask, "Where did you get your education?" And if, when talking to people, they say things that are dull, inarticulate and misguided, people will ask, "Where did you get your education?"

4 As some parents seem willing to pay for an intractable learner to "get" a degree, we can only wonder at what Socrates would have thought about trying to teach people who themselves are not even willing to pay.

5 A high school mentality is such that you should be able to do your homework, and if your homework is done correctly, you deserve an A. This is so different from a university mentality: here the homework is never complete; one should always be asking for additional readings. In an unpublished manuscript, Lee Thayer provides useful discussion of saturating the learning environment. He thus expresses a bit of skepticism regarding the desirability of identifying 100% of the content of a course and then attempting to deliver over that 100% to 100% of the students. This is perhaps acceptable to some degree for some kinds of instruction, but for classes such as human communication theory, media studies, and the humanities broadly sketched this is highly misguided. I remember too when someone asked Thayer about what was needed to earn an A in the class. He responded by saying, "Oh, that's an easy one. Don't worry about it. Simply be head-and-shoulders above everyone else in the class--and I mean clearly stand out as superior--and then, if an A is distributed, you can be sure that you're the person who got it."

6 In class I sometimes open the lecture on this essay by setting up the following scenario: imagine that you have a 13 and 15 year-old at home and they're going to have some friends over for the night, and that you are going to be away for the evening until late. Now, also imagine that you trust your kids and have a great relationship with them, and what is more, you have a large and well-stocked liquor cabinet. The question is: do you lock the liquor cabinet? Students, commonly taking the obvious bait, quickly reply that to lock it would be too distrusting. The essay, on the contrary, seems to imply the following bit of advice: Lock the cabinet. If you do, you can explain to your children that you do not want to leave them without an easy explanation to their peers. If someone tried to "pressure" them, they can always respond, "It might be fun but the cabinet is locked."

7 How about we imaginatively consider a comparison between two kinds of professors: a professor who assumes a role similar to a travel-agent/tour-guide and a professor who assumes a role similar to a mountaineer/ expedition-leader. The former wants people to get a good deal, have a safe, and well-packaged tour. The tour guide feels obligated to ensure that the customer is satisfied and enjoying the trip. The latter is someone who scales mountains and is willing to help those who are qualified and committed to the task. It is about organizing a group experience of great aesthetic accomplishment. It is perhaps worth noting that nestled within both of these metaphors is another metaphor: text as physical space. Admittedly, this does help to offset the unfortunate reduction of reading to the act of "information transfer." If we commonly think of texts as containers that are more or less transparent to the ideas they contain and transmit, we can imagine information transfer to be the issue. But what if we take the metaphor of a "A text is a city." To travel to a new city, say one where we'll be staying at least a few days perhaps even a few weeks or months, there is a long time of "getting to know the place," also phrased as "learning one's way around." We may come to build up an internal map of the city, having a sense of what is there, where one's favorite restaurants are, where there are places to rest and enjoy the scenery. In general, we come to know a city by spending some time in it: driving through it, walking around within it, getting a sense of what is available, where it is, and how to get there. All of this takes some time, and in fact, at first it is easy to get lost, be confused, and travel up and down the same road. In many ways, then, to study a text is to attempt to become familiar with a city. It is to spend time in there, walking through its many streets. Any text that someone has a solid command over has grown familiar in the same ways that the city is familiar to a native urbanite. This so helps to explain entailments such as:

> "I was lost in that book."
> "The text took many unexpected turns."
> "It was hard to make it through that article."

8 The chieftain in Antoine Saint-Exupéry's magnum opus *The Wisdom of the Sands*, writes, "If you would learn to understand men, begin by never listening to them."

9 There are many fronts of the "stick it to myself" under the auspice of sticking it others. Some people overeat at lunch buffets all the while they believe that they are sticking it to someone. Some students try to "skate through" by doing as little as possible. A primer for this is Dan Greenburg's humorous book, *How to Make Yourself Miserable*.

10 On another front this should turn us to the importance of solid study of communication theory. As Robert M. Hutchins, in *The Learning Society*, tells us: "The more technological the society is, the more rapidly it will change and the less valuable ad hoc instruction will become. It now seems safe to say that the most practical education is the most theoretical one" (p. 19).

11 William Carlos Williams writes, "It is difficult to get the news from poems, yet men die miserably everyday for lack of what is found there."

Part II:

Explorations in General Semantics

"A fundamental difference between 'man' and 'animal' is found in the fact that a man can be conscious of abstracting, and an animal cannot. This last statement could be reformulated: that animals are 'unconscious of abstracting.' Now consciousness of abstracting is not inborn as a rule, but becomes a semantic reaction acquired only by education or through very long, and usually painful, experience in evaluation...The world of the animal, as well as of man, represents nothing else than the structural results of abstracting, without which life itself would be totally impossible. Man alone has the power of extending the orders of abstraction indefinitely...In building a $\bar{A}$-system, we have to stress *differences*, build a 'non-system' on 'non-allness,' and reject identity." (Alfred Korzybski, *Science and Sanity*, pp. 500, 507, 514)

Chapter 3: Playing with Bateson: Denotation, Logical Types, and Analog and Digital Communication[1]

"Let me put it to you like this:
We live in a universe of namables.
Within that universe we make classes.
Let me here make the class of chairs.
I now want you quickly, without thinking too much about it,
to name for me some of the 'not chairs.'
You have suggested 'tables,' 'dogs,' 'people,' 'autos.'
Let me suggest one now: 'tomorrow.'
Does it make you a little uncomfortable
when I say tomorrow is not a chair?"
— *Bateson, 1956, p. 145*

"My personal interest in the abstract problem of play
is a desire to know about those processes
whereby organisms pull themselves up by their bootstraps."
— *Bateson, 1956, p. 216*

Setting the Stage[2]

In his essay "A Theory of Play and Fantasy," Gregory Bateson (1955 [1972]) argues that an important evolutionary event occurred when some creatures, specifically humans, became able to take their signs "as signs." His point is that humans talk about talk, and in doing so, can call it into question. In fuller bloom this implies that we can advance formulated propositions (or even gainsay propositions) about what is or what is not. Bateson notes that such denotative utterances always operate on "many levels of abstraction" (Bateson, 1955 [1972], p. 179). The levels he refers to range from "metacommunicative" references (for example, "I am telling you the truth" or "You are taking me too seriously") to "metalinguistic" references (for example, "The word 'cat' does not have whiskers" or "2+2=4 is a true statement"). Even more broadly characterized, Bateson's essay on play and fantasy intends to "illustrate a stage of evolution--the drama precipitated when organisms, having eaten from the Tree of Knowledge, discover that their signals are signals" (Bateson, 1955 [1972], p. 179). Bateson elsewhere echoes this underlying orientation where he states,

> I became interested in the whole problem of play through realizing
> that there must have been an extraordinary step in the evolution of
> communication...It seemed to me that when the human species ate
> of the fruit of the Tree of Knowledge, it discovered that automatic
> signs could be turned into signals and emitted with conscious or
> unconscious purpose. With that discovery, of course, also came the
> possibility of deceit, and all sorts of other possibilities. (1956, pp.
> 157-158)

Obviously, then, Bateson suggests that denotative messages, messages which bear propositional content, are unique to human language and are an evolutionary achievement. They are *different from* other types of communication, but one for which we can find the evolutionary rudiments within mammalian play. Bateson thus backgrounds the evolutionary development from animal signals to humans' denotative utterances by asking us to consider first an "intermediate" stage: play. In his orientation toward play, he is not merely addressing theoretical difficulties associated with all sorts of framing behaviors including that class of behavior called "playing."[3] Although Bateson was interested in the emergence of classes of behavior, in how different organisms codify their environments, and especially, in how organisms exchanged and understood metacommunicative messages, all these interests nevertheless fit into his more overarching concern: how humanity (specifically denotative utterances and human epistemologies) became evolutionarily possible.

In this essay I bring out the relevance of Bateson's ideas on play to contemporary communication theory. His work contributes to the growing debates on epistemology, representationalism, and post-semiotic conceptions of language. In the wake of John Stewart's (1995, 1996) recent criticisms of "two-world hypotheses," Bateson's insights regarding the evolutionary emergence of denotative utterances offer needed considerations and give instructive further direction. Bateson's ideas well accommodate for the sense desired by two-world hypotheses without sacrificing the constitutive character of language, and his thinking furthers non-representational approaches to communication without falling into overly textual post-modernist conceptions, or overly idealist social-constructionist ones (cf. Stewart, 1995, 1996). He offers an ontology of human speech, one which blurs the distinction between communication and epistemology without falling into either naive realism or idealistic nominalism.

This paper is divided into two sections. The first section, "Playing with Bateson," highlights key points in Bateson's (1955 [1972]) essay, "A Theory of Play and Fantasy." I here integrate two concepts from his writings: first, the relation as well as difference between "analog communication" and "digital communication," second, the importance of studying processes of abstraction. The second section of the paper, "'These are Un-Speakable Complexities,' I Said," illustrates the nettlesome character of the paradoxes of abstraction. I try to demonstrate Bateson's insight that humans can "know" that their signals are signals and yet, more often than not, syntactically "forget" their status as human creations. Subtle syntactical magic, linguistic conjuring through the use of the word "not," operates below and within our epistemologies, constituting the very "objects" of those epistemologies. Thus, the denotative aspects of language embody what Bateson, for the purposes of discussion, calls an "onionskin" (See Figure 1). And, the paradoxes of abstraction are the fundamental processes whereby humans, as Bateson nicely puts it, "pull themselves up by their bootstraps" (Bateson, 1956, p. 216).

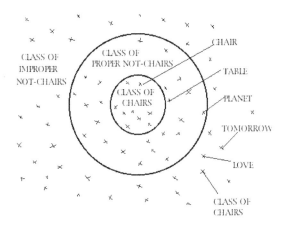

CHAIR

CLASS OF
IMPROPER
NOT-CHAIRS

CLASS OF
PROPER NOT-CHAIRS

CLASS OF
CHAIRS

TABLE

PLANET

TOMORROW

LOVE

CLASS OF
CHAIRS

Figure 1 : Onionskin

Playing with Bateson

Bateson recounts that his original insights occurred while he watched monkeys at the Fleishhacker Zoo. The young primates seemed to be playing with each other, implying that they were sending metacommunicative messages about their interactions; they were signaling that their actions were not fighting. Bateson initially attempted to clarify this complex issue by suggesting that: "The playful nip denotes the bite, but it does not denote what would be denoted by the bite" (Bateson, 1955 [1972], p. 180). Further delineating this idea, Bateson writes, "The statement, 'this is play' looks something like this: 'These actions in which we now engage do not denote what those actions for which they stand would denote'" (Bateson, 1955 [1972], p. 180). But this is not to say that we consistently distinguish between these levels. In fact, the borders of metacommunicative frames such "play" or "pretend" commonly slip and slide ambiguously around, and this increasingly is the case, as Bateson points out, in the frame, "Is this play?". Moreover, serious difficulties emerged within Bateson's initial attempt at clarification.

Bateson claims that he subtly committed what he has chosen to call a "logical typing" error: the phrase "nip denotes the bite" and the phrase "what would be denoted by the bite" both use the word "denote" but do so in very different senses. They (nip and bite) refer to different orders of abstraction, and, he argues, paradoxes of abstraction occur if we conflate this difference. It is here, precisely, that the difficulties in following Bateson's thinking become most pronounced. In fact, in a critical doctoral dissertation John Moran takes pains to demonstrate that Bateson's argument, from a strictly logical analysis, generates neither paradox nor even a violation of Russell's Theory of Logical Types. Moran's well informed account shows that Bateson's uses of the Theory of Logical Types are too loose, too imprecise, and too incomplete. Regarding Bateson's discussion of the differences between the meanings of the word "denote," Moran writes,

> The simple fact that two different senses of a word occur in an expression does not violate the Theory of Logical Types...the two senses of "denote" in Bateson's expanded version of "this is play" are perfectly valid and admissible...Bateson, then, does not demonstrate that "this is play" generates paradox of "Russellian or Epimenidies types." (Moran 1979, p. 76)

Moran's account is both accurate and clear, and yet, it unfortunately underestimates Bateson's overall concerns. Moran correctly takes both "nip" and "bite" as words which refer and which can be made subject to strictly logical analysis. This makes some sense at first but less so if we stick closely to Bateson's own goals. When Bateson talks about the relation of the nip to the bite, claiming that the nip is at a higher order of abstraction, we should not forgetfully take both as simply words referring to different, "already given," classes of action in the world. Bateson, on the contrary, is trying to address something much more complicated than this: how such propositional referring (i.e. a denotative utterance) becomes at all possible. He wants us to consider developments necessary for propositional language to emerge as a possibility. Quite paradoxically, Bateson must use language in his attempt to talk about how it emerged, and such framing by abstraction precipitates an ineradicable slipperiness. Bateson, for example, states,

> Human beings have evolved the 'metaphor that is meant,' the flag which men will die to save, the sacrament that is felt to be more than 'an outward and visible sign, given unto us.' Here we can recognize an attempt to deny the difference between map and territory, and to get back to the absolute innocence of communication by means of pure mood-signs. (Bateson,1955 [1972], p. 183)

Although Bateson here focuses upon particular examples, he is not characterizing rare and occasional occurrences, something that happens every once and a while. Not at all; language itself *is* the "metaphor that is meant." Consider an almost too simple case: A toddler asks, "What is an apple?" I might go into a refrigerator and pull one out. Handing it to the child, I say, "This is an apple." Notice the naturalness of the expression, "This is an apple." Still, later in life the child will learn that "apple" is a noun in the English language. Indeed, we seem to make sense of the illustration that "*this* is an apple," even though apple is but a word. Other than general semanticists, most people don't worry about such everyday oddities, and yet, this smacks of the paradoxical mystery Bateson tried to bring into explicit clarity.

To advance Bateson's concerns, as well as clarify the logic behind his argument, we need to recognize the differences between bite and nip as differences between "analog" communication and rudimentary "digital" communication.[4] As I will try to make clearer, the bite neither affirms nor denies because it is not *about* anything; it simply is what it is. "The bite" is continuous with all other movements and thereby remains installed in the non-repeatable once-occurrent context. It is an analog moment of mood-signs, the signs which are its relations [and hence, we have been making category mistakes as we have called it "it"]. On the other hand, the meaning of the term "denote," as applied to the playful nip, means something akin to "signifies" or "refers to." The nip, therefore, is metacommunicative to an original relation, and so play, metaphorically considered, resembles the seminal structure of denotative utterances. The differences here are well summarized as: "A digital code is 'outside' the sender and receiver and mediates their relationship; an analog code IS the relationship" (Wilden, 1972, p. 173). This implies first that the propositional content within acts of speech is necessarily of a different logical type than that to which it refers. Second, the propositional aspects of language operate with logical types. Third and finally, because we habitually and forgetfully pass-over the difference between differences and distinctions (and also conflate distinctions between logical types), opportunities abound for what Bateson called the "paradoxes of abstraction." As Bateson summatively states, "The message, 'This is play,'…represents a rudimentary beginning at least of what we call an onionskin structure" (Bateson, 1956, p. 158).

Analog and Digital Communication

My analysis of analog and digital communication draws heavily upon Anthony Wilden's chapter "Analog and Digital Communication: On Negation, Signification, and Meaning," from his excellent *System and Structure*. Wilden's reads of Bateson's work (Bateson and Jackson, 1968 [1964]) lay out the wide range of issues at stake, and, his tables of the analogic and digital aspects of communication are worth careful consideration (also see Watzlawick, Beavin, and Jackson 1967).

Most broadly addressed, analog communication includes all events and actions which are irrevocably contextualized within irreducibly concrete and once-occurrent (i.e. non-repeatable, non-decomposable) situations (cf. Bakhtin, 1993). Analog communication registers *differences within* existing relation-states according to actual goal-seeking. An endless array of examples could be offered to illustrate analog communication: as we move, the perceived though unmeasured distances that continuously change between ourselves and the rest of the surround, pressing a foot upon an accelerator pedal, disentangling an intricately snarled knot, watching the visible growth of a balloon, the specific actions which comprise any athletic sport, and most generally, non-linguistic communication through the senses (between organisms or between organism and environment). And even speech, it must be observed, always holds much that is analogic, much which cannot be weaned from its original context of occurrence (e.g. there is always a certain volume, a certain intonation, and a certain rate, etc.). Thus, analog communication operates within all behavior, all action, all haptic spatio-temporal arrangement of material conditions, and as an ineradicable emotive underbelly to the spoken word (cf. Bateson, 1966 [1972]). It meaningfully regards and manages those *differences within* existing relation-states.

In all of these diverse cases of analog communication, *there are no differing levels of abstraction, and so, there are neither classes nor different logical types.* We find only concretely situated differences within existing (i.e. once-occurrent) relation-states. These aspects of our communication remain without definite gaps, holes, or discrete boundaries; all differences occur within and along continuous and contiguous positive values. This means that there is no equivalent to "not," even if we could find the rudiments of a kind of negation in acts of refusal or withdrawal. Analog communication, given its dense concreteness, is *not* denotative and is *not* propositional (cf. Watzlawick, Beavin and Jackson (1967, p. 101). Moreover, syntax and temporal tenses, such as are provided by language (e.g. the prepositional phrase, the future conditional, the perfect past) are wholly absent. All registered relations, as always fully what they are, remain submersively within the present and within infinitely thick prepositional possibilities. Because language isolates, delineates, and basically delimits, any uttered prepositional phrase is a selection from infinite other prepositional possibilities which thereby are down-played or even ignored. For example, a cup is never only "on" the table. It also is "next to" the computer, "behind" the mouse-pad, to the "left" of the window," "in front of" the wall, "under" the ceiling, "above" the floor, "inside" the office, "diagonal to" the wastebasket, etc. Additionally, analog communication seems without the capacity for communicating *about* itself; this level of communication is not "*self*-reflexive." Clearly, a disapproving frown or a particular vocal tone can metacommunicatively 'frame' a linguistic statement. Still, analog communication is not reflexive to itself. Analog differences, it must be remembered, are too concretely situated for such ideal free-play; they cannot be selected out and brought into "proposed" combinations, short of actual spatial-temporal alterations. As having no gaps, no holes, no lines separating distinct "things," there are merely differences *within* continuity. Thus, I cannot by way of analog communication show that I am one thing and the world is something else; all is within concrete once-occurrent installment in the analog. Ultimately, because analog communication is not denotative and is void of propositions, we can characterize it most tightly by saying that it *is* the regard and management of *differences within* relation-states.

Whereas the analogic aspects of communication meaningfully manage concretely installed differences within actual once-occurrent relation-states, the digital aspects register *differences between* relation-states, and thereby, seem to render discrete *distinctions* (i.e. classes, types or essences) which are thereby iso-latable and detachable from their dense analogic installment. Digitalization transcends the dense continuity of analog differences. In fact, we digitalize analog aspects of speech by merely being able to hear spoken *words* out of the analogic qualities of voice. The digital aspects of speech rely equally upon eidetic gaps in acoustical continuities and the syntactical synthesis that meaningfully combines distinctions. Moreover, distinctions increasingly can be recognized at higher and higher levels of abstraction (e.g. cat, mammal, organism; table, furniture, object, etc.). Thus, not only are the differences within analog sounds transcended to register words (e.g. discrete lexical things), but also, words, given syntax, become the condition for punctuating any analog continuum within scaffolded hierarchies of abstraction (e.g. within classes and categories). With the digital aspects of communication we can isolate and delimit, contextualize and analyze.

Digital aspects of speech (i.e. linguistic *distinctions*) are spontaneously and pre-reflectively managed according to the principles of substitution and combination (e.g. phoneme, word, and phrase selection).[5] "Selection (the relation of similarity) and combination (the relation of contiguity)—the metaphoric and metonymic ways—are considered by Jakobson to be the two most fundamental linguistic operations whether at the level of the phonemes (like the *Fort! Da!*) or at the level of sentamemes or words" (Wilden, 1968, p. 245). Granting both selection and combination, we should not imagine language as a collection of word-things which are consciously and thematically selected from, nor should we imagine that pre-existing words are reflectively brought into combination with one another. Rather, denotative speech is an emergent digitalization. It occurs atop a more primary digitalization, the one by which we transcend differences within once-occurrent relation-states—including the very sounding of acoustical differences. Maurice Merleau-Ponty addresses these issues within his general phenomenology of speaking. He writes,

> Speaking is possessing language as a principle of distinction, whatever number of signs it permits us to specify…In other words, the linguistic value of each word is defined only through the presence or absence of the words surrounding it…Moreover, the words and very forms for an analysis of this kind soon appear to be secondary realities, the results of a more originary differentiation. The syllables and letters, the turns of phrase, and the word endings are the sediments of a primary differentiation which, this time, precedes without any doubt the relation of sign to signification, since it is what makes the very distinction of signs possible. The phonemes, too, which are the real foundations of speech, since they are reached through the analysis of spoken language and have no official existence in grammar and dictionaries, by themselves mean nothing one can specify. But for this very reason, they represent the originary form of signifying. They bring us into the presence of that primary operation, beneath institutionalized language, that creates the simultaneous possibilities of significations and discrete signs. (1969 [1973], pp. 32-33)

Utterances bearing propositional content occur as we transcend the eventful gesticulations of analog differences to apprehend digital distinctions at higher levels of abstraction. Furthermore, linguistic distinctions (i.e. signifiers) are brought into syntactical combination with others and thereby enable signification more broadly applied; with digital aspects of speech we can state propositions *about* differences within relation-states.

Distinctions (i.e. classes or types) require boundaries, and, boundaries require the "not." In other words, we classify by inclusion (what is to be regarded as within the class) and by exclusion (what is *not* to be taken as a member of the class). And the "not," as already implied, can be found only at the level of digital communication. Moreover, we should not assume that the "not" is merely one sign among others, just one more word. Such an assumption distorts or even obfuscates how the "not" functions syntactically: it is a metacommunicative rule for introducing gaps into analog continuums. Wilden stresses the importance of the *syntactical* "not" where he states,

We have to distinguish the syntactical "not" of a digital statement from

> the commonsense idea that negation is equivalent to the absence
> of something, to nothing, or to absence in general...It seems that
> saying "not" about some possibility or concept or state of affairs is a
> logical operation of a different logical type from that which relates
> two statements (etc.) by exclusion. "Not" is in a metalinguistic re-
> lationship to what it negates...In other words, boundaries are the
> condition of distinguishing the "elements" of a continuum from the
> continuum itself. "Not" is such a boundary...In number theory, set
> theory, and language, "zero," "ø," and "not" are the rules for punc-
> tuating boundaries. "Not" is of a higher logical type than zero or ø,
> if only because it is the logical prerequisite for zero or ø. (Wilden,
> 1972, pp. 184-186; 188)

The "not," therefore, is *essential* to the digital aspects of speech. Such negativity
operates at a different level of abstraction than that which it negates; it is similar
to the "line" that enables us to see that a figure is *not* its background, or to the
space disclosing that one word is not another. The syntactical "not" thus holds the
necessary requirements for introducing distinctions into analog continuums, and
even more significantly, for using those distinctions within asserted propositions.
We create the possibility of employing logical types within a moving hierarchy of
abstractions.

　　We can say, as Bateson pointed out, that a table is not a chair, and moreover, that the class of chairs is itself not a chair. But it is also the "not," Bateson
suggests, that leads to logical typing errors. When Bateson began his 1956 discussion with the question, "Does it make you a little uncomfortable when I say that
tomorrow is not a chair?," (1956, p.145) he was trying to illustrate that the syntactical "not" can be used in radically different senses (see Figure 1). We can use
it when speaking of those namables ("proper non-members") that are the ground
for the members of a class, and secondly, we can use the word to speak of all of
those namables ("improper non-members") which are not so much the ground
for the class as are of a wholly different logical type. In the course of that group
discussion, Bateson demonstrates that saying "tomorrow is not a chair," even if it
is a violation of the Theory of Logical Types, may make a kind of sense. In fact,
and this is a critical point, it makes no less sense than the claim that the class of
chairs is not a chair, no less sense than saying that the word "chair" is not a chair.

　　To speak is to categorically delimit the continuity and contiguity of analog
continuums. By selection, combination, and negation of distinctions, we condi-
tionally delimit the indefatigable density--the once-occurrent concreteness--and
thereby can signify *particular* relation-states. Taking the infinity of prepositional
possibilities, speech introduces boundaries; it punctuates relation-states at higher
orders of abstraction. We digitally codify concrete contexts and therein disclose
categorical apprehensions (i.e. things as *in* classes). Given this, we can systematically imagine how "things" are and could be related. In stark contrast, we should
recall that the analogic elements of communication can manage only concrete,
actually present differences within relation-states. Digitalization transcends such
installment in sensory immediacy.

　　Denotative utterances depend upon digital distinctions; they require classes or essences, idealities that cannot be concretely installed in "real" space and time (Anton, 2002, 2001). This means that words *qua signification* do not have an actual (i.e. empirically concrete) spatial nor temporal location.[6] They are not installed within the concrete nexus of analog continuums. Erving Goffman well addresses this issue where he writes, "And among all the things of this world, information is the hardest to guard, since it can be stolen without removing it" (1967, pp. 78-79). As a more direct illustration, consider the following two sentences: "Apples are my favorite fruit." And, now, "Apples is a word in English." Why do we change the verb to a singular when talking about the word, "apples?" Surely, millions of people have used the word, and yet, it remains as one, singular. Would it even make any sense to say that there is a certain word that has not been used by more than one person (not even *heard* by more than one) and which has been used only once by that person? Would this even be a word? The sticking point is that speech can make statements bearing propositional content (it can signify) because the realities it draws upon (digital distinctions) have no concrete spatial nor temporal location; they are classes and/or types, objects which can be found only in abstraction (Anton, 2002). Again: such realities exist only at the level of digital distinctions, and as such, these cannot be found at the level of analog differences.

Some Examples

We continually use both analog and digital communication. We integrate and coordinate these different aspects of the whole communication process. We switch between and translate across, often without explicit awareness of how we are able to do what we do. Consider, as an initial illustration, an unmarked stereo volume knob. The knob provides a continuous adjustment in volume and allows one to make "more or less" of it. At a certain point, we might actually speak the words, "The sound is too loud," that is, "It is *not* quiet enough." This kind of sense-making (a spoken proposition) exemplifies how we can digitalize an analog continuum of differences. Taking the sheer differences in "more or less" sound, we, at a higher level of abstraction, propose an "either/or categorization." Employing digital distinctions to express the proposition, we can claim that it is "loud," which also signifies "not quiet." Notice that the actual sound, at whatever specific volume, *is neither denotative nor propositional*. We should grant that two individuals can "dispute" the sound level silently. For example, each adjusts the knob in one direction only to have the other person adjust the knob in the other direction. Here, without saying a word, two people can seem to disagree over the level of sound. Nevertheless, the actual volume always and simply is what it is, and, as should be apparent, only propositions *about* it can be asserted or denied. This helps to further illustrate Wilden's claim that, "Because the analog does not possess the syntax necessary…one can *refuse* or *reject* in the analog, but one cannot *deny* or *negate*" (1972, p. 163).

Consider, as a second example, a large room filled with 100 round balloons, each of which is a different size and a different shade of blue. In such a room we immediately perceive and register these differences; we see them instantly. If asked, we may be able to arrange the balloons in sequenced orders according to size or shade. Still, our semantic resources for "talking about" such differences, thereby employing linguistic distinctions, are quite limited. For size, we are mostly limited to tiny, small, medium, large, huge, and, of course bigger than or smaller than. With regard to color, few persons have lexical resources to name over twenty shades of blue, even though hundreds of shades can be visually discriminated. Additionally, it is over which names are to be given to which size and shade that we would most likely argue, not which are larger or smaller, nor which shades are lighter or darker. Indeed, speakers of radically different languages could reasonably agree upon size and shade arrangements, though their respective resources for talking about these kinds of differences could vary greatly. This shows how analog communication is rich in "semantic" meaning, yet this can remain ambiguous when we attempt to signify it (i.e. speak about it).

To conclude this discussion of the analogic and digital aspects of communication, consider a final example. Imagine a series of ten large identical documents. Each page of each document holds complex line marks that closely resemble the others. Now also imagine that the pages are in a definite sequence and are designed to remain in that particular order. So far, this is not too different from any document collated according to page numbers. But this set of texts has a unique form of "pagination."

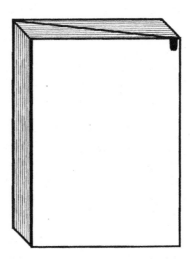

Figure 2. An Analogic Attempt at Pagination

Figure 2. An Analogic Attempt at Pagination depicts a top and side view of one document from the collection. Rather than standard pagination (page numbers on each page), the document is "notched and branded" from front to back diagonally across the top of the pages.

Each page now noticeably holds a unique relationship to the others. Given such markings, if we accidentally were to drop the document, we would have some means of placing the pages back into their intended sequence; we could gain the needed sense of seriality for the task. Nevertheless, each page remains held in relation to contiguous others. These are analog differences not digital distinctions. Each text is a series of *differences within continuity*. Consider how situated and imbedded this kind of contiguous relation remains. Individual pages, although they can be placed into their intended order, cannot be referred to independently. They are not, in Dewey's words, "liberated from local and accidental contexts," and so, at this level, they are not "subject to ideal experimentation" (1925 [1988], p. 132). Thus, traditional pagination, as a mode of digitalization, offers much more power for organization and interaction. Given the capacities of digital communication (i.e. the functions of substitution, combination, and negation), we can *signify* relations rather than manually, actually, arrange them. For example, we now can cite any individual page. We also can say how each could be related to any other (e.g. which ones are *not* contiguous with each other). Moreover, we easily and quickly could turn to the same page on different copies. Even though both establish relations between pages and operate with a kind of "identity," traditional pagination uses discrete *distinctions* rather than relational *differences*. Said otherwise, page numbers, as digital distinctions, are fundamentally *about* something. They operate as discrete signifiers and so generate self-standing pages, *things*, meaning that each and any page can be referred to in isolation.

These brief examples demonstrate how the analogic aspects of communication are installed in the "once-occurrent non-repeatable context," whereas the digital aspects of communication operate with abstract classes, repeatable essences. We found that the difference between analog *meaning* and digital *signification* helps delineate the differences between what Wilden calls, "concrete goal-seeking" and "denotation and concept-transferal," respectively. Thus, only the digital aspects of communication are propositional and, as about something, are thereby capable of being asserted or denied.

Analog and Digital in Review

Wilden's analysis of Bateson's work on play and fantasy directively summarizes the present discussion:

> It is possible to see animal play as a primordial metacommunication--in the strict sense of a MESSAGE ABOUT A MESSAGE--of a different logical type, about the analog communication of fighting. In play, the nip is the METONYMIC SIGN of the bite (part for the whole), but not the bite itself (which is a signal). Whereas the bite is what it is, the nip represents what it is not. The nip signifies the absence AND the presence of the bite...The introduction of the second-level sign into a world of first-level signs and signals detaches communication from existence as such and paves the way for the arbitrary combination of discrete elements in the syntagm. It is thus a discovery of difference at a higher level of communication or organization... Once the digital signal or sign (a distinction) has been constituted out of a world of analog differences, the way is open for the linguistic signifier (which must be digital in form). The amorphous domain of play provides a sort of bridge to conceptualize the digitalization of the analog which is the necessary condition for language. (1972, pp. 172-173)

We, unfortunately, all too often fail to regard the radical difference in logical type between analog differences and digital distinctions. In fact, the scope of Bateson's considerations remains difficult to grasp because the bite is intended to be taken as lower in abstraction than the nip, and yet, both verbal expressions, "bite," and "nip," are much higher in abstraction than that which Bateson was trying to address. Wilden accounts for this slipperiness, the slipperiness that inheres in trying to talk about how talk became possible, by arguing that natural language is a kind of "double articulation." This is, what he calls "second-level digitalization,"[7] or more specifically, the employment of "linguistic signifiers." He suggests that natural language, "is the level of double articulation (duality of patterning) and negation. It is capable of taking over or replacing the analog in terms of both form and function" (Wilden, 1972, p. 165). It is here, with Wilden's concept of double articulation, that Bateson's point regarding the logical type difference of the term "denote" (regarding the "nip" and the "bite") can be explained most effectively.

If we try to adhere to the logic of Bateson's insights, there is no discrete "thing" such as "the bite" within analog communication. Without classifications made possible through digitalization, analog differences remain locally installed and once-occurrent (not yet grasped categorically). Thus we make errors of abstraction by simply using articles such as "an," "a," or "the" in characterizing any "moment" or "part" of analog continuums; to do so is to treat the moment or part as if it were in a class of acts rather than concretely what it is. We confuse the ongoing flow of continuous and contiguous relation-states with symbolic combinations of discrete distinctions. Wilden, once again, nicely summarizes these issues:

> Whereas in the bite, energy and information are one (as in the brake pedal of a car), in the nip the information is distinct from the energy…The world of communication of the bite is full of real differences; with the nip, gaps begin to appear, something akin to the zero-phoneme or to the space between one and two. And whatever else the nip may be, it is NO-THING. The nip begins as a real metonymy (a part for the whole, related by contiguity) and becomes a symbolic metaphor (something standing for something else, related by similarity). (1972, p. 251)

Hence, the nip, as Bateson employs the term, represents the rough evolutionary beginning of the metacommunicative capacities needed for denotative language to emerge. Bateson's actual verbal expressions "the bite" and "the nip" are, therefore, necessarily of a different logical type than that to which he was attempting to refer. Indeed, the degree of abstraction (i.e. degree of difference between energy and information) between these signifiers and what they refer to is vastly greater than the degree of abstraction between what Bateson originally tried to mean by the analogic communication of "bite" and "nip." Said otherwise, what Bateson tried to refer to by the words bite and nip (recall that he was attempting to talk about the conditions necessary for talk to emerge as a possibility) do not appear anywhere on or in the "onionskin," even though we now, by digital distinctions, can speak of the class of behaviors called bites and those called nips. The nip, as he intends it, offers a rudimentary difference of logical type, a difference which becomes the ground upon which an onionskin could become possible.

Alfred Korzybski, father of the General Semantics movement, adamantly maintained that training in "consciousness of abstracting" would lead people beyond the paradoxes of abstraction. In contrast to this belief, Bateson's position continually stresses the inability to achieve this thoroughly. As Bateson states, "Korzybski was, on the whole, speaking as a philosopher, attempting to persuade people to discipline their manner of thinking. But he could not win. When we come to apply his dictum to the natural history of human mental process, the matter is not so simple" (1979, pp. 30-31). Additionally, consider that Bateson elsewhere admits,

> We do not, any of us, achieve rigor. In writing, sometimes, we can take time to check the looseness of thought; but in speaking, hardly ever...I know that I personally, when speaking in conversation and even in lecturing, depart from the epistemology outlined in the previous chapter; and indeed the chapter itself was hard to write without continual lapses into other ways of thinking and may still contain such lapses. I know that I would not like to be held scientifically responsible for many loose spoken sentences that I have uttered in conversation with scientific colleagues. But I also know that if another person had the task of studying my ways of thought, he would do well to study my loosely spoken words rather than my writing. (1968, p. 230)

Toward the end of his career Bateson argued that, "It seems to be a universal feature of human perception, a feature of the underpinning of human epistemology, that the perceiver shall perceive only the product of his perceiving act. He shall not perceive the means by which that product was created" (Bateson, 1977, p. 238). We take that which emerges only because of digitalization as if it were merely discovered "in" analog continuums. We simultaneously use and then forget about our linguistic resources. But, if we did not forgetfully confuse logical types, we would not get lost in novels, we could not suspend our disbelief within movies, we would remain unable to recognize the genre of any utterance, and ultimately, we never would have been able to take our utterances seriously.

"These are Un-Speakable Complexities," I Said

Recurrent difficulties occur whenever we try to talk about the relations between words and things, or between language and the world, or between the verbal and the nonverbal (i.e. whenever and wherever we conflate the difference (and distinction) between analog differences and digital distinctions). But similiar difficulties occur throughout the scaffolded hierarchies of logical types within digital communication. In such cases we purchase sense through the use of higher and higher abstractions, and all the while we seem to presume that our subject matter becomes less abstract. The difficulty here, Bateson points out, is that, "As soon as sufficient complexity is reached to permit of two or more levels of abstraction, the organism becomes able to treat abstractions of a higher level as though they were equivalent to abstractions of a lower level" (1968a, p. 191; also cf. Bateson, 1968b [1972]). This especially seems to be the case because we so quickly and forgetfully employ "metalinguistic" terms (cf. Anton, 1998). Therefore, we take the syntactical redundancy that emerges from our use of overlapping reference on multiple levels of abstraction as if this enabled empirically sound statements regarding things independent of language. We easily forget that what can appear to be an empirical statement (e.g. how the verbal relates to the nonverbal), is, in fact, a linguistic redundancy created by syntactically combining, in an overlapping reference, differing logical types. By combining multiple levels of abstraction in a given proposition, we become able to make sense of empirical assertions of the naive realist type.

Although full analysis of these pervasive difficulties surpasses the scope of this essay, I here can provide a few heuristic considerations. I begin with Bateson's (1956) lecture/group discussion, published as, "The Message, 'This is Play.'" One of his opening statements is, "We live in a universe of namables." Even if we grant to this proposition its clear and immediate sense, we should observe how subtly it suggests that "we" and "a universe" are not an *already named*. The syntax of the sentence lends the sense that "we" and "a universe" are not yet included within the "namables." It implies that *we* and a *universe* are already given and would be in addition to what is namable.

Second, Korzybski's *Science and Sanity* discusses at length the non-identification between "words" and the "un-speakable objective level," and he succinctly summarizes the general spirit with his pithy one-liner: "Whatever one might *say* something 'is,' it is not" (cf. 1933, p. 409). In this instance, Korzybski's utterance cuts against his insights as he states them. The utterance syntactically implies that the words "something" and "it" are not already something said. Obviously, Korzybski would defend himself and say that this exactly is his point, as he sums it up elsewhere: "It is evident that every time we mistake the object for the event we are making a serious error, and if we further mistake the label for the object, and therefore for the event, our errors become more serious" (Korzybski , 1949, p. 245). Notice the same difficulties again: he uses the words "object" and "event" to state his insights and thereby uses the resources he calls into question; he cannot propose a non-identification--nor call identification into question--without subtly making the mistakes that he wishes to challenge.

Third, Kenneth Burke's essay, "What are the Signs of What: A Theory of Entitlement," offers relevant considerations. Burke suggests that the socio-political order "depends upon the verbal order in a way that the natural order does not" (1966, p. 375). He attempts to clarify what he means by writing,

> If I say "table," and you don't understand me, there is at least the possibility of my using the physical object as the source of communication between us. Or, at once remove, I might show you a picture of a table. But if I say "democracy" or "dictatorship" or "rights" or "crimes" or "obligations," despite the vast institutional backing that such words may come to have, there is no clear "natural" counterpart to the word. (Burke, 1966, p. 375)

A difficulty here is how to make sense of Burke's words "physical object." It would seem that all abstract words for the natural order, words such as "physical" or "object" or "thing" or "entity" or "natural" or "something," likewise depend just as vitally upon the verbal order. How, we might ask Burke, could someone present a picture that means the "'natural' counterpart" of the words "object" or "thing" or "entity"?

Finally, consider this: if asked to clarify what the general semanticists meant by the term "abstraction," we might explain as follows: "To abstract is to classify things according to commonalties. The higher the level of abstraction, the greater and the more diverse are the things within the class; the lower the level of abstraction, the smaller the number and less diverse are things within that class." If this seems a fair account, take a moment to notice its slipperiness. In this definition the word "things" is used as if it refers to what is not already in a class. It seems that we abstract by noting commonalties across things, but such a description pushes from attention the fact that the word "things" refers to what already is classified. Even if we speak of entities that are "not yet" classified, we may lead ourselves to overlook the fact that we already have classified them. In the previous sentence, for example, the words "entities" and "them," if they refer at all, refer to what are already within the class of "entities." Whenever we say what something is called, we can seem to think that the thing thereby referred to is not yet classified, or perhaps identified as eligible for classification. Our sense making, that is, enables us to forget that we already have called it "something" and also "thing." And even here, we likewise may forget that we called the thing "it." And now "thing" again. All said, we slide from one word to another, obliviously taking some to be labels for things while taking others to be things referred to (i.e. not more labels). Indeed, we might further imagine someone trying to explain the term "abstraction" in this way: The person, holding a cup of coffee, states that the thing she is holding and drinking from is *not* a "cup." "'Cup,'" the person then says, "is the English word we use to refer to this thing; the actual thing in my hand is not a 'cup,' but rather, 'cup' is a linguistic convention that enables us to categorize this thing." Note here that the talk about it, as funded by digital aspects of communication, *increases* in abstraction: we take the word "*cup*" as an abstract label and simultaneously take the word "*thing*" as if it were the thing more directly, as if this were a less abstract term.

By syntactically combining different levels of abstraction in an overlapping reference, we paradoxically produce the sense that we can talk about what is independent of language. Such paradoxes of abstraction arise mainly due to the conflated difference in logical types between general or abstract words (e.g. "things," "entities," "objects") and metalanguage or words that refer to the verbal order (e.g. "speech," "language," "words"). Whereas the word "things" makes a categorical reference, the word "language" makes a categorical reference to linguistic referencing per se. This means that even though non-metalinguistic words can imply that their referents preceded the words we used to refer to them, this sense is facilitated only through the powerful syntax that digitalization enables: whenever used in combination with metalinguistic terms the obvious sense carried is that the referent is already related to language. Terms such as "language," or "words," or "speech," when used in syntactical combination with abstract words such as "object" or "thing," enable a mode of "overlapping reference" (Holenstein, 1976). They open a "code to message" reflexivity that allows us to make sense of the idea that "objects" and "things" preceded the words by which we grasped them. Hence, linguistic signification not only facilitates a digitaliz-ing of analog relations, but, as holding metalinguistic references, enables a self-reflexivity that becomes forgotten (taken-for-granted) in the claim that "things came before language." By the workings of the very syntax we can say that things precede language, and, this can make sense, but only because we have used metalinguistic references and so *already* have referred to the verbal order.

Similar kinds of difficulties emerge from any overly literal attempt to sepa-rate a class from its name. Clearly, logical-typing errors occur if we confuse a class with its name. But the question is: how could this thoroughly be avoided, for doesn't an unnamed category seem not to be a category at all? What would an unnamed category be a category of? A more illustrative example may be needed: Common sense dictates that particular individual apples must have preceded the class of apples. But, if we do not yet have the class of apples, how could any one apple be counted *as* an apple? The difficulty here, as Lee Thayer suggests, is that "To have *one* of anything, we already must have a category" (Thayer, 1997, p. 75). Thayer's point is that individual things do not precede the categories by which we categorize them. Take, for further example, Bateson's entries into the problem of play. Even these subtly seem to underestimate how deeply run the difficulties of what he calls an "onionskin," (i.e. how higher levels of abstractions can be taken as if they were lower levels). Bateson (1956, p. 145) states, "We live in a universe of namables. Within that universe we make classes." But could the namables come before the classes? Are not the namables thereby already within a class, the class of namables? (also cf. Scheffler, 1967, pp. 12-14). In this sense, any denotative utterance already displays the root paradox of abstraction.

Someone following in traditional realism still might try to argue that lan-guage is not needed for the existence of kinds of things. On the contrary, it is only for our convenience (it merely aids us) in labeling naturally occurring types. Com-mon sense says: "I don't care what you call the things. Whether you call some-thing a 'cup,' a 'drinking vessel,' or an 'object' does not matter; the actual thing is still here. The words are simply different labels for it." This makes sense, at least at first. But, as I have tried to illustrate in many ways, we have not so much made good sense as we have enabled ourselves to overlook our non-sense. Recall that when the White Knight meets Alice, in *Through the Looking Glass*, he prepares to cheer her up by playing some music. But first he states,

> 'The name of the song is called "*Haddock Eyes*."'"Oh, that's the name of the song is it?' Alice said, trying to feel interested.
> 'No, you don't understand,' the Knight said, looking a little vexed. 'That's what the name is *called*. The name really is "*The Aged Aged Man*."'
> 'Then I ought to have said "That's what the song is called"?' Alice corrected herself.
> 'No, you oughtn't: that is quite another thing! The *song* is called

"*Ways and Means*": but that's only what it's *called*, you know!'
    'Well, what *is* the song, then?' said Alice, who was by this time completely bewildered.
    'I was coming to that,' the Knight said. 'The song really *is* "A Sitting On A Gate": and the tune's my own invention.'

We may feel that Alice, eventually, got to the bottom of all this (also cf. Wilden, 1978). But did she? How could it be that the song <u>is</u> 'A *Sitting On A Gate*'? Is this not a kind of category mistake, a subtle act of taking the words for the thing? Can we now hum a few bars from, '*A Sitting On A Gate*'? That is, do we now know the song and not the title of the song? And, more critically, what does the White Knight mean by "the tune"? Now, I am not interested in what the name of the tune is called, nor in what the tune is called, nor even in the name of the tune. I want to know if the White Knight is simply calling his song "the tune" or if the song is the tune. I also want to know how I know (or why I seem to think) that the tune is the song. And, more practically and perhaps along with all, I want to know (i.e. to be able to "re-produce," even if only partly and in memory) the actual song.

    Carroll's textual imbroglio forces our attention to the "premise intransitivity" which Bateson suggests characterizes naturally communicative rather than strictly logical frames. As Bateson suggests, "It is conventional to argue that if A is greater than B, and B is greater than C, then A is greater than C. But in psychological processes the transitivity of asymmetrical relations is not observed. Proposition P may be a premise for Q; Q may be a premise for R, and R may be a premise for P" (Bateson, 1955 [1972], p. 185). The critical implication is that we in our everyday talk habitually fail to notice how quickly we hop around and between various abstract words and, in doing so, leave such intransitivity strangely forgotten. Bateson's diagram for discussion referred to as "onionskin" also well signifies the premise intransitivity that necessarily characterizes syntactical digitalization (see Figure 1). His diagram signifies not that language "is making it all up," but simply that, without precipitating a paradox of abstraction, we cannot say what is or what is not in analog communication. And, this is why, as Bateson suggests, "It is excessively difficult to talk about the structuring of an onionskin system, because our language is always within one or another system of that kind, and we ourselves are faced with the problem of being inside that whole which we are trying to talk about" (1956, p. 155). Thus, when Bateson suggests that he has a "desire to know about those processes whereby organism's pull themselves up by their bootstraps" (1956, p. 216), he addresses communication as an evolution of digital communication from within on-going analog communication, and moreover, he turns our attention to how digital communication syntactically imbricates intransitive yet asymmetrical distinctions and thus in-builds layers of abstraction.

    Finally, the difficulties discussed throughout this paper seem to emerge whenever someone uses the logic of set-theoretic classification (i.e. "members" and "sets") to understand the relations "between" words and things. George Lakoff and Mark Johnson (1980) persuasively argue that definitions are better grasped though "protoytpes" and "family resemblances" than by "set-theoretic" orientations. They therefore call into question the entire problematic that Bateson encumbers in moving out from The Theory of Logic Types. Granting this, Bateson's work stands in agreement with Lakoff and Johnson's stress upon the "interactional nature of properties," and moreover, Bateson has the advantage of demonstrating how shifting logical types are employed nonetheless and how syntactical redundancies can appear under the guise of empirical assertions about relations between verbal and "nonverbal" realms. All of the above is made evident, though only symptomatically, where Burke suggests that "we gravitate spontaneously toward naive verbal realism" (1961, p. 18). We forgetfully slip back into the belief that there is first a world of things and then, also, as a convenient happenstance, a set of words for labeling or referring to them. Notice how problematic such thinking becomes if we explicitly deal with the fact that all sets can be nested in multiple other sets. For example, the set of soup spoons can be a member of the set of silverware. Also, the set of silverware can a member of the set of utensils, which, in its turn, can a member of the set of things. But now, if I were to suggest that things (and in fact utensils, silverware as well as spoons) are all members of the set of words, a critic may accuse me of making a category mistake (that of confusing the name with the thing named). This critic might suggest that my mistake is easy to point out: "the words 'spoons,' 'silverware,' 'utensil,' and even 'things' can be said to be members of the set of words, but, that to which the words refer are not." "The things themselves," the critic would argue, "are not members of the set of words." Now, I completely agree that I am making a logical-typing error, and, I happily grant that this is an obvious one. Nevertheless, for those who would speak of such things, there appears to be little escape from such mistakes! For surely *"things"* is a word and the neglect of this fact enables much more subtle category mistakes. Within the critic's critique for example, notice how quickly we made sense of the higher abstractions (e.g. "that" and "things") as if they were not simply more words. Such a move inevitably traffics in the *same* paradoxes of abstraction. Not only do paradoxes of abstraction occur because "things" is a word of a different logical type than that to which it putatively refers, but additionally—and more subtly—because the word "words" is a metalinguistic term. Each word ("spoon," "silverware," "utensil," "things") never referred to an original real one "thing" per se (sic!). Rather, each is a moment within the constitutive underbelly of propositional language and denotative utterances. If words were but one natural set of things that exists independent of and in addition to other natural sets of things, how could something, say a pen in my hand, also be a utensil as well as an entity, an object, and a thing? Where is that which determines the lines of inclusion and exclusion, of taking-apart and bringing-together, of division and merger? That which makes something a thing, but even more specifically, "a utensil but not a spoon," cannot be found within the thing per se.[8]

We Speak Nonetheless

Gregory Bateson concludes his essay, "A Theory of Play and Fantasy," with the following words:

Our central thesis may be summed up as a statement of the necessity of the paradoxes of abstraction. It is not merely bad natural history to suggest that people might or should obey the Theory of Logical Types in their communications; their failure to do this is not due to mere carelessness or ignorance. Rather, we believe that the paradoxes of abstraction must make their appearance in all communication more complex than that of mood-signals, and that without these paradoxes the evolution of communication would be at an end. (Bateson, 1972, p.193)

Our ability to signify, to speak *about* something, is funded by and always rests imbedded within the world of analog communication. The paradoxical sense that "things precede language" is, at root, a tacit recognition that digitalization is inseparable from the analogic world. The world of analog communication is without classes; it is the total action within the absolute non-repeatable once-occurrent context (i.e. the meaningful goal-seeking-within-environment). Thus, when we say that things could not have preceded language, this does not attempt to reduce world and all therein to language.[9] Instead, it advances Bateson's ideas of play, framing, and analog and digital communication to show how things, *qua things*, become possible only given linguistic signification.

A most profound and ubiquitous "category mistake" is the sheer ability to speak *about* aspects of the world. We are able to make sense of the claim that "things preceded language" because we are comfortable with paradox. The propositional aspects of human speech, as Bateson observed, have the character of an onionskin. This is a useful guiding metaphor for the digital aspects of language. It is not that there is nothing outside of what we talk about; it is that we cannot, without paradox, say what that something is. Better said, denotative speech, because of our comfort with paradox, allows us to take seriously our attempts to *say* what lies outside of speech. Obviously, much lies before our utterances and much comes after them, and certainly, much is permanently other than them. Nevertheless, we never can say what all or any of that "much" is without making a kind of category mistake.

It would be foolish to deny that there are the many different things in the world, but we should not maintain that they—*those things that we could or do talk about*—can be grasped independently of how we grasp them. It is not that there are no things in the world; rather, there is denotative speech. Things appear as things because we can speak *about* them. Therefore, if we say that there are no things without language, this is not an attempt to deny the vast and all-too-present un-speakable. Not at all. It is an invitation for a direct confrontation with the paradoxical character of denotative utterances.

Endnotes to Chapter 3

1 Abstract from the original: This paper critically develops the ideas of Gregory Bateson. Bateson's work on play led him to conclude that paradox is the ground of propositions and/or denotaton. Working through various problems of "framing" and focusing on forms of meta-discourse, Bateson's work broadly illustrates how what he came to call "the paradoxes of abstraction" inevitably arise within denotative utterances. In addressing the root paradoxes of framing and denotation which Bateson's work on play identified and sought to elucidate, this paper outlines and advances some of Bateson's main contributions to communication theory.

2 I want to express my gratitude and thanks to William K. Rawlins, John Stewart, Mark Pestana, Dewey Hoitenga, Maria Cimitile, Robert Mayberry, and Valerie Peterson for their many helpful criticisms and suggestions. I also need to

thank the Josiah Macy Jr. Foundation for their kind permission to reprint the "Diagram for discussion purposes referred to as 'onionskin,'" taken from Bateson's 1956 lecture/group discussion.

3 Readers interested in "framing" also should see Erving Goffman (1974).

4 Rawlins (1987) more strictly adheres to Bateson's position in suggesting three kinds of codification, (analog, gestalt, and digital). For consistency and simplicity, I have followed the lines traced by Wilden (1972) and as a consequence have taken gestalt and/or iconic codification as a kind of first-order digitization.

5 For provocative analyses of language via Jakobson's structural approach [the axes of selection and substitution (vertical or paradigmatic operations) and contexture and combination (horizontal and syntagmatic operations) see Elmar Holenstein (1976) and Richard Lanigan (1992).

6 For an excellent address of these issues see Susanne K Langer's (1942, pp. 83 -116) discussion of the emergence of denotation in the chapter "Language." Also see Hans Jonas's (1966, pp. 157-182) "Image-making and the Freedom of Man."

7 By "first-order" digital operations Wilden (1972) mainly addresses decision-making processes, especially where simple feedback is needed (e.g. the on-off setting for a thermostat, a circuit breaker on a stereo speaker, a neuronal decision to fire or not, the automatic shut-off on a coffee pot).

8 Bateson writes, "Difference, you see, is just sufficiently away from the grossly materialistic and quantitative world so that mind, dealing in difference, will always be intangible, will always deal in intangibles" (1977, p. 240). And also: "'Information' and 'form' resemble contrast, frequency, symmetry, correspondence, congruence, conformity, and the like in being of zero dimensions and, therefore, are not to be located" (1967 [1972], p. 408).

9 Wilden (1972) nicely counters the reductive tendencies that can come from too much attention to propositional aspects of language. He states: "This is not to say that all knowledge is digital, although many philosophers seem to think so, or at least to behave as if it were. Most knowledge is analog...Most of our knowledge or understanding (in the usual sense) is communicated analogically, by imitation" (p. 166).

Chapter 4: A Levels Orientation to Abstraction, Logical Typing, and Language More Generally

> *"No communication can be properly defined or examined*
> *at the level at which the communication occurs...*
> *This sentence is in English."*
> — Wilden, 1972, pp. 113; 172

Grounded in Alfred Korzybski's program of "consciousness of abstracting" as well as Gregory Bateson's appropriations of Bertrand Russell's theory of logical types, Linda Elson's project constructs a working definition of a "levels-perspective" on discourse and communication more broadly. She argues that Korzybski and Bateson, for all they have done in turning attention to processes of abstraction and levels of logical typing, have nevertheless failed to provide a coherent definition of levels-phenomena (either of abstraction or logical typing or even communication more broadly). Her definition emerges as she explores levels-phenomena that arise in paradoxes across a wide range of contexts: the liar's paradox, prediction paradoxes, interpersonal framing troubles (including double binds and paradoxical injunctions), and a broad spectrum of jokes and humorous plays on words. The span of contexts considered--the range of examples and illustrations regarding the phenomena explored--is a main strength of Elson's early arguments. Additionally, by focusing her analyses upon levels-paradoxes, Elson is able to: (a) provide a coherent and unified definition for understanding a wide range of levels-phenomena and (b) reveal how levels-phenomena share in a few basic characteristics. The kernel of the paradox in each case, Elson maintains,

> ...can be located in a (mainly) verbal message, conveyed by a single individual or by a group of individuals with a single "voice." Invariably, this message is self-referential, and it is "antithetically compound" (it can be separated analytically into two antithetical components). Furthermore, in each instance, the message invites a choice between two alternatives, which turn out to be illusory in that each entails the other. (2010, p. 152)

She clarifies these relationships further and notes their common occurrence throughout the five types of paradoxes. She writes:

> ...each of the five paradoxes arises when the components of the paradoxical message are processed separately and sequentially. The result in each case is an alternating sequence of antithetical conclusions, a theoretically interminable succession wherein each interpretation perpetually displaces and entails the antithetical counterpart, which invalidates it. In all of the paradoxes with the exception of humor, we process the lower level first—possible evidence of an unconscious bias which favors lower levels as more "real." (Elson, 2010, p. 154)

We find, then, that all of the paradoxes occur because some message components can be at different levels than other components. And, if we attempt to reveal the conditions of possibility for such levels-paradoxes, we find a peculiar property of levels more generally: "aboutness."

By the notion of aboutness, I refer not merely to the fact that discourse has levels, but rather that it has levels *only because* of aboutness. As Elson thoughtfully suggests, "The relationship of "about" distinguishes one level of abstraction from another" (2010, p. 191). Further delineating the nature of the relationship between meaning, levels, logical typing, and "aboutness," Elson writes,

> Meaning might even be redefined, from a levels-perspective, as the relationship of (what Korzybski calls) a "thing/event" with emergent higher-level patterns. Maybe our failure to acknowledge levels is implicated in the paradox, in our failure to distinguish the relationship of "about" from other relationships between message components, and in our consequent failure to appropriately process messages with disparate levels-components. The failure to distinguish the relationship of "about" is equivalent to the failure to acknowledge the levels-dimension. (2010, p. 189)

Without such aboutness, we would not experience levels nor could we experience messages as antithetically compound. Indeed, it is the multi-leveled nature of language--the many different ways that 'component parts' can be about other parts--that most needs attention and study in contemporary scholarship.

Interestingly enough, although Elson found a unity in the sense that all of the paradoxes hold some relationship of "aboutness" within them, the solutions to the various paradoxes were found to be of more than one type (i.e. at more than one level). In fact, Elson makes clear that, in contrast to her originally anticipated conclusions, two *kinds* of levels-solutions emerged. She differentiates between a "hierarchy of representation" which refers to levels of abstraction that are hierarchically and successively imbricated (e.g. the Liar's Paradox) and a "hierarchy of transformation" which refers to a composition of three levels of abstraction where, from the opposition between two adjacent levels, a new level emerges. Summarizing these distinctions, Elson writes,

> *Levels of abstraction* refers to the hierarchical organization of levels of information, such that a higher level represents, organizes, transforms lower-level information, and not vice-versa. Relative to absolute disorganization and infinite detail, a higher level is at a further remove.
>
> A *hierarchy of representation* is comprised of successive levels of information, such that information at the higher *level of representation* classifies information at the next lower level.
>
> A *hierarchy of transformation* is comprised of three levels of information such that from the opposition between two adjacent levels of representation, a qualitatively new feature emerges at a higher *level of transformation*. (2010, p. 171)

Looking back now on her many examples, we can see the usefulness of this discovery. And, if only for further illustration of the usefulness of this distinction, let me quickly offer an original example of each.

Consider an illustration of what Elson means by "hierarchy of representation." The example I provide here has the benefit of being a bit more contextually dense than the free-floating Liar's paradox [more on this in later sections], though it equally introduces an infinity of antithetically compound entailments. The riddle/puzzle is one that I remember from my childhood. It goes: "Their our three errors in this sentence."[2] List the errors.

1. The word "Their" should be spelled "There."
2. The word "our" should be spelled "are."
3. The third error is that there are only two errors in the sentence.

So, if all of those are true, then are there three errors or not? If there are three then the third listed error is not an error (it is false), but, if there are not three, then that is the third error. In this example of "hierarchy of representation" we see the on-going succession of levels such that each new level classifies the former at the next lower level.

A fine example of "hierarchy of transformation," on the other hand, can be found in a practical joke that children sometimes play upon one another. One person says to an unsuspecting target, "Hey, do you want to take an idiot test?" The second person replies, "Alright, I'm ready." The first person says, "How much is two plus two?" Other person: "4." The first person, "How many items are in a dozen?" Second person, "12." First person, "From which direction does the sun rise?" Second person, "The East." First person, "What was the first question I asked you?" Second person, "How much is two plus two." Second person, "No it wasn't; the first question I asked you was, 'Do you want to take an idiot test?' So you failed; you're an idiot." At first pass we assume the expression "the first question" to refer to the first question after we agreed to take the test. The victim does not suspect that the invitation to the test is the first question of the test (i.e. does not suspect that the line/premise that constructs the set can be treated as if included within the set). It is only because words can be caked with multiple meanings, an encrusted meaning (*du mechanique*) which is upon a *du vivant*, that such humor is possible. Said otherwise, the person "proves" to be an "idiot" but of a different sort (level) than the one first imagined.

In what follows, I advance and fortify Elson's levels-perspective by supplementing it with lines of scholarship that have explored similar issues as well as scholarship that can be fruitfully integrated into a levels-perspective. To set the stage for arguments to come, my first move is to contextualize some possible explanations for why Bateson failed in (or perhaps refrained from) providing a comprehensive definition of different "levels." Then, I advance a levels-orientation to language that is largely inspired by Elson's overall project. The general strategy is to track down the phenomena of levels as they occur within the code itself; more specifically, I explore two kinds of words that, as providing the ground for a "code to message overlapping reference," disclose levels of aboutness which emerge because the code per se is, in fact, multileveled (cf. Holenstein, 1976). For clarity and focus, I examine the emergence of "*syntactical negation*," (i.e. the use of "not" as metalinguistic rule), and I also examine how "shifters" such as "this" and "I" (words whose referents are made evident through indexicality) are used in combination with other words that are themselves at different levels. Ultimately I try to highlight and illustratively clarify a range of levels-phenomena as they operate within everyday mundane language.

One of the reasons that the multileveled phenomena of language have been passed over is because of what might be called, "the explicit challenge to naive verbal realism." Basically, in contrast to any views which presupposed a transparent or unmediated access to things in the world, the challenge that General Semantics brought to naive verbal realism unfortunately cast a kind of dichotomy between the "objective/event level" and the "abstract level of symbols" used to talk about the world.[3] In this way, levels-phenomena within discourse were conflated--bundled and passed over--as the main distinction that took attention was between the "verbal level" and the "nonverbal level."

A related difficulty is that language includes and uses multiple levels of abstraction, but here again the levels themselves seem to occur all on the same plane of discourse: (i.e. Jakobson's paradigmatic/vertical axis of "selection," "substitution," and "similarity").[4] For example, we can note that a given item of the world can be labeled at different levels of abstraction. The same organism might be referred to as a Beagle, or as a dog, or as a mammal, or as an animal or entity, or even just, "Rover." Here, even though we find many different levels of abstraction, they remain as levels within or along one plane, and, in that sense, we have different levels of abstraction for semantic reference but not yet levels within and across discourse itself. Consider too the kind of levels of abstraction that occur where we note that Rover[1] is the not the same as Rover[2] nor as Rover[3]. Here levels of abstraction refer to abstraction over time, the way that the word "Rover" can unify and hold together the many physical changes that occur from pup to dog to deceased pet.

There, admittedly, have been other senses of levels of abstraction, but these too seem to suffer from similar limitations. Consider Kenneth Burke's (1966) masterful essay, "What Are the Signs of What?" where he addresses how any talk about something always encumbers the inherent problem of framing by placement (also cf. Goffman, 1974). All events, that is, must be "placed," and they take their placement within different scopes or circumferences according to the terms used. As Burke provocatively writes,

> For instance, I am writing these words "in Florida this January," or "during a lull in the bombing of North Vietnam," or "in a period following the invention of the atomic bomb but prior to a soft landing of electronic instruments on the surface of the moon," and so on. Thus that "same" act can be defined "differently," depending upon the "circumference" of the scene or overall situation in terms of which we choose to locate it. (1966, p. 360)

Even though Burke well recognizes that anything talked about will need to be framed by the terms we choose to use,[5] the important point for present purposes is simply to recognize that all such operations still move mainly along the vertical axis: Burke is describing how the same thing can be framed from different levels of contextual involvements. This line of awareness of abstraction is still not the study of different levels being coordinated and calibrated horizontally within the language.

We basically reviewed two orientations to levels of abstraction that, though insightful in their own regard, somewhat inhibited the development of an overall levels-perspective to language and communication. Those two orientations are: separating the "non-abstract objective level of event" from the "abstract level/ realm of symbols," and second, recognizing that an item of the objective/event level can by referred to and/or framed by various levels of abstraction.

The kinds of levels that Elson's scholarship brings so clearly to light, on the contrary, are more like levels-phenomena on more than one plane, themselves of more than one level. They are, as I try to illustrate in later sections, emergent within the oscillations and reverberations of grammar and syntax (i.e. Jakobson's syntagmatic/horizontal axis of "contexture," "combination," and "contiguity").

Now, clearly, Bateson was well aware of the issue of "aboutness" and he advances farther than does Burke (or Korzybski) in recognizing kinds of levels as well as logical typing problems/solutions. But, as Elson rightfully suggests, he had not fully developed a working definition of levels or even of logical types. I will return to the issue of Bateson's reluctance to formulate a definition of levels, but let me first quickly review the move that signified his first major shift toward a different orientation to levels, one that paved the way for a thoroughgoing levels-understanding.

A new kind of awareness of levels dawned upon Bateson when he tried to account for the playful nips of monkeys in the Fleishhacker Zoo. Bateson initially characterized what he observed by writing, "The playful nip denotes the bite, but it does not denote what would be denoted by the bite" (1972, p.180). Or stated more generally, "The statement, 'this is play' looks something like this: 'These actions in which we now engage do not denote what those actions for which they stand would denote'" (Bateson, 1972, p. 180). This seemed at first to be insightful but not without its own shortcomings, for Bateson discovered that he had used the word "denote" in two very different degrees of abstraction. In fact, he claimed that he subtly committed what he called a "logical typing" error in doing so. They (nip and bite) referred to significantly different orders of abstraction, and paradoxes of abstraction occur, he argued, if we conflate this difference.[6]

Much as Bateson (1972) suggested that the word "denote" was being used in two different degrees of abstraction, so, too, he focused upon the word "not" and how it was used in different degrees of abstraction. It is here, in noting that the word "not" is inattentively or unwittingly used in multiple levels, that we find Bateson most thoroughly approaching a rigorous levels-orientation. I will try to show that it is the word "not," more precisely the process of "syntactical negation," that opens the doorway to a levels-perspective to language itself.

Syntactical Negation as a Different Kind of Level

Bateson (and Korzybski too) recognized that communication always occurs on a range of levels that vary from simple denotation. The range Bateson first had in mind spanned in two directions: first toward metacommunicative framings (e.g. "Are you kidding?"; "You can trust what I'm telling you"), and second toward metalinguistic references (e.g. "In English, the word 'roast' rhymes with 'toast'"; "The word 'teeth' cannot bite you"). Bateson also understood that denotation (e.g. an utterance bearing propositional content) is itself fundamentally *about* something. Indeed, the very definition of denotation is a statement bearing propositional content about which we can ask the question: 'Is that true?' So Bateson clearly acknowledged that levels of abstraction change whenever we move from seemingly simple direct denotation or "object language" to metacommunicative framings or metalinguistic references. What he had not yet fully schematized, however, is the different levels of language within given messages, in particular at the *levels of the code itself*.

Admittedly then, Bateson never committed to an explicit definition of levels, but perhaps that partly can be explained. In 1955, in front of a range of noted scholars including Margaret Mead, Ray Birdwhistle, and a host of others, Bateson gave a lecture entitled "The Message, 'This is Play'" (1956). In this address Bateson explicitly resorted to using a picture-frame orientation and/or a set-theoretical approach to clarify his thinking. It should be underscored that just a year earlier, in his more well known chapter from *Steps to an Ecology of Mind*, "A Theory of Play and Fantasy," he openly argued against the metaphors of either picture frames or mathematical sets. He then held that, "while the analogy of the mathematical set is perhaps overly abstract, the analogy of the picture frame is excessively concrete. The psychological concept which we are trying to define is neither physical nor logical" (1972, p. 187). Granting such earlier reservations, in his 1956 lecture he decided to graphically represent the line that must not be drawn if we are to avoid Russellian paradoxes, that line which keeps items of different logical types separated. Trying to illustrate what he then called an "onion-skin" (perhaps his most "level-like" expression), Bateson prefaces his lecture by drawing Figure 1 on a blackboard.

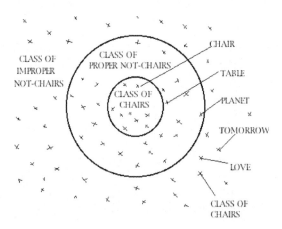

As he was making his drawing, he was also stating the following:

> Let me put it to you like this: We live in a universe of namables.
> Within that universe we make classes. Let me here make the class
> of chairs. I now want you quickly, without thinking too much about
> it, to name for me some of the "not chairs." You have suggested
> "tables," "dogs," "people," "autos." Let me suggest one now: "to-
> morrow." Does it make you a little uncomfortable when I say to-
> morrow is not a chair? (Bateson, 1956, p. 145)

It is also worth recalling that to his question, "Does it make you a little uncomfortable when I say that tomorrow is not a chair?" someone in the audience yells out
"Schizophrenic," to which Bateson replies, "Thank you," and then proceeds to
formally introduce and overview his lecture.

The above diagram (Figure 1) attempts to represent how the word "not"
operates on more than one level, and, as such, how "syntactical negation" inerad-
icably introduces the very line that the Russellian Rule disallows. The outer line-
-the line that attempts to handle different logical types--is not permitted, though
for all kinds of reasons we do draw precisely this line. As one humorous example,
I recently received a coupon good for a "buy one, get one free" meal at a local
restaurant. The coupon had a stipulation though, one that was clarified by words
typed out in bold-faced print: "**Not Valid on Holidays or Lobster**."

Anthony Wilden and Tim Wilson (1976) help to clarify the critical role that
the "not" serves in sorting out not only different items of the same logical type but
also items of different logical types:

> Between items of the same logical type, "not" serves the sorting
> function of distinguishing them from each other. However, as Bate-
> son has pointed out (1972, pp. 188-189), there is invariably a *sec-
> ond* kind of boundary involved in all such processes: the boundary
> between the set of items of the same logical type we have selected
> out and the "background" set of all other items belonging to sets of
> any number of different logical types. (p. 278)

The point here is that mental processes (psychological frames) cannot help but
draw the line that precipitates into paradoxes.[7] Even more intriguing still is the
fact that the word "not" is more like a metalinguistic rule for introducing boundaries (i.e. gaps into continuums) than some "thing" to which we make reference.
Said otherwise, syntactical negation is always at a different level of abstraction
than that which it negates. Consider, for quick illustration, the following sentence:
"This statement contains five words." In this example, we attend to the difference
in levels by focusing our attention between the statement conveyed by the proposition and the actual materials used to convey the proposition (i.e. the code). Now
comparatively consider the following sentence: "This sentence does not contain
eight words." This second sentence not only displays the difference in levels between the code and the proposition conveyed by the code, but it further illustrates
how the "not" introduces yet another level which is reducible to neither the level
of the proposition nor "the code" per se.

Residual Resistances to a Formal Definition

Although the above discussion illustrates how the "not" played a critical role in the advancement toward a levels-orientation--and we can find more extensive analysis in Wilden's (1972) work on syntactical negation as well as analog and digital communication--we should underscore that Bateson himself was unhappy with such visual representations. He seemed unsure of how to best represent or clarify the kind of psychological levels he had in mind. There are three reasons for his ambivalence.

First, Bateson suggests that psychological frames, as both inclusive and exclusive, are more like premises than physical frames or categorical sets, and yet those premises stand in asymmetrical yet intransitive relations to each other. Thus, his first concern over the problem of levels is that we often fail to find a bedrock level or a next lowest level of abstraction. In fact, Bateson argues that, in contrast to strictly logical analysis, frames within natural everyday communication exhibit a kind of "premise intransitivity" even though they are asymmetrical. As Bateson writes, "It is conventional to argue that if A is greater than B, and B is greater than C, then A is greater than C. But in psychological processes the transitivity of asymmetrical relations is not observed. Proposition P may be a premise for Q; Q may be a premise for R, and R may be a premise for P" (Bateson, 1972, p. 185). This means that we routinely hop around between various levels and unwittingly neglect the fact of such intransitivity (cf. Anton, 2003). In this way, higher-order abstractions can be (and often are) treated as if they were the thing more directly. For illustration, imagine someone trying to explain the term "abstraction" in this way: The person, holding up a piece of chalk, states that the thing she is holding is not "chalk." "'Chalk,'" the person then says, "is the English word we use to refer to this; the actual thing in my hand is not 'chalk,' but rather 'chalk' is a linguistic convention that enables us to categorize this thing." Note here that the talk about it, as incorporating more than one level of abstraction, actually increases in abstraction: we take the word "chalk" as an abstract label and simultaneously take the word "thing" as if it were the thing more directly, as if this were a less abstract term, as if it were less of a label. Thus, when Bateson suggests that he has a "desire to know about those processes whereby organism's pull themselves up by their bootstraps" (1956, p. 216), he turns our attention to how communication syntactically imbricates intransitive yet asymmetrical levels within language. For this reason, Bateson was rather reluctant to solidify his definitions and examples of levels.

A related and additional part of the problem, one that needs at least some mention here, is that much of Bateson's thinking makes recourse to Freud's distinctions between "primary process" and "secondary process." This means that the asymmetrical yet intransitive premises often fall below the operations of strictly reflective analytical thought. It also implies that most of the processes by which we confuse logical types are themselves below the level of conscious reflection. As Bateson writes, "It is, however, a characteristic of unconscious or 'primary-process' thinking that the thinker is unable to discriminate between 'some' and 'all,' and unable to discriminate between 'not all' and 'none'" (Bateson, 1972, p. 184). These terms, it should be observed, constitute the very lines of discrimination, the boundary conditions, which give form to frames of inclusion and exclusion.

The third difficulty here (i.e. a final factor that kept Bateson from offering a formal definition of levels) is that there are indeed different kinds of levels, and one of the challenges is that it is exceptionally difficult to define the relationship between levels of logical types and levels of organization. In some ways this third restraint is more implied in Bateson's work than it is spelled out. It is spelled out, though, by Wilden where he writes, "The relationship between levels of logical types and levels of organization is not easy to define (because the explanations are of different types)" (1972, p. 171). As he further suggests,

> 'This message is in English' can be called a metacommunication of a higher logical type than the message to which it refers. It is the class of all messages in English. But the message to which it refers is of a more complex level of organization…(A rule of a code is a higher logical type, but of a less complex level of organization, than the messages it gives rise to). (1972, p. 171)

Within situated moments of discourse, therefore, it makes pretty good sense to suggest that, "Any message which 'frames' another message is, synchronically speaking, of a higher logical type than that which it frames" (Wilden, 1972, p. 171). Nevertheless, the matter is not settled so simply. Part of the difficulty is that different kinds of levels, as emergent, can alter the entire patterning of *organization*, including the system of logical types.[8] As Wilden stresses,

> …in ontogeny and phylogeny, the negentropic emergence of more and more complex levels of organization requires that we decide whether a new level of organization…'frames' or 'is framed by' whatever diachronically preceded it…Every diachronic emergence of a new level of organization must necessarily require the reorganization of the logical typing of the system. (1972, pp. 171-172)

It is for all of these reasons: the difficulty of characterizing the nature of psychological frames, the intransitivity of asymmetrical relations, the failures of analytical discrimination within primary process, and the challenges posed by emergent levels of organization that, cumulatively, Bateson was either reluctant or unable to offer a clear and fully consistent definition of levels-phenomena.

Thus far in this chapter, I have sought to review some of the basic orientations that Elson's project opened up and I have sought to give a little background on how Bateson both advanced the notion of levels but also refrained from offering an explicit definition. In what follows, I attempt to further illustrate and develop the insights Elson provides by more focally attending to multiple levels within language itself.

The Level of Shifters and Indexicality

Levels-phenomena are implied in all language use, and this is highly evident if we turn to Roman Jakobson's theory of "linguistic axes." The vertical or paradigmatic axis (selection, substitution, similarity) and the horizontal or syntagmatic axis (combination, contexture, contiguity) are both drawn upon as persons engage in discourse. Something happens and we are called upon to say what happened. Not only must we select words and expressions (signs) from all possible ones, we also need to combine those signs with other signs. Elson's work, broadly construed, illustrates how different levels open by way of horizontal reverberations that then impact the vertical axis. Such an account offers a substantial addition to Jakobson's thinking on encoding and decoding. It was his extensive studies of linguistics, and in particular his examination of Luria's work on aphasia, that led him to a model of encoding and decoding which insightfully addresses the multi-level meaning in discourse. He argued that encoding moves from parts to whole while decoding moves from whole to parts.[9] What Elson's work makes more than evident is that we move, and oftentimes even oscillate, between being both the encoder and decoder. She broadly illustrates how listeners (or readers) suffer reverberations in both directions and it is precisely such sequential reverberations that allow a word to be "simultaneously" at more than one level of abstraction. One way to say this is to say that parts must be encrusted and then broken, for that is one of the main ways that we re-interpret what we thought we knew. But reverberations allow not merely one word to appear in multiple levels nor different words at different levels to refer to ostensibly the same item; they bring into conscious attention the ways that different levels of the code are calibrated.

One way to contextualize this issue, therefore, is to see that at each level of analysis, we have revealed the conditions of possibility of the next lower level. Levels are found to have levels within them, and there are many different kinds of levels too. Perhaps obviously, then, any proposition can be subject to reflective scrutiny: it can be analyzed as comprised of a code that is at a different order of abstraction than the proposition conveyed by it.[10] Here we find not various words being used at different levels of abstraction to make reference, but rather, messages appearing before our eyes as we consciously experience the difference between a code and the proposition stated by way of it. Moreover, as Wilden suggests, "The mediating function of a code derives from the fact that it is necessarily of a different *logical type* from the messages it permits..." (p. 269). One way to illustrate how even straightforward statements (i.e. not paradoxical mundane utterances) have multiple levels of meaning is to re-consider the quotation used to open this essay: "This sentence is in English" (Wilden, 1972, pp. 113; 172). The statement in English is at a different level of abstraction than the proposition stated about it. Note, too, the impossibility of directly translating that statement (switching the code) while retaining the truth of the proposition. And an even more critical point here is that there must be some kind of indexical meaning, for it is by riding between levels that we are able to assess the truth-value of the proposition. The only way to determine the veracity of the proposition is to examine it in terms of its *contiguous relations* to the factual/actual code. The general points thus far are: (a) we find a factual statement at one level and a proposition about that statement made at a different level, all conveyed by the one sentence, and (b) it is only because we can attend to the indexical level of language that we are able to check the veracity of such self-referential statements.

Not only are we able to distinguish between the level of the code and the propositions conveyed by the code, but we gain that ability largely through those parts of the code that are *about* the message. This implies that one of the most imbedded and unregistered "level of levels" can be found within the code itself, as the code is not of one level. The kinds of levels at issue here, once more, are not different levels of abstraction used to make semantic reference, nor are they the same words being used in more than one level of meaning. The code itself is multileveled, meaning that the routine functioning of some words is to operate at a level other than the words with which they are combined. We have already explored how the word "not" is one such case, but there are others that need some mention in this context.

The case that most demands our attention here is the role played by "shifters." Words that linguists sometimes call "shifters," words such as "this," "here," or "I" when used in combination with words such as "says," "lies," "read," "told," allow for a "code to message" reflexivity that on-goingly etches levels into the code per se. But we need to be very cautious here, for this is not to say that words such as "this" or "I" are in fact indexicals whereas other words are not indexicals. The point is that words themselves always exist on multiple levels and we can turn attention to, and meaningfully take reference from, their status as *pointers*. Again, I am not suggesting that some words are arbitrary and that some are indexicals, rather, we can use some at the level of their indexicality to make a reference.

The levels-orientation found in Jakobson's approach is partly attributable to his appropriations of Peirce's triadic division of signs into icons, indices, and symbols. Holenstein summarizes Jakobson's thinking here:

> The icon rests on a "factual similarity," the index on a "factual contiguity," and the symbol on an "imputed, learned contiguity"…Of significance here is that this trichotomy is not a division of individual signs, but consists rather of three different modes of signs. Each sign owes its name to the preponderant component. The index character dominates the shifters, whose reference changes with every situation of discourse…Shifters differ from all other constituents of the code by virtue of their compulsory dependence on the given message. This situational and contextual dependence, however, does not mean that they are denied general meaning, as frequently claimed in traditional language theory. (1976, p. 158)

Some words are misunderstood if we believe that all words are simply "arbitrarily related" to a referent. Such a reduction of words to one level misses the ways that indexicals make certain kinds of "aboutness" possible. Consider the example of one kind of shifter, pronouns. If I were to say, "Jill went to the store, and she bought some milk," the word "she" refers to Jill and does so indexically. There are factual contiguities that enable me to determine this, as I have not "learned" the referent by convention. If anything, I have learned the rule for using some sound/images at their indexical level (i.e. as context-dependent pointers). Said quite otherwise, if we were non-native speakers and were reading the sentence but did not recognize the word "she," the dictionary's meaning for the word, "feminine personal pronoun in the third person of the nominative case" would not in any way help us gain the word's referent.

It must be understood that, from within a native tongue, some of the words operate more as pointers than as sounds whose referent is arbitrarily signified by the sound/image. They are a part of the code that takes its meaning from being *about* relations of contiguity to the code per se. That is, the relations that are operative in allowing indexicals to point out their referents are relations of contiguity, not mere historical convention. As Holenstein suggests,

> In clarifying reference, Jakobson decidedly rejects the Saussurian principle of arbitrariness. Citing Boas and Benveniste, he…extends Saussure's own attenuation of this principle through recognition of the relative motivation based on the relations of the signs to each other. A language may at most be arbitrary only "from the point of view of another language (Boas)." (1976, p. 156)

The motivation comes from other signs, often those signs that relate by factual contiguity. We must also recall on this point that Jakobson, whose model is multileveled, employs the term "context" to signify what is commonly termed "referent." He does so because he argues against any atomistic orientation to reference. Holenstein points out that Jakobson, in his later publications, argued in contrast to both Frege and Husserl regarding the issue of reference. Holenstein summarized this view where he writes, "Every object always appears in a situation, in a network of relations that is defined temporally, spatially, or by its content and that must be taken into account in determination of the referent. We cannot designate an object without, at the same time, introducing it into a situation or a context" (1976, p. 88). The relevance of such situations/contexts becomes even more pronounced as we also understand that, for Jakobson, absolutely everything imaginable is a sign at some level. Holenstein is thus able to show how indexical meaning within the spoken word relates to factually contiguous signs (not exclusively linguistic ones): "It is possible in language to refer to something (factually) extralinguistic. But it is quite impossible to use language to refer to something absolutely extrasemiotic, to something that is not itself already semiotically staked" (1976, p. 159).

In real everyday life, where we find a thick density of analogical qualities and relationships that concretize the digital aspects of speech and where we have neither a first word nor a final word, the sheer statement, "I am lying," seems less than genuine. Wilden and Wilson, in discussing the relationship between analogic and digital communication argue that,

> …hidden within this relationship lurks one of the oldest logical paradoxes: the so-called Cretan paradox: "I am lying." …The oscillation is dependent on the binary alternative of "truth" and "falsehood" linked by the boundary or null set represented by syntactic "not." The paradoxical injunction involved here stems from the fact that all messages in any system are simultaneously reports and commands (McCulloch)—as well as questions. (1976, p. 275)

Perhaps not surprisingly, the "I am lying" paradox seems a bit fake, an artificial façade that is produced only because writing, decontextualizing the language and carrying but the digital aspects, can seem to sever any necessary or analogically factual relations.[11] "I am lying" seems to be a paradox mainly because we can imagine it in total isolation; we can imagine it as not making reference to something already said or something about to be said.

But the paradox is also vexing for reasons "internal" to language itself. Of the many shifters in discourse including pronouns and demonstratives, it is the first-person singular pronoun "I" that is both paradoxical and yet utterly mundane.

> Logicians distinguish the "I am lying" paradox from other paradoxes in different ways, but, precisely because it includes the term "I," it appears to be the ground of all possible paradoxes…The "I" in the statement is a rule about membership in the class of "I" by a member of the class of "I." It both makes a distinction in a universe of discourse and defines the locus of intervention into that universe… We have to conclude that the paradox of paradox is the result of the self-referring characteristics of the human subject—as represented in the (digital) discourse by the linguistic shifter "I"—the subject of both the proposition "I am lying" and of the goalseeking, time-dependent subsystem that proposes it. (Wilden, 1972, p. 124)

One of the insights of chaos theory is the notion of self-similarity. Self-similarity refers to various patterns or shapes that appear at different levels or scales of analysis. Benoit Mandlebrot, a founding figure in chaos theory, illustrates the natural occurrence of self-similar phenomena by turning our attention to a head of cauliflower. If we break off a small piece of the cauliflower, the piece is self-similar to (has morphological similarities to) the entire head, and if we further break off an even smaller piece, it too displays a self-similarity to the whole. As the concept of self-similarity has been applied to a wide range of phenomena, including fractal geometry, migration patterns, models of weather systems and population growths, it seems to be highly relevant to the levels phenomena that Elson has explored.

And yet despite all of this similarity, we do well to simultaneously remember that language itself is comprised of many different kinds of words. A major advantage of a levels-orientation to language is the recognition of the diverse kinds of actions that different words do. One of Wittgenstein's great insights was to open awareness to the neutralizing effects of dictionaries. If we were to try to understand the nature of language by simply looking at words on the page, we might get the sense that all words are of the same kind and on the same horizon line (in a word, at the same level). The problem is that words in the dictionary do not a language make; there are maneuvers of grammar and syntax, discourse practices, many kinds of sounds that are meaningful but not found in any dictionary, and, obviously, that indefatigable density of noise and analogic relations factually surrounding us at all points (cf. Lingis, 1994).

Wilden and Wilson summarize the double bind theory in terms that seem to equally fit to the levels-perspective that Elson develops. They write what could be taken as a fitting summation of her project, and what should be recognized as a great summation of the kinds of insights that we are only beginning to understand:

> The epistemology implicit and explicit in the double bind theory is

the only approach we know of that has been able to deal at all adequately with the problematic of semiotic levels: levels of logic, levels of communication, levels of coding, levels of complexity, levels of organization, levels of structure…In going beyond the closed-system basis of ordinary logic by its illumination of the paralogical, it provides us with new ways of dealing with context, closure, and punctuation in open systems. (1976, p. 273)

Endnotes to Chapter 4

1 I want to thank Valerie V. Peterson for her assistance in the preparation of this manuscript, and I also want express thanks to the Josiah Macy Jr. Foundation for their kind permission to reprint the "Diagram for discussion purposes referred to as 'onionskin,'" taken from Bateson's 1956 lecture/group discussion.

2 There is another variation on this one that states, "Their our four errors in this sentence." List the errors. #1 and #2 are the same but #3 is the actual word "errors" (it is one of the errors in the sentence), and #4 is that there are only three errors.

3 For an interesting discussion and criticism of how Korzybski's view makes reality always one step removed cf. Hilary Putnam's (1990) ideas of "internal realism" in *Realism with a Human Face*.

4 This can be noted in Korzybski's work. Korzybski writes, "It is evident that every time we mistake the object for the event we are making a serious error, and if we further mistake the label for the object, and therefore for the event, our errors become more serious" (Korzybski, 1949, p. 245). This indeed may make some kind of sense: what we label an "apple" is an event and neither the event nor the object should be confused with the symbol. Still, what are we to say of the multileveled combinations that incorporate words as "not" or "this" or even "I"?

5 His point is well taken, and to this we must acknowledge Burke's insights about how such mediations occur in both directions, leading us to ask what are the signs of what? Great illustrations of the dialectical framing of verbal by nonverbal and nonverbal by verbal can be found in the television sow: "Whose Line Is It Anyway?"

6 It is here that Bateson's thinking becomes most subtle and challenging to follow. It must be underscored that in a critical doctoral dissertation John Moran demonstrates that Bateson's argument, from a strictly logical analysis, generates neither paradox nor even a violation of Russell's Theory of Logical Types. Moran's astute account shows how Bateson's uses of the Theory of Logical Types are too loose, too imprecise, and too incomplete. Regarding Bateson's discussion of the differences between the meanings of the word "denote," Moran writes,

> The simple fact that two different senses of a word occur in an expression does not violate the Theory of Logical Types…the two senses of "denote" in Bateson's expanded version of "this is play" are perfectly valid and admissible…Bateson, then, does not demonstrate that "this is play" generates paradox of "Russellian or Epimenidies types." (1979, p. 76)

Moran's account is both clear and defendable, and yet, it underestimates Bateson's overall project. Moran correctly takes both "nip" and "bite" as words which refer and which can be made subject to strictly logical analysis. This is sensible at first but less so if we adhere closely to Bateson's goals. (Also cf. Anton, 2003).

7 Bateson writes, "This double framing is, we believe, not merely a matter of 'frames within frames' but an indication that mental processes resemble logic in needing an outer frame to delimit the ground against which the figures are to be perceived" (1972, p. 188).

8 Wilden's (1972) main illustration seems to be how the emergence of the ability to digitally say "I" reorganized the logical typing of such global and pervasive natural systems as "human/environment" and "cooperation/competition." Well beyond the scope of the present essay, future research might explore how alphabetic literacy is the exemplar case of an emergent level of organization that changed the logical typing of oral noetics. Havelock's (1963, 1986) work on the emergence of abstract nouns is a case and point. Also relevant is David Olson's (1994, 1996) work, for example, on the many ways writing and speech frame each other (are about one another). Useful guiding questions might be: In what ways is speech more abstract than writing and in what ways is writing more abstract than speech? Where, when and how, does which serve as the frame of which?

9 Holenstein cites Jakobson on this point: "First the decoder is faced with the context, second, he must detect its constituents; combination is the antecedent, selection is the consequent, that is, the ultimate aim of the decoding process. The encoder begins with an analytic operation which is followed by synthesis; the decoder receives synthesized data and proceeds to their analysis" (1976, p. 145).

10 All of this was implied by Bateson where he writes, "this evolution occurs when the organism gradually ceases to respond quite 'automatically' to the mood-signs of another and becomes able to recognize the sign as a signal: that is, to recognize that the other individual's and its own signals are only signals" (1972, p. 178).

11 To illustrate how the written word travels "context free," and thus produces the horizon for an unending succession of antithetical conclusions, I recall something from my youth: I once found a small slip of paper upon which it was written, "The other side is true." And, then, when I turned the paper over, I found the message: "The other side is false." Here is the liar, saying the lie over and over.

Chapter 5: Korzybski and Bateson: Paradoxes in 'Consciousness of Abstracting'

Alfred Korzybski's project adamantly maintained that training in "consciousness of abstracting" would lead people beyond the paradoxes of abstraction. Gregory Bateson, on the other hand, argued for the inability to achieve this thoroughly. He writes, "Korzybski was, on the whole, speaking as a philosopher, attempting to persuade people to discipline their manner of thinking. But he could not win. When we come to apply his dictum to the natural history of human mental process, the matter is not so simple" (1979, pp. 30-31). This point can be brought out more generally, where Bateson suggests,

> We do not, any of us, achieve rigor. In writing, sometimes, we can take time to check the looseness of thought; but in speaking, hardly ever...I know that I personally, when speaking in conversation and even in lecturing, depart from the epistemology outlined in the previous chapter; and indeed the chapter itself was hard to write without continual lapses into other ways of thinking and may still contain such lapses. I know that I would not like to be held scientifically responsible for many loose spoken sentences that I have uttered in conversation with scientific colleagues. But I also know that if another person had the task of studying my ways of thought, he would do well to study my loosely spoken words rather than my writing. (1968, p. 230)

Finally, toward the end of his career, Bateson concluded that, "It seems to be a universal feature of human perception, a feature of the underpinning of human epistemology, that the perceiver shall perceive only the product of his perceiving act. He shall not perceive the means by which that product was created" (Bateson, 1977, p. 238).

I will not, as if by fiat and pronouncement, take sides on this issue. Rather, I here attempt to explicitly walk through a series of illustrations that help bring out how the "logic or method" of Korzybski remains correct but the conclusion of Bateson should not be underestimated. I try to demonstrate that we, in our warnings and suggestions regarding the troubles with abstraction, inevitably make the very kinds of mistakes that we attempt to extirpate.

Even if we desire to speak about entities which are "not yet" classified (such as the concepts of "the unspeakable level" or perhaps "the infinity of 'things' not yet talked about"), we so easily neglect how we already (i.e. therein) have classified them.[1] I apologize for my utter literalism here, but I would like you to carefully examine the previous sentence. In particular, the words "entities" and "things," to the extent that they make reference, refer to what are already within a class. This means that if we say what something is "called" rather than address what the thing "is," we might thereby conclude that it is not yet classified. Syntax is such that it enables us to forget that we already have called it "something" and also "thing." And even there, in that previous sentence, we seemed likewise to forget that we called the thing "it." And *there* it was called "thing." Across these few simple sentences, we hop from one word to another, obliviously taking some to be labels for things while taking others to be not more labels; it is as if we make reference to what we then pretend we didn't talk about.

Consider an even more direct and immediate manner of explaining the term "abstraction." I could stand before people, hold a cup of coffee in my hand, and then state that the thing I am holding and drinking from is not a "cup." "'Cup,'" I further say, "is the English word we use to refer to this thing." Then, silently tapping the cup and dramatically wrapping my hands around it, I say, "*This*, what I now am holding in my hands, is not a 'cup,'; 'cup' is a word, a kind of mapping, that enables us to categorize things, in this case what I am holding." What is critical is that although my silent action accompanies my words, the words themselves actually increase in abstraction: The word "cup" is labeled as an abstraction while simultaneously the word "thing" seemed to be used as if it were the less abstract term. By syntactical combination, integrating different levels of abstraction though an overlapping reference, we produce utterances in which we seem to talk about what would be independent of our talk about it; higher abstractions are thus taken as if they were the "thing" more directly.

These paradoxes of abstraction occur because we conflate the difference in logical type between abstract words (e.g. "things," "entities," "objects") and metalanguage or words that explicitly refer to the verbal order (e.g. "speech," "language," "words"). Although non-metalinguistic words (abstract words) can posit that their referents preceded the words we used to refer to them, we are able to do so only because of syntax: Terms such as "language," "words," "speech," or even "verbal level," when syntactically combined with abstract words such as "object" or "thing," operate as a mode of "overlapping reference" (cf. Holenstein, 1976). They function as a "code to message" reflexivity that allows us to make sense of the claim that "objects" and "things" preceded the words by which we refer to them. Hence, metalinguistic references enable a reflexivity that becomes taken-for-granted in the claim that "things came before language." By the very syntax of our utterances, we say that things precede language, and, this does make sense, but only because we have used metalinguistic references and thereby *already* have referred to the verbal order.

The roots of such difficulties can also be found where we attempt to thoroughly separate a class from its name. If we confuse a class with its name, we obviously suffer from logical-typing errors. But the question remains: is it even possible for this to be thoroughly avoided? Doesn't an unnamed category seem not to be a category at all? What, that is, would an unnamed category be a category of?

Perhaps a more illustrative example would help: Common sense suggests that actual physical apples must have preceded the abstract class of apples, and yet, if we do not yet have the class of apples, then how could any one apple be counted *as* an apple? As Lee Thayer (1997) suggests, the difficulty is that "To have one of anything, we already must have a category" (p. 75). Thayer's point is that individual entities do not precede the categories by which we classify them. Take, as one more example, Bateson's opening remarks regarding the problem of "play." Bateson (1956) states, "We live in a universe of namables. Within that universe we make classes" (p. 145). This is certainly clear enough, but could the namables come before the classes? Is it not obvious that the namables are already within a class, the class of namables?

At this point, a critic still might try to argue that language is not needed for the existence of kinds or classes of things. 'It is only for our convenience, it merely aids us in labeling naturally occurring types,' the critic might argue. The critic may further state: "It does not matter what you call the thing. Whether you call something a 'cup,' a 'drinking vessel,' or an 'object', the thing is still here." This does seem to make sense at least initially. And yet, as I have tried to show in several ways, we have not made good sense as much as we have enabled our-selves to overlook our non-sense. It is worth recalling that when the White Knight meets Alice, in *Through the Looking Glass*, he tries to cheer her up by playing some music. But first he states,

> 'The name of the song is called "*Haddock Eyes*."'
> 'Oh, that's the name of the song is it?' Alice said, trying to feel interested.
> 'No, you don't understand,' the Knight said, looking a little vexed. 'That's what the name is called. The name really is "*The Aged Aged Man*."'
> 'Then I ought to have said "That's what the song is called"?' Alice corrected herself.
> 'No, you oughtn't: that is quite another thing! The *song* is called "*Ways and Means*": but that's only what it's *called*, you know!'
> 'Well, what is the song, then?' said Alice, who was by this time completely bewildered.
> 'I was coming to that,' the Knight said. 'The song really is "*A Sitting On A Gate*": and the tune's my own invention.'

It appears that Alice eventually got to the bottom of all this (also cf. Wilden, 1978), but did she? Could the song be '*A Sitting On A Gate*'? Is this not a kind of er-roneous identification, a subtle act of taking the words for the thing? Do we now know the song rather than its title? More critically asked: what does the White Knight mean by "the tune"? My inquiry focuses not upon what the name of the tune is called, nor what the tune is called, nor even is it an attempt to know the name of the tune. I would like to know how I know (or why I seem to think) that the tune is the song. And, end of the day, I would like to know (i.e. to be able to "re-produce," even if only partly and in memory) the actual song.

The textual imbroglio we find in Carroll's humorous tale forces our atten-tion to what Bateson called the "premise intransitivity" that characterizes naturally communicative frames. Bateson (1955) argues, "It is conventional to argue that if A is greater than B, and B is greater than C, then A is greater than C. But in psychological processes the transitivity of asymmetrical relations is not observed. Proposition P may be a premise for Q; Q may be a premise for R, and R may be a premise for P" (p. 185). Our everyday talk habitually hops around and be-tween various abstract words and, in doing so, we leave such intransitivity covered over. Thus, when Bateson suggests that he has a "desire to know about those processes whereby organisms pull themselves up by their bootstraps" (1956, p. 216), he turns our attention to the ways that communication syntactically imbricates intransitive yet asymmetrical distinctions and thus in-builds different layers of abstraction.

Now, obviously, Korzybski's *Science and Sanity* (1933) discusses at length the non-identification between "words" and the "un-speakable objective level," and he succinctly summarizes his ideas with the pithy one-liner: "Whatever one might *say* something '*is*,' *it is not*" (p. 409). In this very quotation, Korzybski's actual utterance goes against his insights as he states them. By the syntax of the utterance he implies that the words "something" and "it" are not already something said. Korzybski undoubtedly would defend himself and say that this exactly is his point, as he sums it up elsewhere: "It is evident that every time we mistake the object for the event we are making a serious error, and if we further mistake the label for the object, and therefore for the event, our errors become more serious" (Korzybski, 1949, p. 245). Here we again find the same difficulties: he uses the words "object" and "event" to state his insights and thereby is forced to use the very resources that he calls into question.

We cannot propose a non-identification--nor call identification into question--without subtly embodying the errors that we wish to challenge. Regarding the paradoxes of abstraction, we thus continue to make the mistakes--and thereby to illustrate--the very difficulties that we attempt to bring under critical attention.

Endnotes to Chapter 5

1 This point is nicely brought to a head by Alan Watts, who compares Korzybski's views with Zen Buddhism. Watts writes, "However, it would seem that Korzybski still thought of the 'unspeakable' world as a multiplicity of infinitely differentiated events. For Zen, the world of 'suchness' is neither one nor many, neither uniform nor undifferentiated... it teases the mind out of thought, dumbfounding the chatter of definition" (1957, pp. 130-131). This issue is taken up also by Walker Percy (1954).

Chapter 6: Is There a Territory Without Maps?

> *"The collision of two galaxies
> and the salivation of Pavlov's dog,
> different as they are, are far more alike
> than either is like the simplest act of naming.
> Naming stands at greater distance from Pavlov's dog
> than the latter does from a galactic collision."*
> —— Walker Percy, 1954, pp. 154-155

We *say* that the map is not the territory. But we must remember that there is no territory without maps. To think otherwise is to believe that, in both the first and the second sentences of this brief essay, the word "territory" is not just that, a word. "The pencil is itself unspeakable. True; but insofar as it remains unspeakable—that is, unvalidated by you and me through a symbol—it is also inconceivable" (Percy, 1954 p. 262). If I make reference to what is not yet referred to (i.e. unspeakable), am I not thereby referring to *it* nonetheless?

We *say* that the map is not the territory. But we must remember that there are no maps which are not, *de facto*, part of the territory. The reason the territory is always larger than the map is because all maps are part of the whole to which they refer. But we need not try to imagine some kind of paradoxical map that would be so all inclusive in its details that it would include the map itself. We simply need to stay with the question: if maps were not part of the territory, if they were not basically terrain, then where would they be?

Maps, said quite otherwise, are a particular intentional attitude that we can adopt toward certain parts/aspects of the terrain. Take this case: Five students stand in a line before a large classroom. Moving down the line from left to right each student says the name "Alfred Korzybski." Although each student utters the words (i.e. produces acoustic signs) at a different place, at a different time, using different pitch, timbre, rate and intonation, the same words (immaterial symbols) were said. *Where*, I am asking, is that which is the same? Even if we grant for the sake of argument that these words may have multiple meanings and even changing ones, we also must grant that to say as much is to assume that the word per se stays the same. Indeed, it makes only literary and poetic sense to say that a *word* changes.

It is not simply that the 'word is not the thing,' it is that *words are not things*. If they were things they'd be subject to entropy and decay. Erving Goffman (1969) nicely points out one implication: "Among all things of the world, information is the hardest to guard, since it can be stolen without removing it" (pp. 78-79). Imagine, for further illustration, someone approaches you on the street and whispers, "Shhh. Try not to use the word 'apple'; there's a shortage." Such an obviously crazy statement reveals with considerable clarity that a word which is not a principle of repeatability is no word at all.

Conceptual assistance regarding these issues comes from Walker Percy's (1954) *The Message in the Bottle: How queer man is, how queer language is, and what one has to do with the other*. He identifies the phenomena of naming and denotation as the exemplars needing our attention. He initially attempts to clarify his ideas by considering a toddler who one day points to a balloon to which the father says, "Balloon." In this seemingly simple case, Percy notes "three mystifying negatives."

> Where, what is the word balloon?...Where is the word itself? Is it the little marks in the dictionary which you point to when I ask you to show me the word balloon....What about the balloon itself?...It is precisely the nature of the boy's breakthrough that the object he points to is understood by him as a member of a class of inflated objects. A few minutes later he might well point to a blue sausage shaped inflated object and say, "Balloon." What about the boy himself?...He couples *balloon* with balloon. But who, what couples? (pp. 43-44)

This passage holds at least the following aspects: first, denotative words, as principles of repeatability, convey a content that cannot simply be identified with the form of their spatio-temporal expression (also cf. pp. 217-222). Second, by their very nature, ideas deal in general content, classes or types. They apply categorically and are kinds of promises of intelligibility for an indefinite future (also cf. Royce, 1967). Furthermore and finally, Percy's account of persons suggests that they somehow couple by "equating the unequal": on the one hand, the particular balloon with the general concept of a balloon, and on the other hand, the particular and fleeting sounds in the air or the visible marks on the page with the word "balloon."

He thus characterizes denotative utterance, speech employing the word "is," as a kind of valuation; it is an act of *identification* whereby we demonstrate our ability to "equate what is not equal." By this account, denotation holds both a kind of category mistake as well as an easily overlooked creative potential. The category mistake is most thoroughly spelled out by Korzybski in his *Science and Sanity*, and is nicely summed where he writes, "Whatever you say something is, it is not" (1933, p. 409). The point here, said otherwise, is that "the word is not the thing." Granting initial insight to the general semanticists, Percy nonetheless maintained that the word "is" casts more than a spell of delusion. For, if we are able to *equate* the unequal, then are they unequal or not? He writes,

> When a man appears and names a thing...something unprecedented takes place. What the third term, man, does is not merely enter into interaction with the others--though he does this too--but stand apart from two of the terms and say that one "is" the other. The two things which he pairs or identifies are the *word* he speaks or hears and the *thing* he sees before him...A is clearly not B. But were it not for this cosmic blunder, man would not be man; he would never be capable of folly and he would never be capable of truth. Unless he says that A is B, he will never know A or B; he will only respond to them. (p. 157)

He further suggests, "We might therefore reverse Korzybski's dictum: It is *only* if you say what the object *is* that you can know anything about it at all...The thing is intended through the symbol which you say and I can repeat, and it is only through this quasi identification that it can be conceived at all" (p. 263).

The map is not the territory; the word is not the thing; we cannot eat the menu. Fair enough. Even if it is true that we cannot say what things *are*, it is just as true that *only* by our sayings can we say what things are not. In fact, only by speech can we conceive of that which we say is more and/or less than what is said about it.

Chapter 7: The Thing Is Not Itself: Artefactual Metonymy and the World of Antiques

General Semanticists routinely draw attention to the non-identification between the symbolic realm and first-order processes of reality. This distinction underlies many different expressions within GS: "Whatever I say a thing is, it is not," "The map is not the territory," "Symbols are not what they symbolize," "Representations are not the things they represent," and even Alan Watts' comical refrain: "The word is not the thing, the word is not the thing, Hi Ho the Derry-O, the word is not the thing" (Watts, 1974, p. 8). Not only do GS scholars commonly note the differences between the realm of words and the realm of first-order processes of reality (i.e. realm of not-words), they also commonly acknowledge that words operate at multiple and varying levels of abstraction. Consider, for example, a few illustrations from Irving Lee's *Language Habits and Human Affairs:*

These illustrations are clear and helpful, and they are representative of the images throughout Lee's book. At many different places, Lee illustrates not only varying levels of abstraction, but he demonstrates the kinds of confusion that emerge from failing to stay vigilant in these distinctions. He advocates a careful practice of moving from observation to description to inference. All said, Lee differentiates many layers of abstraction: an event-process level, an objective level, a descriptive level, and finally, an inferential level (cf. 1941, p. 204).

For all that Lee's depiction does in clarifying the nature of abstraction, it unfortunately seems to suggest that inferential aspects should or ought enter with speech and description. First order abstractions are cast as sheer processes of sense organs and the nervous system transforming the silent eventfulness, the "electronic dance," into a stable appearance of things, objects, and the world more generally. In this account, people use language too inferentially and too commonly fail to take the opportunity for careful observation and description prior to making their inferences. Stated a bit reductively, Lee's program seems to suggest that semantic confusions can be alleviated by always ensuring that description precedes inference.

If at first pass this appears to be little more than a residual difficulty, it grows into a pernicious one as we consider the degree to which we remain unable to bracket out all of the aesthetic connections within our social and physical worlds. Part of the problem with the many means of human abstraction is therefore not merely that "the word is not the thing;" it is that even things are never simply themselves.

The issue is not merely that the word "apple" is not an apple or that we can't eat a picture or painting of an apple. It is that everyday objects transcend themselves, and when we attempt to describe them prior to making any inferences about them, we are, ironically, attempting to de-contextualize and de-realize the ways that items of the world actually show themselves. Aren't there, for example, inferential relations that are nearer to the objective level than to the verbal descriptive level? In such cases (perhaps the average and most likely case for everyday household artifacts), items are contextually imbued and transformed into vestiges of unseen relations. It is not then, as Lee suggests, as if we jump past the descriptive level to the inferential level: on the contrary, it is rather that we jump over the nonverbal inferential level when we attempt to liquidate something into a careful objective verbal description that would precede all inference.

It might help to consider the ways that sets and verbal classifications are easily recognized as multileveled but too commonly are contrasted with a kind of unified What Is Going On, WIGO. The process-level of reality, the unspeakable-only-showable, the immediate, all of these seem to imply that the phenomenon of levels is largely an issue of the verbal realm. That is, I can hold an object such as an apple in my hand and then show how all of the verbal classifications of it operate at different levels: "organic matter," "edibles," "fruits," "apples," "granny smiths." At no point, we commonly say, are we ever able to say the thing itself, the actual item I can hold, eat, etc. Then, we may even point to one given apple and start to show how even this one apple is ever changing, and we index it by henceforth calling it, "apple$_1$," "apple$_2$," "apple$_3$," etc. The subtle difficulty is that we seem to unify or totalize into a non-leveled phenomenon all that is not verbal. It is as if reality itself is all of the same level, and then the senses filter and engage in a kind of first-order abstraction, and then language breaks the sensory world into a hierarchy or ladder of abstractions for everything else.

Wendell Johnson's notable book, *People in Quandaries*, offers a discussion of levels of abstraction that advances but moves beyond the account found within Lee. Johnson identifies multiple levels of abstraction already at the level of "not words" and thereby helps to illustrate how we routinely fail to register the many different levels within the silent operations of the senses. Johnson writes, "...ordinary food dislikes are as good an illustration as one could want of the confusion of one level of abstraction with another—of the failure, that is, to differentiate the levels, and to *act* as if one knew that the sense-data levels were different from the inferential-data level" (1946, p. 108). His point is that our food preferences (as well as the reasons we like or dislike them) often have less to do with the physical or actual properties of the food than they do with other matters such as associations and inferential data to which we all too commonly act as if we were reacting purely to sense data or first-order reality. He accordingly opens resources for dealing with the many different levels of abstraction that occur even at nonverbal levels. Indeed, for Johnson, there are many different levels of abstraction within the not-words process-level; as he maintains, "Abstractions on all these levels are *unspeakable*" (p. 109).

I am belaboring and haggling about this rather nuanced point because codifications of reality—and management of different levels of communication—are to be found at various "levels" below the verbal, that is, within visual, vocalic, and 'nonverbal' realms (also cf. Gregory Bateson, 1972). To help to clarify this difference between Irving Lee and Wendell Johnson—and to help fortify Johnson's line of argument, we might turn to the ideas of Susanne K. Langer. Langer outlines modes of abstraction and forms of symbolic inference that operate prior to (or beneath) any verbal description. She documents the many ways that human life blazes with aesthetic character according to presentational forms and participative processes.

In *Philosophy in a New Key*, Langer accounts for how metonymy operates at the presentational (i.e. nonverbal) level; she basically discusses the forerunner of articulate speech and addresses what she calls "artefactual metonymy." Putting the beginnings of the operations of language into the pre-verbal or silent realm, Langer writes:

> ...'the tendency to see reality symbolically,' is the real keynote of language... presentational forms are much lower than discursive, and the appreciation of meaning probably earlier than its expression. The earliest manifestation of any symbol-making tendency, therefore is likely to be a mere *sense of significance* attached to certain objects...It is like a dawn of superstition—a forerunner of fetishes and demons, perhaps. (1942, p. 110)

Further clarifying her ideas, Langer states, "One of my earliest recollections is that chairs and tables *always kept the same look*, in a way that people did not, and that

I was awed by sameness of that appearance." In this particular example, Langer is suggesting a kind of symbolic transformation nestled within vision itself, and she is not taking this "visual significance" from inferring out of verbal descriptions. On the contrary, if we were to attempt to suspend all symbolic transformations and presentational forms, as if objects could be isolated and rendered as merely available for objective description, we actually neutralize and sever them from the countless relations implicated by their participations in particular situations and engagements.

At one point Langer discusses the ape, Gua, and the manner in which Gua was anxious and alarmed when her trainer left the area but also how Gua could be pacified fairly quickly by receiving the trainer's overalls. The overalls, Langer suggests, served as a kind of artefactual metonymy: they stood in as a kind of surrogate. Gua would drag them around as a "fetish of protection." Langer writes, "Gua was using the coveralls even in his presence as a help to her imagination, which kept him near whether he went out or not" (p. 114). To better understand the artefactual metonymies all around us, we can consider how everyday objects are often more than the material items that they seem to be. In fact, if we were to limit our experience of objects to what could be had solely by observation and description, we would actually de-world them as we break them from their dense and largely aesthetic participation in lived existence. As a point of comparison, we might turn to the human world of antiques and antique collecting.

In the world of antiques, we find a kind of "non-identity" at the non-verbal level but one that is at a different level of abstraction than any previously mentioned. For example, consider the difference between walking into both a grocery story and an antiques store. In each case, we might simply look at (or even carefully observe) all of the different items and be tempted to reduce them to one level: the level of immediately available objects with one's perceptual field. For all the objects, aesthetic qualities might be recognized and judged bereft of any historical awareness.

But, to recognize an antique as the particular antique it is, we need to change the way we look at things. We come to see the object in terms of what is no longer here; the item itself hints and alludes to a mysterious otherworldliness. Indeed, what makes an antique an antique is not merely how old it is, as if antiqueness were a property or quality of the object itself. "Antiqueness" is a register of the change in the world around the things; the world in which they were designed to fit is now absent and this change in the larger world changes the things themselves. It is, again, the changes all around an item that make the item an antique; the antique is made into an antique when its world disappears. And so, even if the thing seems to be fully intact and functional—and by that I mean nearly unchanged from its original condition, the thing is thereby even more "other than itself," for in such cases we speak of an "antique in mint condition." Antiques, and ancient relics even more so, are things that represent worlds that have long since passed away, and it is this representing whereby things transcend their merely physical properties and become, at another level, surrogates or stand-ins for times now bygone.

In contrast to all of the ways that "the word is not the thing" and the ways that inferential statements get inattentively carried over into observation and our reactions, I think that Johnson's (and Langer's) important contribution to our understanding is that even at the level of the not-words we always already have introjections of inferential data. This means that items of the human world are not simply themselves. They inevitably get transformed into nonverbal metonymies in accordance with the situations in which they are imbedded and in which they have participated.[1] To say that even the thing is not itself is to recognize that many forms of inferential symbolism occur below the verbal and prior to the descriptive realm.

In this very brief paper, I have tried to draw a rather fine and nuanced line between the ideas of Irving Lee and Wendell Johnson. Granting to Irving Lee a great deal of practical wisdom concerning the relations between the verbal and the nonverbal, it is Johnson, I have suggested, who most helps to clarify the inferential levels of abstractions even within the world of non-words, particularly as exemplified in antiques.[2]

Endnotes to Chapter 7

1 Well beyond the scope of the present paper, future work might explore how sexual desires and fetishes, various kinds of bodily appetites, emerge as artefactual metonymies.

2 Part of this point can be driven home if we go comparatively to the spoken word for just a moment. One of Walter Ong's contributions was to recognize how the language we use everyday, our mother tongue, is overpopulated with meanings, so much so that the meanings of words come into play beyond speaker intentions. Of the penetrating examples offered by Ong is the fact that sir Isaac Newton wrote his major works in Latin. Ong further contends that the historically developed scientific distinction between knower and known critically depended upon Learned Latin. He writes:

> It would appear likely that a textualized chirographically controlled language such as Learned Latin aided greatly in establishing the distance between observer and observed, between the knower and the known, that science and especially modern science, required. No longer a mother tongue, Learned Latin left all its users free of the rich, emotional, unconscious, but often confusingly subjective involvements of a language learned orally from infancy, where knower and known, subject and object, formed a kind of continuum that could be broken up only gradually and perhaps never completely. (1984, p. 8-9)

The words we use hold subterranean significations: many words are ineluctably over-populated; they surpass and overflow the original intention. Graphic illustration of this fact can be seen on the television show, *Beavis and Butthead*, where the two main characters twitter and laugh any time someone says a word which has any, and by that I mean only the slightest or remotest, association with sex or sexual encounters: "crack of dawn," "screwdriver," "wood," or even "penetrating." Words themselves cannot be expunged of all of their repressed meanings, suggestions, innuendos, and past associations and involvements. Many words even hint at the words with which they rhyme, and so, tongue twisters such as, "Mother hen pheasant plucker, plucking mother pheasant hens" can be quite humorous even when correctly pronounced.

Part III:

Media Ecological Studies

"People have long supposed that bulldog opacity, backed by firm disapproval, is adequate enough protection against any new experience. It is the theme of this book that not even the most lucid understanding of the peculiar force of a medium can head off the ordinary 'closure' of the senses that causes us to conform to the pattern of experience presented. The utmost purity of mind is no defense against bacteria, though the confreres of Louis Pasteur tossed him out of the medical profession for his base allegations about the invisible operation of bacteria. To resist TV, therefore, one must acquire the antidote of related media like print." (Marshall McLuhan, *Understanding Media*, p. 436)

Chapter 8: History, Orientations, and Future Directions of Media Ecology

"Man is an extension of nature
that remakes the nature that makes the man."
— McLuhan & Nevitt, 1972, p. 66

"There is no way to write 'naturally.'…but --paradox again—
artificiality is natural to human beings."
— Ong, 1982, p. 83

"A new technology does not
add or subtract something.
It changes everything."
— Postman, 1992, p. 18

Introduction

Media ecology is a broad-based scholarly tradition and social practice. Most generally characterized, media ecology understands the on-going history of humanity and the dynamics of culture and personhood as intricately intertwined with communication and communication technologies. It spans the study of communication between and among the earliest peoples to the exploration of emerging communication technologies. Both historical and contemporary, it slides across and incorporates ancient, modern and postmodern discourses. Located comfortably within secular as well as sacred spaces, media ecology takes as relevant both humanist and theological concerns. Although some media ecologists hold degrees in areas of communication studies, media ecologists can be found in nearly every discipline. Media ecology is thus multidisciplinary, as it draws upon and contributes to anthropology, archeology, economics, history, literacy and orality studies, literary theory, rhetorical studies, systems theory, phenomenology, and theology, to name only a few. It is sometimes called "the Toronto School," or "medium studies," or even "North America Cultural Studies."

Although media ecology traces its roots all the way back to ancient history, it first became coherent and solidified in the writings of Marshall McLuhan, Walter Ong, Harold Innis, Lewis Mumford, Edmund Carpenter, Dorothy Lee, Eric Havelock, Jacques Ellul and many others. The expression itself, "media ecology," emerged in a 1967 discussion between Marshall McLuhan, Eric McLuhan and Neil Postman (see Strate, 2005). Postman then started using the expression in public talks as early as 1968, and by 1971, New York University (NYU) had launched a doctoral program by that name. Like an increasing number of scholars, Postman recognized a need to systematically address the organic nature of communication, media, and human life. He also sought a term that would well represent the perspective and field of inquiry that was becoming increasingly evident. This was solidified even further in 1998 when NYU, the Toronto schools of media studies, and St. Louis University joined resources and founded the international organization known as the "Media Ecology Association" (MEA). With annual conferences drawing scholars from around the globe and representation at national and international communication conferences throughout the year, the MEA [www.media-ecology.org] actively supports one of the more significant traditions in media and mass communication research in North America.

Some basic or core ideas within media ecology are wrapped up in aphoristic statements such as: "The medium is the message," "The medium is the metaphor," "Media are environments and environments are media." And, "the user is the content of any medium." What these different quotations try to make clear is that communication and communication media are environmental and that we, ourselves, are mediated by those environments. The printing press, for example, is not so much a technology within an environment as it is that by which we have come to live inside a literate culture. Money, as another example, is not a mere thing that can be held within one's wallet; it is part of a larger environment (the economy) in which those who have money can be. Likewise, a watch is not a mere object that rests within an already existing sense of time; we are able to find ourselves within the temporally synchronized environments that watches make possible. Microscopes, telescopes, mirrors, lenses, all of these technologies have not simply added something to the human world; they have changed both it and us. The same could be said of all dominant communication technologies.

Three Key Figures: Marshall McLuhan, Walter J. Ong, Neil Postman

Orientation to the field of media ecology comes from considering some of the main ideas of a few of its central figures. Although many scholars have played a vital role and have made substantial contributions, the present discussion focuses upon three: Marshall McLuhan, Walter Ong, and Neil Postman. In his summative and authoritative review of the media ecology tradition, founding MEA president Lance Strate, writes "media ecology can be understood as an intellectual network in which McLuhan, Ong, and Postman constitute the prime nodes" (2004, p. 3). Additionally, Strate points out that McLuhan's *Understanding Media*, Ong's *Orality and Literacy*, and Postman's *Amusing Ourselves to Death*, are "of the most frequently cited works in the media ecology literature" (2004, p. 19). What follows is a brief review of some of the main ideas of these three thinkers. Then, I discuss a few additional contributors and some of the different medium areas that have been studied and researched. I conclude with future directions.

Before proceeding any further, I must make clear that what follows is a rough and very abstract summary of a complex multidisciplinary field of study. The few addressed are treated quickly and incompletely and countless authors are omitted. Moreover, some scholars might contest the presence or absence of some thinker or important work. Despite these obvious shortcomings and space limitations, the goal is to deliver the spirit and flavor of media ecology. More thorough review also can be found in Lum (2005).

Marshall McLuhan

Marshall McLuhan, for some media ecologists, is the key or central figure within the field of media ecology. McLuhan was so innovative and groundbreaking that media scholar Paul Levinson found it appropriate to write: "What did

McLuhan contribute to Media Ecology? …Without his work in the 1950 and 60's there would be no field of study that sought to explain how the nuances and great sweeps of human history are made possible by media of communication" (2000, p. 17). This may or may not be an over-statement, but it is clear that North American media study would never be the same after McLuhan. Many contemporary scholars, suggests Tom Wolfe in his video "The Video McLuhan," begin explaining their own position by stating first whether they agree or disagree with the ideas of McLuhan.

Formally trained in English literature, especially well versed in the works of Shakespeare, Thomas Nashe, and James Joyce, McLuhan style is dense and aphoristic, both challenging and playful. His books present mosaics rather than linear arguments, and he always maintained that his grand sweeping claims were to be taken as "probes" rather than as literal assertions. "I explore; I do not explain," he would stress.

Not only was McLuhan a prolific and innovative scholar (writing over a dozen books), he also was involved in many collaborative interdisciplinary projects. These projects included works on art and perspective with Harley Parker and Quentin Fiore, works on modern organizations with Barrington Nevitt and Peter Drucker, and various projects with anthropologists such as Edmund Carpenter, Ray Birdwhistle, and Dorothy Lee. Part of what becomes apparent in McLuhan's books, especially *Counterblast* (1969) co-authored with Parker, and his best selling work, co-authored with Fiore, *The Medium is the Massage* (1967), is the very meaning of the book as a medium. These books, for example, break protocols of uniformity, linearity, and seriality. Some of the sentences change font or type size; some sentences are written in swirls or loops. Some pages need to be held at a tangential angle or viewed in a mirror's reflection. By way of these texts, McLuhan shocked and suddenly awakened readers to the psychological and visual sensibilities that are conditioned by the printed word.

One of McLuhan's most definitive probes, already mentioned above, serves as the main theme for the first chapter of his most studied book, *Understanding Media: The Extensions of Man* (1964). The chapter title and recurrent idea is "The Medium is the Message." This was his pithy response to what seemed to be the dominant view at the time (and perhaps still is in some scholarly traditions). This popular view is that media are simply objects out in the environment and that the impacts or effects of a given medium come from the 'content' it conveys or the use to which it is put rather than from the medium per se. McLuhan, on the contrary, argued for a need to study the many-leveled alterations and modifications encumbered by any pervasive communication technology. For example, just as the emergence of a staple crop within a society alters patterns of living and social organization, so a dominant communication medium will shape and alter the lives of those who depend upon it (McLuhan, 1964). In this very simple way, the medium is the message. But the expression implies much more than this.

For McLuhan, media are extensions of the human body, and those extensions alter and modify the senses and ratios among them; they alter our sensibilities of space and time. The expression, "The medium is the message," therefore, partly means that any medium alters the sensory and the spatio-temporal biases of persons and cultures (also see Anton, 2005). Said otherwise, the noetic and sociological character of a society and its members *is* the message of any dominant communication medium (also see Dance, 1989). Another meaning to the expression "the medium is the message" is that the content of any medium is an earlier medium; new and emerging technologies hold previous technologies as their content (McLuhan, 1964). For example, the book holds writing and writing holds speech. Film carries photographs, and TV holds both radio and film. And finally, one last meaning of "the medium is the message" deserves mention and brings us full circle. McLuhan writes,

> Technologies begin as anti-environments, as controls, and then become environmental...To say that a technology or extension of man creates a new environment is a much better way of saying that the medium is the message. This environment is always 'invisible' and its content is always the old technology. (McLuhan, 1967, pp. 30-31)

To suggest that media, as extensions of the human, become environments in their own right is a different way of saying that the user is the content of any medium. This suggests that basic sensibilities of space and time—the underlying order in and by which we experience the world, others, and ourselves—are mediated by various communication technologies. All of these different meanings and ideas are nicely suggested in the opening epigram to this paper: *"Man is an extension of nature that remakes the nature that makes the man"* (McLuhan & Nevitt, 1972, p. 66).

A more progressive analysis comes by noting that McLuhan identifies the alphabet, the movable-type printing press, and the telegraph as three of the most significant communication technologies in the development of history and the modern world. Each of these media of communication, as it has become dominant within a given culture, has introduced radical and sweeping changes in all areas of life: personal, private, secular and sacred.

McLuhan characterizes earliest tribal life as having an integration of the senses, and he suggests that tribal humans experienced speech as part of sacred and acoustic space. Such early people were nomadic hunters and gatherers who lived in the sacred resonance of oral tradition. Non-specialist integration into the tribe and depth involvement were other general characteristics. McLuhan also suggests that earliest oral peoples did not know of a private "inner" mind as is known today, though as tribal life became less nomadic and more sedentary, psychological characteristics and the patterns of social organization changed accordingly (also see Berman, 2000). These changes, which took millennia, brought more inward differentiation, specialization of role, and a greater reliance upon writing. Various forms of writing in fact played a critical role in bureaucratic record keeping, but more importantly, it was the particular invention of the Greek alphabet that, McLuhan says, was the key to the development of Western culture.

Prior forms of writing (e.g. ideographic, syllabic or consonantal systems) were fairly difficult to read and this difficulty worked to keep literacy and individual cultures somewhat closed. The Greek system, as economical and exhaustive, was, in McLuhan's terms, "explosive": the basic units and all the signs necessary to read any alphabetic script could be mastered quickly. The explosive power of the alphabet was witnessed in modern times by Carothers' (1959) studies of the dissemination of alphabetic literacy in Africa, where a single generation of alphabetic literacy was enough to challenge and disrupt more traditional oral-modes of culture (McLuhan 1963, 1964). Additionally, the Greek alphabet enabled various attempts at "universal" language translation, and it held the nascent possibility of globalism, a possibility that was pursued partly through early Roman conquests and expansions. As the phonetic alphabet laid the groundwork for de-tribalizing oral societies, so the printing press was the architect of nationalistic, public individualism.

McLuhan's second single-authored book, one that won him much scholarly acclaim, was *The Gutenberg Galaxy: The Making of Typographic Man* (1963). This book documents the drift from oral/sacred/acoustic space to the neutralized secular space of the visual alphabeticized word. McLuhan identified the psychic impacts of the printed word, and suggested that it intensified fixed point of view and perspective, fostered the sense that space is visual, uniform, and continuous, gave the ability for detachment and non-involvement, and enabled the separation between thought and feeling. The printing press, as he states elsewhere, brought "nationalism, industrialism, mass markets, and universal literacy and education" (1964, p. 173).

It helped to foster a total homogenization and orderliness by carrying the general message of uniformity, exact repeatability, and standardization. Typography and the printing press brought forth publics comprised of private citizens who maintain individual points of view. The printing press, McLuhan argues, was one of the most significant communication media in changing and altering all aspects of human life.

Whereas the printing press was a kind of culmination of the potentialities of the alphabet, the telegraph was almost a total reversal. Its only rival, according to McLuhan, was the original extension of all the senses that occurred with the very dawn of human language. Whereas earlier forms of mechanical technology were centralist, electricity is fundamentally decentralist. We can appreciate the significance of the telegraph by putting it in the context of its emergence. McLuhan thus begins his *Understanding Media* with the sentence: "After three thousand years of explosion, by means of fragmentary and mechanical technologies, the Western world is imploding." By implosion he means that electric forms of media collapse space and liquidate time. With electric media we find the emergence of the mass person, the re-tribalized person. We are now, to use one of McLuhan's well-known probes, living "in a global village." The emergence of the possibility of a global consciousness came with the telegraph and the ensuing electric communication technologies. In sum: McLuhan suggests a drift first from oral/tribal life to publics comprised of private citizens and then on to the mass humans who live in a global village. Eric McLuhan, Marshall's son and colleague, has followed up on this line on thought and recently identified the emergence of the Paleolithic hunter within the information jungle (2005).

Although time has proved McLuhan right more than some early critics could have imagined, he nevertheless remains a controversial figure. He is celebrated for his keen insight and originality, though he is often criticized for grand and sweeping statements that defy empirical testing. In any event, his writings are excellent beginnings and explorations meant to help us attend to the ways that technology may be mediating our self-relations, our interpersonal relations, and our relations with the larger world.

Walter J. Ong

Walter J. Ong was a graduate student at St. Louis University when he first met Marshall McLuhan. McLuhan's influence upon Ong was evident not only in Ong's selection of Gerald Manly Hopkin's poetry for his master's thesis but even more so in his much celebrated doctoral dissertation on Peter Ramus. In his dissertation, completed at Harvard University under Perry Miller, Ong detailed and documented how the rise of Ramism was related to developments in visual technologies and ran concurrent with the decline of dialogue as a model of knowing (Ong, 1958). This initial work also, as Strate emphasizes, "established Ong's reputation as an impeccable scholar, and serves as a model for research in media ecology and cultural history" (2004, p. 12).

Although Ong is perhaps best known for his book *Orality and Literacy* (1982), he has approximately 400 publications—and over 10 books. These writings span the history of consciousness, the nature of the person, the relations between shame-based cultures and guilt-based cultures, the nature of dialogue and dialectic, the origin of the scientific world-picture, the nature of the electric and recorded word, and finally, the contestations over the definition and meaning of "life." Across these diverse works, Ong pioneered a phenomenologically informed media history, bringing historical depth and breadth together with phenomenological sensibilities to explore how various communication technologies have altered and modified human psychodynamics, social structures, and cultural practices (also see Gronbeck, Farrell, & Soukup, 1991).

Ong's works carry a phenomenologically attuned media history as a kind of method or orientation throughout, but his scholarship as a whole is perhaps better understood as Thomas J. Farrell suggests, as "broadly interested in working out an adequate personalist philosophy" (2000, p. 7).

For Ong, this means studying the ways that interiority and exteriority intertwine in the person. In his *The Presence of the Word* (1967), Ong stresses the primacy of sound, suggesting that "sound itself thus of itself suggests presence. Voice is not inhabited by presence as by something added: it simply conveys presence as nothing else does" (1967, p. 114).

Persons are present in voice and voice conveys the presence of the person, but voice, it must be understood, is never a mere object over and against us within neutral visual space. Therefore, when Ong says that voice conveys the presence of the person, this does not imply that words or persons are extended spatial (i.e. visible) wholes. Writing both about the person and about spoken words, Ong argues that they refuse to "submit completely to any of those norms of clarity or explicitness (which means 'unfoldedness') such as we derive through considering knowledge and communication by analogy with sight" (1962, p. 29).

For Ong, the presence conveyed by voice does not literally go into or "inside" others. On the contrary, it is we who always already find ourselves within another's voice. As Ong puts it,

> When we speak of a presence in its fullest sense—the presence which we experience in the case of another human being...we speak of something that surrounds us, in which we are situated. "I am *in* his presence," we say, not "in front of his presence." Being in is what we experience in a world of sound. (1967, p.130)

Human voice conveys the presence of the person, a presence that is an interiority in which we can find ourselves and with which we can commune. And so, speech does not simply occur within a given situation. It is part of the situation in which we find ourselves, not only in the case of a conversation or argument but especially in the case of a pledge, oath or vow.

In the modern literate world, words (living vocal cries) came to be taken as if they were but things. How did this come to pass? That is, what transpired historically to lead people to think and believe that words and persons are basically visible things or objects? Ong suggests that simple naming is the most basic operation for intellectually separating the known from the knower. From that beginning, phonetic writing facilitated a kind of control that helped to solidify, intensify, and perhaps overdraw this distinction. Prior to objectifying their speech, earlier peoples experienced interior and exterior as inseparable or somehow intermingled. After the wide dissemination of alphabetic print, however, interiority and exteriority seemed separable if not wholly and completely separate. With print, persons could grasp their speech at arms length and get a firmer handle on it. As Ong suggests in *Interfaces of the Word* (1977),"with writing, the earlier noetic state undergoes a kind of cleavage, separating the knower from the external universe and then from himself" (1977, p. 18).

Whereas older "primary-oral" cultures mainly recognized thought and reason as occurring in dialogue and conversation, literate moderns increasingly imagine that thought and reason occur "in" a silent reader, writer, or thinker. It was thus literacy, Ong argues, that led to the modern solipsistic notion of a silent, psychological thinker. Consider, for example, the common assumption that Rodin's "The Thinker" is an ancient piece of art. Its modern quality should be obvious, because it is moderns, certainly not ancients, who associate thought with the solitary, silent individual. Literacy also introduced the idea of intellectual property rights: the legal notion that someone, a single particular person, could be the originator and source of some given idea. With literacy also came the popular notion that learning by repetition and rote is degenerate and that originality ought to be valued over retention of the past (Ong, 1982).

Although literate sensibilities were imperceptibly slow to develop, we should not underestimate conscious pressures to make language lend greater and greater objectivity. Highly relevant for the scientific revolution was that people eventually learned how to stand in subject-object relations to their own speech, and thereby, learned how to attempt "objective" definitions. One crucial example was Learned Latin. Ong maintains that it was vital to the growing scientific distinction between knower and known:

> It would appear likely that a textualized chirographically controlled language such as Learned Latin aided greatly in establishing the distance between observer and observed, between the knower and the known, that science and especially modern science, required. No longer a mother tongue, Learned Latin left all its users free of the rich, emotional, unconscious, but often confusingly subjective involvements of a language learned orally from infancy, where knower and known, subject and object, formed a kind of continuum that could be broken up only gradually and perhaps never completely. (1984, pp. 8-9)

It was not merely writing and alphabetic text that enabled people to get a firmer grasp upon the difference between the knower and known; it was the calculated employment of a dead language. The more general point is that interior depths of consciousness emerged and developed inseparably from the evolution of communicative technologies, writing and print in particular. As Western culture expanded in reach of and in regard for exteriority, it correlatively grew a more and more intensified sense of each person's absolute interiority.

Within Ong's historical account, then, the increase of depth and detail in our regard for exteriority is tied to increasing recognition of individuation and personal uniqueness—and vice versa—and both of these are intricately tied to developments in communicative technologies. Whether tracing developments in phonetic writing, or discussing differences between primary orality and secondary orality, or unpacking how Ramism or the printing press altered social and psychological patterns, or considering the articulation of Victorian particularism in Hopkins' poetry and prose, or even examining how newer electronic media continue to shape both speech and writing, Walter J. Ong stands as a central pillar in the media ecological tradition.

Neil Postman

It was in the 1950's, while he was pursuing a doctorate at Columbia University's Teachers College, that Neil Postman—then a student under Louis Forsdale—heard Marshall McLuhan give lectures in New York City. The impact of these early encounters is evident in Postman's first book, *Television and the Teaching of English* (1961), and although Postman's views changed as his career matured, the overall influence of McLuhan on this thinking never waned.

A social critic, communication theorist, educational reformer and public intellectual, Neil Postman was the author of at least 20 books, and he produced a lucid body of scholarship that serves as a model of media ecological research (also see Gencarelli, 2000). Of the scholars reviewed so far, Postman is the most pessimistic and most neo-Luddite of the group. Unlike McLuhan and Ong, Postman more aggressively cuts against the seemingly endless popular optimism surrounding technological "progress" and offers resources for recovering the ideals of earlier (and more reasonable) ages. Postman also is the most vocal proponent of the actual expression "media ecology." For brevity and focus, the present discussion is limited to reviewing a few select areas of Postman's scholarship: his contributions to educational reform and pedagogical theory, his analyses of the follies and foibles of everyday language use, and finally, his widely known critical works on television, technology, and contemporary culture.

Some of Postman's early works now stand as classics in educational theory and practice. Although critical discussion of education appears throughout almost all of Postman's books, four books in particular, the first two co-authored with Charles Weingartner, deserve mention. First is *Teaching as a Subversive Activity* (1969), where Postman and Weingartner outline a radically new curriculum, one that is more in step with the emerging electric generation. At this early point in his career, Postman seemed slightly optimistic about the prospects of the educational system "getting with" the televisual revolution. Not yet employing the term "media ecology," Postman back then used the most unwieldy expression: "the Sapir-Whorf-Korzybski-Ames-Einstein-Heisenberg-Wittgenstein-McLuhan-Et Al. Hypothesis" to convey the sense that communication and communication technologies transform the ways we act and understand the world and ourselves. By 1971, with the publication of *The Soft Revolution* (1971), the term media ecology had emerged. This book, a piece of "soft activism," has a styling and layout reminiscent of McLuhan's *Counterblast*. Additionally, this work includes a brief prospectus for a Ph.D. program in media ecology. The third work deserving mention is *Teaching as a Conserving Activity* (1979), where Postman considerably revises the position he had taken earlier with Weingartner. He now advocates a more critical view of electric media, and outlines a media ecological position called the "thermostatic view of education." He here calls attention to consequences of unchecked cultural biases regarding technology and education. He also includes a curriculum that intends to balance the trend of televisual culture and provide resources against "media fallout." Finally, in *The End of Education* (1995), Postman claims, "there is no surer way to bring an end to schooling than for it to have no end" (p. 4). His point is that we, as human beings, need ends—meaning life-giving narratives to "give point to our labors, exalt our history, elucidate the present and give direction to our future" (p. 7). Further suggesting that the contemporary "technology-narrative" is failing, Postman outlines some promising narratives regarding our life on this planet, the nature of democracy, and the importance of attending to everyday language use and technology.

Postman was the editor of the journal *Et Cetera: A Review of General Semantics* for 10 years, and although the influence of the general semantics movement is evident in many of his works, it is most noticeable in his *Crazy Talk, Stupid Talk* (1976). Postman here addresses language use in everyday affairs and employs the expression "the semantic environment" to discuss how speech itself is ecological. In contrast to theories where

> ...communication is conceived of as a discrete quantifiable piece of stuff that will move from one source to another and then back again...The metaphor of a semantic environment...says that communication is not stuff or bits or messages. In a way, it is not even something that people do. Communication is a situation in which

people participate, rather like the way a plant participates in what we call its growth. (1976, p. 8)

Throughout this witty book on language, Postman documents how we routinely "defeat ourselves by the way we talk" and also outlines "what we are to do about it." At the end of the book, Postman identifies the origin of his commitment to clarity of thought where he says it was his ambition in life "to grow up to be George Orwell" (p. 257).

Of his works on contemporary culture, I here mention only two. First, in his most widely known book, *Amusing Ourselves to Death* (1985), Postman discusses how television has made all aspects of U.S. culture reflect the image of show business and entertainment. Two significant theoretical chapters are, "Media are metaphors" and "The epistemology of media." In arguing that "the medium is the metaphor," Postman adds an addendum to McLuhan's "the medium is the message." He argues that the word "message" still trades upon some notion of a content conveyed, whereas when we use the word "metaphor," we refer to words that "classify the world for us, sequence it, frame it, enlarge it, reduce it, color it, argue a case for what the world is like" (p. 10). The purpose of the book is to scrutinize the epistemological transformations occurring since the second half of the twentieth century in U.S. culture. He critiques the sense in which "politics, religion, education, and anything else that comprises public business must change and be recast in terms that are most suitable to television" (p. 8). Television, he suggests, does not merely convey entertainment as its content; all that is shown on television is, at best, entertainment. This book also includes insightful analyses of the differences between word and image, and analyses of how notions of truth and communication media intertwine. In another polemical text against technology, *Technopoly* (1992), Postman suggests that modern history might be explored as a development from "tool-use to technocracy," and then, from "technocracy to technopoly." By "technopoly," Postman means when all aspects of culture are pervaded by a faith in technological improvement and progress.

Toward the end of his book *Teaching as a Conserving Activity* (1979), Postman not only summarizes the spirit of McLuhan and Ong but also encapsulates the central ideas of media ecology. He writes:

> Media ecology…is concerned to understand how technologies and techniques of communication control the form, quantity, speed, distribution, and direction of information; and how, in turn, such information configurations or biases affect people's perceptions, values, and attitudes…such information forms as the alphabet, the printed word, and television images are not mere instruments which make things easier for us. They are environments—like language itself, symbolic environments—within which we discover, fashion, and express our humanity in particular ways. (p. 186)

From here, we can now turn to other scholars of the media ecological tradition.

Additional Media Ecological Roots

We can find ideas congruent with media ecology in early civilizations and ancient sacred texts (e.g. early religious cautions over the use of symbolic images or Socrates warning Phaedrus about the false sense of wisdom that writing will bestow). We also find media ecological sensibilities increasingly evident in the contemporary field of anthropology. A few anthropologists who were highly influential on McLuhan and the early beginnings of media ecology include Edmund Carpenter, Dorothy Lee, and Edward Hall. Carpenter's *Oh, What a Blow that Phantom Gave Me!* (1973), and his *They Became What They Beheld* (1970) are both media ecology classics. The first is an account from 1967-1969 of the introduction of various communication media to indigenous peoples in the most remote areas of New Guinea. Hired by the government of New Guinea to modernize native peoples, Carpenter studied how photographic images, audiotape recordings, mirrors, radio broadcasts, films and other technologies related to the emergence of new sensibilities toward self and personhood. The second book visually explores the relationship between image and identity. Two other anthropologists who had a significant influence on the development of media ecology were Dorothy Lee and Edward Hall. Lee, author of *Freedom and Culture* (1959) and *Valuing the Self* (1976), was a first generation Greek-American and is most known for her scholarship on "lineal and non-lineal languages." She also made many contributions to the nature and dynamics of symbolism, the experience of self, and the unique character of Greek identity. Hall wrote works on context, and on different sensibilities of space and time across different cultures. Hall's *The Silent Language* (1959), *The Hidden Dimension* (1966), and *Beyond Culture* (1976) are standard readings in cross-cultural understanding, much of which addresses space and architecture as kinds and modes of communication. Some of the basic terminology that Hall provides includes the distinctions between "high-context" and "low-context" communication, between "fast messages" and "slow messages," and between "monochromatic time" and "polychromatic time."

Three other preeminent scholars also deserve at least brief mention here: Harold Innis, Lewis Mumford, and Jacques Ellul. Innis was a colleague of McLuhan's at the University of Toronto, and he is often noted as one of McLuhan's more significant influences (cf. also Carey, 1989). It was later in his career, well after completing a Ph.D. in Economics from University of Chicago, that Innis turned his attention to the role media play in world history. In *The Bias of Communication* (1951), Innis outlines how the physical properties of the media that people use impact their orientations to space and time. He distinguishes between "heavy media" (e.g. stone) and "light media" (e.g. papyrus), suggesting that societies with only the former at their disposal may remain time-biased whereas societies that rely primarily on the former become space-biased. Space-biased societies also become oriented to outward expansion and the development of empire. Part of what makes Innis's insights so provocative and noteworthy is that his early research on economic staples such as fur and timber, which show how money and goods function as communication media, helped to orient the subsequent media ecological tradition (Strate, 2004). Other important works include, *Empire and Communications* (1972) and the recently re-released, *Changing Concepts of Time* (2004).

Another significant figure in media ecology is Lewis Mumford, a cultural historian who published about 30 books spanning broad topics such as architecture, art, the city, human development as well as technics and technology. Particularly influential is *Technics and Civilization* (1934), where Mumford outlines how different phases of history are characterized by the materials they employ, the means by which they use and generate energy, and the particular kind of worker they bring into existence. Rather than divide Western history into pre- and post- Industrial Revolution, Mumford looks at the last 1,000 years, taking the development of the clock in the tenth century to be the most significant invention in Western development. He then explores the succession of three "*over-lapping and interpenetrating phases*: eotechnic, paleotechnic, and neotechnic" (1934, p. 109). The first phase is characterized by crude handicraft materials (part of the water-and-wood complex); the second is characterized by increased durability and economical mass-distribution (part of the coal-and-iron complex), and the third is characterized by refined and organic products/processes (part of the electricity-and-alloy complex).

Finally, Jacques Ellul is perhaps the most radical in his views on the pervasiveness and negative impact of technology. Author of many works on technology, sociology and theology, Ellul is most known for his book, *The Technological Society* (1964), in which he explores not the history and impacts of particular media, but rather the nature of *technique* per se. He writes, "The machine is now not even the most important aspect of technique (though it is perhaps the most spectacular); technique has taken over all of man's activities, not just his productive ones" (1964, p. 4). His point is that technique no longer needs the materiality of the machine. It now pervades all aspects of life including the economy, the arts, education, government, and our understanding of human relations.

Media of Ecological Interest: From Orality to the Internet and Beyond

The latter half of the twentieth century witnessed a flood of research into the nature and character of literacy as well the nature and character of wholly oral cultures and minds. Among scholars at the center of this research is Eric Havelock, whose many books include *Preface to Plato* (1963), *Prologue to Greek Literacy* (1971) and *The Muse Learns to Write* (1986). Havelock covers topics such as how Plato's theory of forms and abstract thought (e.g. the Beautiful or Good *per se*) depended upon noetic changes made possible by writing and how tolerance for novelty in thought relied upon the sense of permanence that writing conveys. He also outlines distinctions between three main types of writing (logographic, syllabic, and alphabetic) and clarifies the difference between "craft literacy" and "general literacy." Overall, Havelock provides a wealth of scholarship on the nature of early Greek literacy and its impact on sociological structure and psychological functioning.

Another significant orality/literacy scholar is cultural anthropologist Jack Goody, whose *The Domestication of the Savage Mind* (1977) identifies the nature of the earliest forms of writing to be mostly lists of gifts and debts rather than narratives or stories. From this, Goody argues that abstract representational thought gains practice in decontextualization by way of written accountancy (also see Denny, 1991). Among Goody's many other books, some of interest to media ecology include: *The Logic of Writing and the Organization of Society* (1986), and *Interfaces between the Written and the Oral* (1987), where Goody traces the common ancestry shared by all European and Indo-European alphabets.

Other scholars relevant to the media ecology tradition include archeologist Denise Schmandt-Besserat (1992, 1996), who has shown how the development of writing was accompanied by a change in orientation of images on ancient pottery. Physicist and media ecologist Robert K. Logan, drawing upon Havelock's work, explores the developments of legal systems and the social/political world in *The Alphabet Effect* (1986). Developmental psychologist and orality-literacy scholar, David R. Olson studies how literacy in childhood impacts the strategies and nature of interpretation. Among his main arguments in *The World on Paper* (1994) is the claim that writing does not represent speech, but rather, it allows speech to enter into conscious awareness in particular ways. In other words, writing systems provide models that people use to interrogate and experience their own speech (also cf. Anton, 2005).

In addition to the boom in scholarship regarding the nature of orality and the influences of literacy upon human development both historically and individually, some lines of scholarship attend to technological developments within scribal and manuscript culture. For example, Saenger (1997) tracks the transition from the writing form known as "scriptura continua" to a form of writing that has gaps between letters to signify word breaks. He argues further that silent reading became prevalent only after styles of writing inserted gaps or spaces, thus forming something akin to the modern notion of word (also see Illich, 1991). Other significant scholarship has addressed the use of engravings and woodcuts. William Ivins (1953, 1954), for example, documents how prints and exact replication of visual drawings made possible a diffusion of scientific knowledge. He also details the "visual syntax" in the composition of lines, points and spaces that enable images to appear through wood-cut engraved and etched media.

Elizabeth Eisenstein's *The Printing Press as an Agent of Change* (1979) is recognized as an authoritative study on the printing press and its overall impact on early Europe. It follows up and give support to many of McLuhan's basic claims about the printed word. With regard to other media, scholars have explored the use and social consequences of mirrors (see Carpenter, 1973; Mumford, 1967; Berman, 1989) and the historical impact of the clock and mechanical synchronization upon patterns of life and leisure (de Grazia, 1964; Hall 1976, 1983; Mumford, 1934). Susan Sontag's writing explores the meaning and nature of photographic images (1977). James Carey (1989) has documented the rise, development, and impact of the telegraph, including the development of standardized time-zones, the creation of the futures market, the possibility of live-time weather prediction, and in general the creation of "the News" (also see Czitrom, 1983). Scott McCloud (1993, 2000) has done interesting media ecological work on the nature of comics and iconic imagery, and equally interesting work has been done on radio, mass media, and advertising by Tony Schwartz. Of particular relevance is his *The Responsive Chord* (1974), where he develops a theory of communicative "resonance."

Of more contemporary media, a good deal of media ecological scholarship has addressed television and the electric revolution (Boorstin, 1978, Gumpert & Cathcart, 1979; Meyrowitz, 1985), the many-leveled implications of online communication, computer-mediated communication, and cyperspace interactions (see Barnes, 2001, 2003; Baron, 2000; Bolter, 1991; Strate, Jacobson & Gibson, 2003). Considerable contemporary research also has explored the meaning and impact of cell phones (Gergen, 1991; Levinson, 2004; Rheingold, 2003), the epistemological and pedagogical implications of hypertext (Bolter, 1991; Landow, 1997), the way that electric word processing shapes our understanding of the word (Heim, 1987), and the implications of virtual reality (Heim, 1993). On the very forefront of emerging and new media research in media ecology are Robert K. Logan and Paul Levinson. In his book, *Digital McLuhan*, Levinson examines McLuhan's ideas and shows how digital technology and online communications were well anticipated within McLuhan's basic framework. Logan has published several books on new media (1997, 2000) and is currently innovating a notion of the "blook," a hybrid between the book and the blog. His blook, currently in progress, is tentative titled, *Understanding New Media* and is intended to update and re-vise McLuhan's classic *Understanding Media (*1964).

Before closing this review, some mention should be given to the reader, *Communication in History* (2003, 4th ed.), compiled by David Crowley and Paul Heyer. It holds many classic pieces of scholarship in the history of communications technologies, all of which serve as excellent background and introductory reading in media ecology. Main themes addressed in their collection include: why new communication media emerge, how they impact prior media, how they exert an influence on everyday life, and how societies, in their own turn, exert an influence back on media practices (p. xv).

Future Directions for Media Ecology

Today, many media ecologists try to cultivate a media ecological awareness in everyday life. Such awareness helps people develop a critical attitude regarding the nature and impact and the social and psychological consequences of communication media, especially new and emerging ones. Urban development, educational practice, political structure, and overall media consumption—all of these need attention and vigilant scrutiny.

A second direction regards new media per se. Marshall McLuhan and his son Eric formalized a media ecological model in their *Laws of Media* (1988). This model had become increasingly evident in Marshall's corpus. The model suggests that each new medium (with medium defined very broadly) can be examined as holding four different kinds of effects, and the four "laws of media" are posed as questions that can be used to examine any new medium. The four questions are: 1. What does the medium enhance or extend? 2. What does it obsolesce? 3. What does it retrieve that an earlier medium obsolesced? 4. And what does it reverse or flip into when pushed to its extreme? This tetradic model may provide some assistance in anticipating the impacts of new technologies and the changing technological environment (McLuhan and McLuhan, 2011; Logan, 2011).

Finally, with the founding of the Media Ecology Association, media ecology has become more than an academic tradition and scholarly practice. For an increasing number of scholars, especially those who have always felt a yearning for broad-based, historically and cosmically situated research on how communication and communication technologies are inseparable from the human condition, media ecology offers a long-awaited place to call home.

Chapter 9: Early Western Writing, Sensory Modalities, and Modern Alphabetic Literacy: On the Origins of Representational Theorizing[1]

> *"Until writing,*
> *most of the kinds of thoughts*
> *we are used to thinking today*
> *simply could not be thought."*
> — *Walter J. Ong, 1971, p. 2*

On the Origins of Representational Theorizing

This paper attempts to bring out how modern alphabetic literacy, (i.e. the integration of alphabetic technologies into eye, tongue, and ear) poses significant difficulties for a fully "post-representational" conception of language.[2] By reviewing developments in Western writing systems and also by giving phenomenological consideration to the lived-body's sensory modalities, I account for the origins of the contemporary and postmodern representational crisis and show how many of these "problems" of representation (e.g. "atomism") are just as equally capacities now made real through alphabetic literacy. For clarity and sharp focus, I base my arguments around John Stewart's critique of the bulk of Western theorizing on communication and language. His *Language as Constitutive Articulate Contact* (1995) is a broad *tour de force* that not only indicts and criticizes many influential thinkers (e.g. Plato, Aristotle, Saussure, Peirce, von Humbolt, Cassirer, Langer, Burke, Kristeva, and numerous others), but more importantly offers significant reconsiderations of basic issues in communication theory. Stewart provides many needed criticisms and his work has far reaching implications, so much so that it ought to be central to contemporary theorizing. Despite its scope, range, and contributions, his orientation seems not to have received the attention and recognition it deserves.[3] This project is partly motivated, then, by a desire to recognize and advance Stewart's ideas, even if this means limiting their sweep. Additionally, Stewart's writing is clean, accessible, and provides clear and distinct benchmarks for scholarly contention. I also must stress that although what follows is a largely critical assessment, I applaud and admire Stewart's project. Not only would I identify his work as philosophically akin to my own, but I think that his sketch, in its broad strokes, is outstandingly on-target. But I still want to haggle over some of the fine-tuning. I first briefly review some of Stewart's main arguments and then identify the questionable claims I will be responding to throughout the rest of the paper.

Stewart argues that most Western theorizing regarding language (and hence communication) employs the "symbol model," which means language is treated as an atomistic system of symbols representing discrete items of experience. Spelling this out in terms of five "commitments" that comprise the symbol model, Stewart first suggests that Western scholars begin with the assumption that "there is a difference in kind between the linguistic world, or the world of 'signifiers,' and some other world, that of 'things,' 'mental experiences,' 'ideas,' 'concepts,' or some other 'signifieds'" (1995, p. 7). The second commitment, "atomism," is the belief that "the linguistic world consists of identifiable units or elements...[this] has been most apparent in theorists' dependence on examples of single words to support their claims about the semiotic character of language" (1995, pp. 7-9). Third, "the commitment to representationalism follows directly from the first two commitments. Given two worlds, each made up of units, one is led to ask how units of one relate to the other" (1995, p. 10). The fourth and fifth commitments, "system" and "tool" respectively, simply follow suit; theorists posit both that language is "a system rather than either an event or as a mode of being human...[and that]...language is one of the more-or-less objectifiable tools subjects use to accomplish their goals" (1995, pp. 11-12). In contrast to these five commitments, and the symbol model more generally, Stewart argues that "there can be only one kind of human world, a pervasively languaged kind" (1995, p. 124). This further means that language, as "constitutive articulate contact," is the primary way humans are "who we are...we *inhabit* or live in our language" (1995, p. 126).

　　　Stewart substantiates his position on the symbol model by criticizing various contemporary theorists who come close to overcoming symbol model sensibilities but who, nevertheless, seem to slip back into them. Among the many whom he indicts on this charge is Kenneth Burke (cf. 1961; 1966). He credits Burke for some sympathies toward non-symbol-model conceptions but maintains that Burke's writings have clear moments where language is characterized as if it were an *atomistic* symbol system (i.e. comprised of discrete units [words] which persons use to refer to different units [things] in the non-verbal world). Taking issue with accounts of language that rely too heavily upon analyses of the meaning of individual words, Stewart writes the following:

> An account of the nature of language that begins from or focuses on discrete terms inescapably distorts the lived phenomena it attempts to describe. When Burke chose to discuss the nature of language by emphasizing individual words and word combinations, he risked reducing his analysis to only a reductive and derived account of language as humans live it. (1995, p. 212)

Stewart further tightens and extends his argument: "Speaking and listening, or addressing and responding, are the primary and uniquely human linguistic processes, not choosing and using individual terms" (1995, p. 212). These claims, I maintain, invite a false dichotomy by potentially covering-over our linguistic inheritance. Exploring them in detail, I begin with a series of questions: Is it really the case that within our immediate activities of speaking and listening, we neither choose nor even use individual *words*?[4] Also, if focus on discrete terms distorts the phenomenon of speech, then how much comparatively do we distort the phenomenon if we fail to regard how modern alphabetic literacy has grown into it? Such questions are meant to suggest that Stewart may be caught by a need for some kind of "pure and unadulterated" non-historical phenomenon, what he calls, "speech communicating." It is worth noting that he attempts to avoid a free-wheeling idealism (or a too locally generated social-constructionism) by underscoring historical inheritance. Stewart writes that "features of human worlds do not first exist and then get spoken or written of; they *come into being in talk*. Of course, no individual initiates this process…thus human worlds are not constituted *de novo*, but from what we inherit" (1995, p. 113). We can agree that language is not a thing that humans use; it is never a mere item within experience. And most broadly, Stewart recognizes and powerfully brings out how communication and language profoundly and mysteriously intertwine with our historical existences. Nevertheless, it's difficult to get most literate people to understand (to believe?) that words, as lexical or semantic units, are not consciously selected nor even used in communication. The account we are left with subtly assumes that one can isolate out the historical developments of "constitutive articulate contact." This is a contradiction, or, at the least, a case of wanting it both ways.

Logos is the human condition, but phonetic literacy is the current condition of logos for the bulk of the Western world. Stewart's advances and important contributions might fruitfully be extirpated of their oral purism if we take hold of the roots of our prejudices toward semiotic conceptions of language and display the many ways that "constitutive articulate contact" has grown literate. Seriously, where and when *is* literacy? It certainly is not merely a skill acquired and occasionally employed, nor is it a discontinuous activity that comes into operation only during moments of reading or writing. And "it" is not simply "tacked on" to speech either. Speech communicating, now inseparable from alphabetic literacy, is sociohistorical as well as phenomenologically constituted in ways that may be easily passed over (also cf. Dance, 1989). To flesh out what is at stake here, I draw upon the works of Walter J. Ong, Eric Havelock, Jack Goody, David Olson, Ivan Illich, as well as Hans Jonas, Erwin Straus, Maurice Merleau-Ponty and others, to demonstrate how historical developments in writing and phenomenological differences between sight and hearing reveal a ground of *literate* articulate contact.

A Brief Sketch of Western Writing Systems

Alphabetic writing, Stewart suggests, provided the basic paradigm for the subsequent understanding of language as a symbol system, but his discussions of early Western writing systems and early developments of the alphabet hold the main source of the difficulties in his position. To account for the origin of the commitment to atomism (the analytic tendency to dissect speech into "constituent" elements), he identifies writing as pivotal and suggests the following:

> The first primitive pictographs isolated some visible features of notable events and the letters of the first alphabets designated specific sounds or phonemes. In each case, consequential decisions were made to mark some elements of communicative experience and *to ignore others*…Thus the atomism commitment has…highlighted some kinds of parts and ignored others with as much or more semantic and pragmatic importance. Although it would constitute another major project, it would be illuminating to trace the implications of these early choices through the history of theorizing about language. (1995, p. 9)

This passage is both highly insightful and yet deeply problematic. A review of some of these "early choices" could be very worthwhile and might indeed un-cover the roots of the commitment to atomism, but by treating pictographic and alphabetic writing indiscriminately, this passage also covers over the sensory dif-ferences at play in pictographic writing and in alphabetic writing. Ong pinpoints the difficulty with this conflation when he writes, "A picture, say, of a bird does not reduce sound to space, for it represents an object, not a word....The alphabet... represents sound itself as a thing, transforming the evanescent world of sound to the quiescent, quasi-permanent world of space" (1982, p. 91). Second, and perhaps more significantly, the passage holds questionable or at least unfortunate word choices. Stewart suggests that "decisions were made to mark some ele-ments of communicative experience and to ignore others" and further describes these as "early choices." The insights are well taken but they may lead us into the presumption that people had full and direct access to "the whole" of their speech and then, from that, they decided which aspects were to be marked and which ignored. Here Stewart implies a position he elsewhere explicitly holds, that writing works as a representation of speech (cf. Stewart, 1995, pp. 34-38). If on the con-trary, as David Olson maintains, writing provides the model through which speech enters awareness in particular ways, then "early decisions" were made only *after* writing enabled some "parts" to enter awareness.[5]

A brief review of some of the historical developments in early Western writing systems lends support to Olson's position and helps to contextualize some particular features of *literate* constitutive contact. The few developments I focus upon occurred mainly between the 17th century B. C. E. and the 8th century C.E. Three significant changes are analyzed: first, the movement from logographic script to syllabic/consonantal (i.e. phonetic) script; second, the shift from phonetic writing to alphabetic writing; and finally, the change from "scriptura continua" to self-standing lexical units (i.e. written words separated by spaces). Although the analysis summarizes historical effects and developments, my purpose is not to create a narrative of historical progression and advancement, and certainly not to give support to Gelb's questionable "principle of unidirectional develop-ment."[6] My purpose is to illustrate different developments in Western writing to show how these shaped not only subsequent theorizing on language but the way that speech, as literate, is practiced and undergone.

Early Developments

The radical differences between the earliest forms of Western writing and what is today understood and experienced as writing are less than obvious at first. Pictographs, hieroglyphs, ideographs, rebuses (or "logographs" more gen-erally) preceded alphabetic technologies by thousands, and in some cases tens of thousands of years. The differences between such non-phonetic texts and modern alphabetic texts are numerous, but for brevity and clarity I focus on three distinguishing characteristics. First, for the few who practiced it, logographic writ-ing mainly served mnemonic functions.[7] It referred to that which someone was trying to remember (e.g. debts, obligations, gifts, and ideas).[8] This basic opera-tion of using visual inscriptions to mnemonically recall whole general concepts (or items to be remembered) appears in so many varieties that it can be characterized as naturally emergent within countless human cultures (cf. Jonas, 1966, pp. 157-182). Second, as generated from collectives who used them, logographs were serviceable almost exclusively to those who had something they wanted to remember; they emerged indigenously and operated in relatively local or closed contexts. Third, logographs were ciphered by scribes who would say aloud or express what the logographs meant. Because logographs, for the most part, are not directive with regard to sound, early scribes had to know (i.e. be able to remember) what each visual logograph meant. Exceptions and variations are certainly to be found in many ideographic systems where rebus-like writing styles characterized the most likely precursors to phonetic texts (cf. DeFrancis, 1989). Unlike readers of modern alphabetic script, who are taught to "sound out the words," early logograph readers had no such constancy. As further illustration, some Native American tribes adamantly argued that they had no writing and that their language could not be written down. Such an assumption, which may if only partly be based on the belief that all writing is non-phonetic writing (i.e. is logographic), well highlights the radical break that phonetic writing introduced.

A significant break from logographic to phonetic writing occurred around the 17th century B. C. E. (Goody, 1987). Cuneiforms, made by stylus imprints upon softened clay, correlated syllabic sound units with visual signs. The shift from logographic writing to phonetic writing marked a significant change in interpretative demands. Whereas logographs had to be known to be read and thousands might have to be known (granting that some, as pictographic or rebus-like, could be "figured out," some had 'radicals' which aid in pronunciation), phonetic script provided a model for sound units individually rather than whole ideas. Readers of phonetic script could pronounce a script with less extensive memory use, as phonetic writing employs radically fewer distinct signs. Still, early forms of phonetic scripts, often referred to as "syllabic" and/or "consonantal" writing, demanded high degrees of interpretative competence even for pronunciation. Vowels and consonants are not adequately disentangled, and thus each sign-image holds cognate variations for vowel possibilities (i.e. each syllabic variation). The visual sign "k," for example, had to be read by the scribe as ka, ke, ki, ko, or ku. Also, gaps or spaces between letters had not yet been inserted to demarcate discrete words. Scribes read from unbroken strings of letters, a writing style which Saenger calls, "scriptura continua," and which continued to characterize Western writing and reading for well over a millennium after the invention of the Greek alphabet (Saenger, 1997).[9]

Although syllabic and consonantal writing were the direct precursors to the Greek alphabet, both still assumed the syllable as the smallest unit of speech. The Greeks' main contribution was the imagined or eidetic isolation of atomistic "sub-components" of syllables. To explain this point some scholars maintain that the Greeks basically modified the Phoenician consonantal system by introducing vowels. Jack Goody, for example, writes,

> The proto-Canaanite script is the common ancestor of the Phoenician, Hebrew, and Aramaic variants. In about 1500 B.C.E. it seems to have consisted of twenty-seven pictorial letters which were reduced to twenty-two in the thirteenth century...It was this [Phoeni-

cian] consonantal alphabet that the Greeks in turn adopted, adding their own five characters to represent vowels. (Goody, 1987, p. 46)

A different way to conceptualize the Greek contribution, as both Havelock and McLuhan argue, was that their writing made possible the pure consonant. Havelock explains this point:

> It is easy to see why pre-Greek systems never got further than the syllable. This 'piece' of linguistic sound is actually pronounceable and so empirically perceptible...The Greek system got beyond empiricism, by abstracting the nonpronounceable, nonperceptible components of linguistic sound and gave it a visual identity. The Greeks did not "add vowels" (a common misconception: vowel signs had already shown up in Mesopotamian Cuneiform and Linear B) but instead invented the (pure) consonant. In doing so, they for the first time supplied our species with a visual representation of linguistic noise that was both economical and exhaustive: a table of atomic elements which by grouping themselves in an inexhaustible variety of combinations can with reasonable accuracy represent any actual linguistic noise. (Havelock, 1986, p. 60; also cf. McLuhan and McLuhan, 1988)[10]

This separation of vowel and consonant was *the* radical break that made this system of writing, for some thinkers, the only true alphabet (Diringer, 1953). By generating an *atomistic* and *exhaustive* set of speech sounds, the Greek alphabet further lessened the interpretive demands encumbered in pronouncing syllabic scripts. Readers of alphabetic writing now could see how to say the script instead of having to decide which vowel cognate to pronounce with each consonantal sign. In general, alphabetic writing seemed easier to read than syllabic and/or consonantal script, and also, it began to expand possibilities of people writing texts for other people to read them (i.e., not for aiding memory).

The next development, already alluded to, occurred around the 8th century C.E., about fifteen hundred years after the invention of the alphabet: the introduction of what we might recognize as written words. Saenger characterizes the profundity of this break-through when he writes that: "to most modern readers, the idea of reading lines without word separation is unimaginable" (Saenger, 1991, p. 203). Indeed, many people are surprised to learn that individually written words, as we understand them, did not prevail until monks used them in the 7th-8th centuries. "In both the ancient Greek and Roman books and in the Vai," Saenger states, "the reader encounters, at the first glance, rows of discrete phonetic symbols that first have to be manipulated within the mind to form properly articulated and accented entity equivalents to words" (1991, p. 202).[11] We need but look upon early stone or clay tablets, such as the Rosetta Stone, which holds Egyptian hieroglyphics, demotic script, and ancient Greek, or early parchment to observe the unbroken succession of letters. A few examples of early Roman writing did contain individuated words, but early texts by and large were written in "scriptura continua," as Saenger explains:

> While the very earliest Greek inscriptions were written with separa-
> tion by interpuncts, Greece soon thereafter became the first ancient
> civilization to employ scriptura continua...The Romans, who bor-
> rowed their letter forms and vowels from the Greeks, maintained
> the early Mediterranean tradition of separating words by points far
> longer than the Greeks, but they too, after a scantily documented
> period of six centuries, substituted scriptura continua for separated
> script in the decades preceding 200 [C.E.]. (Saenger, 1991, p. 207)

The shift to self-standing lexical units made reading seem even easier, for prior
to such word breaks, reading aloud had been largely necessary. It enabled the
words most recently said to remain in the ear while the next lexical units to be said
were identified by the leaping-ahead of the eyes. With the invention of written
words, per se, the practice of silent reading not only became possible for the first
time, it eventually became the norm. The following is a brief discussion of some
of the consequences of these developments.

A Few Historical Effects

The Greek alphabet was more easily learned than other forms of Western writing; it was both economical and exhaustive. All of the basic units of the
alphabet could be mastered in a relatively short period of time, enabling people
to acquire all the signs necessary to read any alphabetic script, and, as Carothers'
studies of the dissemination of alphabetic literacy in Africa show, a single generation of alphabetic literacy was enough to challenge and disrupt more traditional
oral-modes of culture (cf. McLuhan 1963, 1964).

Second, logographic writing was generated and used by local communi-
ties and syllabic/consonantal script was demanding and difficult to read. Both of
these facts served to keep prior literacy and cultures somewhat closed. As the
Greek alphabet developed, it enabled language translation as no other writing
system did, as McLuhan explains:

> All other forms of writing had served merely one culture, and had
> served to separate that culture from others. The phonetic letters
> alone could be used to translate, albeit crudely, the sounds of any
> language into one-and-the-same visual code...the phonetic alpha-
> bet, by a few letters only, was able to encompass all languages.
> (1964, p. 87; also cf. Diringer, 1953)

Alphabetic writing, therefore, was the necessary pre-condition for various attempts
at "universal" language translation. Ong and Goody maintain that the Greek
alphabet, Early Hebrew, South Semitic, Phoenician, Aramaic, and all Western
alphabets, Arabic, as well as Indian, and South-East Asian alphabets, all have a
common and traceable origin (cf. Ong, 1982, pp. 85-93; Goody, 1987).

Third, because alphabetic script was relatively easy to read, it lent itself
to applications well beyond the mnemonic functions of earlier systems of writing.
The Roman Empire used alphabetic script upon lightweight papyrus to establish
and exercise of precise power over distant command posts (McLuhan, 1964).
Commands and reports thus could be given and maintained over large distanc-

es. Other empires would do likewise. The easily learned alphabetic script was a central element of various historical expansions, social and political conquests in particular.

Finally, many centuries after the fall of the Roman Empire, the invention of gaps between letters ended the predominant writing style of scriptura continua, and the practice of silent reading came to dominance (Saenger, 1997, 1991). The significance of the change becomes apparent if we contrast silent reading with the practices of reading in early manuscript culture. Scribes, especially those who could read what they copied, learned to isolate and pronounce segments from scriptura continua. Because no written texts were identical, scribes had to become highly familiar with the actual, particular, pieces of writing they encountered. This included not simply mistakes and/or occasional tropist embellishments, but also to the facts of wide variation of the medium (e.g. pieces of parchment were differently sized and shaped), as well as wide variations in handwriting styles. Obviously, to speak of scribes becoming familiar with their "copy" of "a text" is at best an anachronism. Reading and writing within manuscript culture were anything but the widespread individual (i.e., private) activity that we understand as literacy today, not even during the Golden Age of Greece (Havelock, 1963). Reading in manuscript culture had been a vocalized public practice, and scriptoria were places of group learning. One person or a few would read to the many. After the invention of spaces between the letters, this slowly ceased to be the case. "For well over two thousand years," Ivan Illich states,

> the decoding of the alphabetic record could not be performed by the eye alone... The break or empty space between words was unknown...There was almost no other way of reading than rehearsing the sentences aloud and listening to hear whether they made sense...Word breaks were introduced in the eighth century, in Bede's time, as a didactic device...Space between words made silent copying possible; the copyist could then transcribe word for word. (1991, p. 36)

An additional side-effect of silent reading, according to Illich, was that "scriptoria ceased to be places where each one tried to hear his own voice. Neither the teacher nor the neighbor could now hear what was being read and—partly as a result—both bawdy and heretical books multiplied" (1991, p. 37; also cf. Innis, 1952). For McLuhan the rise of silent reading, especially throughout the 17th to the 19th centuries, meant the beginning of the de-poeticization of speech. Because writing increasingly could be written as much for the silent eye as for the public tongue and ear, appreciation for the sheer musicality of the spoken word began to fade. People slowly learned to read for purely propositional content, for that which is wholly separable from the sounds of speech. Not until Joyce and the other poets of the electric age, McLuhan claimed, would soundings of voice recaptivate our attention.

The preceding points, taken together, generate the following sketch. Increasingly, the practices of both reading and writing became more and more privatized, more and more silent, more and more of an individualizing and interiorizing force (Ong, 1958). Historical developments moved toward creating writing systems which *seemed* to lessen the overt and obvious interpretive demands of readers. More developments came to bloom during the later stages of manuscript culture, and more came later. It was not until the invention of the printing press, for example, that punctuation, pagination, headings, spelling, and even titles appeared (Eisenstein, 1979). This makes sense because writing, at least initially, was largely mnemonic in function. As time went on, however, a writer's audiences were able to become more and more of a fiction (Ong, 1971). In Edward Hall's terms, writing systems have progressively become lower and lower context (1976, pp. 85-116; 1983, pp. 59-77).[12] More and more of the non-verbal and extra-verbal context is elaborated explicitly into the code. Examples discussed include providing guides for sounds themselves, eliminating the demand for syllabic cognate selection, introducing empty spaces to enable silent access to word meaning, and various forms of punctuation and spatial organization (Ong, 1958; Eco, 1995). The relevance as well as significance of these shifts to the current representation crisis can be made more evident by briefly considering some of the phenomenological differences between vision and hearing.

Phenomenological Differences Between Vision and Hearing

Phenomenological studies of the body's different sensory modalities articulate the embodied ground upon which modern alphabetic literacy shows its powers. Surprisingly, Stewart says little about sensory differences, despite his reliance upon the ideas of Heidegger and Gadamer and his insistence upon the primacy of the "oral/aural."[13] Such neglect is not all that uncommon in theories of literacy and symbolicity. Both Marshall McLuhan and Walter Ong take phenomenological differences seriously, though McLuhan mainly hints at different sense ratios in the human sensorium and offers little systematic and extended consideration. Ong admittedly gives more thorough and systematic insight, though his discussions also can be advanced in light of contemporary phenomenology. As a final note, in his "reasonably exhaustive" *Spoken and Written Discourse* (1999, p. 1), Khosrow Jahandarie integrates an impressive breadth of scholarship including summaries of the early Toronto school, contemporary cognitive studies, educational and psychological research, historical and anthropological work but gives no mention of phenomenological accounts of sensory modalities and their bearing upon these issues. To remedy this gap in interdisciplinary integration, I now turn to the contributions of Hans Jonas, Erwin Straus, and Maurice Merleau-Ponty.

Spatio-Temporal Characters of Vision and Hearing

If we pause and try to become aware of how "each organ of sense explores the object in its own way" (Merleau-Ponty, 1962, p. 223), the most general difference seems to be, as Erwin Straus suggests, "Experienced sound has a spatial and temporal structure astonishingly different from that of light and color" (1966, p. 56). In other words, each sensory modality orients itself within a particular mode of spatializing and temporalizing. My analysis elucidates this general claim, but I caution in advance against accidental vivisection, for the lived-body always integrates and intermingles different sensory contributions, and this minimally applies to two levels. First, conscious attention drifts in and out of varying degrees of awareness through any one or more sense, and, this drifting itself passes mostly unnoticed, *operative* rather than consciously attended to in its own right (cf. Leder, 1990). Contributions may be parceled out in reflective analysis, but in lived experience the spontaneous and tacit integration of the senses is the predominant mode. Second and perhaps more importantly, the senses grow in their ability to intercommunicate and intermingle. Most relevant to this analysis is that alphabetic technologies train us to *see* speech and thus to be oriented toward it *as if* it has the spatio-temporal characteristics of things seen. Four highly inter-related points are made about this.

First, vision opens to veneers, meaning that extended visual wholes in the distance simultaneously display their beginnings and endings. Short of visual hal-lucinations, extension is the rule, and colors compete for exclusive occupancy of spatial surface. As Straus states, "colors are both bounded and in turn boundary setting; they confine space, differentiating it into partial spaces ordered sidewise and in depth" (1966, p. 7). Sounds are radically distinct from this. They have no surfaces, no veneers, and, because they separate from their sources, sometimes leaving us unable to reliably determine their exact location or origin, they are nev-er over-and-against us as colored surfaces are. Not only invisible, the beginning and ending of an acoustical whole is never given at the same time; such wholes exist only through sequence. Moreover, in the audible sphere, sounds frequently compete with each other for varying degrees of co-occupation; one sound can fill a room and yet still leave room for more sound.

Second, to see is not only to see forms in the distance, it is to see the intervening distances between ourselves and things as well as between the mul-tiple, simultaneous things disclosed. "Sight is *par excellence* the sense of the simultaneous or the coordinated, and thereby of the extensive. A view compre-hends many things juxtaposed, as co-existent parts of one field of vision" (Jonas, 1966, p. 136). Multiple dimensions of distance open as a steady horizon from which more concentrated focus may make varying degrees of selective attention. In the world of hearing--because sounds are invisible, evanescent, and separate from their sources--distances collapse rather than discretely maintain themselves in simultaneous extension (Ong, 1967). "When we hear," as Straus suggests, "we have already heard it" (1966, p. 16). Unlike colored surfaces seen standing over-and-against us, hearing does not disclose intervening spaces both between ourselves and the source, as well as the distances between different sources (cf. some exceptions in Ihde, 1982). Thus, auditory values, even though sources are in the distance, are always intimately near, as sound does "not extend in a single direction; rather it approaches us, penetrating, filling and homogenizing space" (Straus, 1966, p. 7). Hearing thus generates a synthetic sense of space in con-trast (and in supplement) to the analytical sensibilities of vision, both of which are nicely summed by Straus's claims: "Seeing is an analytical sense...Hearing is a synthesizing sense" (1963, p. 337).

Third, visual elements register a sense of permanence beyond the current act of viewing. In the visual sphere, even movement and change convey perma-nence: as an object moves through space, changing its positions, it discloses itself as the same throughout the duration of the changing. In fact, "Motion is visible insofar as a thing, in the continuous progression of time, changes its position in space without changing its identity. In visible motion, an identifiable or apparently identifiable thing passes through locations which are not affected by its motions and which have their place in an unmoving space" (Straus, 1963, p. 376). Not so with auditory phenomena, for here change is change through and through, for sound is naturally evanescent and fleeting. Sounds are symptomatic evidence of activity and action; they are not disclosed characteristics of bodies at rest. Straus further clarifies this:

> Color is the mark of a thing, whereas tone is the effect of an activity. We say, for example, that a cock *is* white or multicolored; on the other hand, we do not mention crowing as one of his attributes, but as his activity….But we do not mean that his color is one of his characteristics because the cock always appears white or multicolored whereas his crowing is observed to be discontinuous. A brook murmurs continuously day and night and can even be heard when both banks and water have disappeared in darkness and become invisible. (1966, p. 8)

Whereas colors are taken as predicates of things, sounds are symptoms of action and activity. This also implies that things seen routinely allow a kind of return to the identical that is unknown to the ear.

Fourth, vision offers "a *dimension* within which things can be beheld at once and can be related to each other by the wandering glance of attention. This scanning, though proceeding *in* time, articulates only what was present to the first glance and what stays unchanged while being scanned" (Jonas, 1966, p. 144). An enduring gaze enables an apprehension of the constancy of a thing across changes of perspective taken on it. Things seen routinely allow us to alter our perspective. We may shift and rotate the position of things or ourselves and thereby we both move them and hold them constant to a scanning eye. In this process, "Seeing and that which are seen are separated…The possibility of seeing again is ordinarily taken to be self-evident. Just as self-evident to us is the impossibility of hearing again" (Straus, 1963, p. 374). That is, a sound cannot be frozen in glass so as to allow us to change perspective on it. Because "sound exists in sequence, every now of it vanishing into the past while it goes on," Jonas states, "to arrest this flow and 'view' a momentary 'slice' of it would mean to have not a snapshot of it but an atomic fragment of it, and strictly speaking nothing at all" (1966, p. 144). Hearing and sound are thus not separated; Jonas explains that, "The duration of the sound heard is just the duration of hearing it. In this regard, sounds are concurrent with the event of hearing, and thus we cannot re-turn to sound the way we can see again an object" (p. 137). More generally stated, the notion of "sameness" is radically different depending upon whether we are speaking of the visual or aural realm. The impermanence of sound means that the moment of return, its "representation," is qualitatively distinct from the "representation" of things seen. Sounds, in this strict sense, can neither represent nor can they be represented; they are repeatable, livingly imitated, perhaps mimetically and kinesthetically re-enacted, but always, they are fleeting and invisible symptoms of *actions*.

Implications of Phenomenological Differences

Maurice Merleau-Ponty suggests that, "the body is a ready-made system of equivalents and transpositions from one sense to another. The senses translate each other without any need of a translator...Similarly any object presented to one sense calls upon itself the concordant operation of all the senses" (1962, pp. 235; 318). These ideas, also sometimes referred to as the "reversibility thesis," hold significant implications for theories of modern alphabetic literacy and current representational quandaries. If all writing were logographic, we might be to some degree more justified in keeping speech, writing, and literacy separate, but this is not the case. Alphabetic script teaches us to intermingle the different sensory orientations of vision and hearing. It thereby shapes our experience of the spoken word. By learning how to hear utterances as they can be seen, people are enabled to render words as things with surfaced boundaries and which retain their identity even as they move into different contexts. This is a fairly clear description of char-acteristics displayed in the movement of things *seen* (see above).

Modern "spelling bees" well illustrate how our senses grow together in their intercommunication. Such oral competitions require orthographic rendering of phonetic values, and by definition, this is possible only by training the ear to hear what the eye would be able to see were the speech written. People have come to recognize the inner boundaries of discrete words, and so, by learning how to spell, they also learn how to tear asunder the audible syllables of pre-given words. Spoken utterances increasingly can be grasped as comprised of both monosyllabic and polysyllabic words, and these can be parceled out from strings of multilexical idea units (e.g. tropes, schemata, clichés and other oral formulas). People thus learn to separate individual words from all these audible syllabic ambiguities in speech. Alphabetic spelling (i.e. the dictionary) encourages ears to disentangle the audible rhythm of syllables and to locate discrete lexical units; spelling practice cultivates the ability to disentangle monosyllabic words from polysyllabic words from multilexical idea units. Only vision's orientation toward surfaces, distances, and permanence makes this possible.

One of the operative concepts in recent cognitive processing models is known as "lexical access." Across extensive research on the issue two broad schools of analysis have emerged: phonological coding and orthographic coding (cf. Jahandarie, 1999, pp. 151-197). People gain lexical access to word meaning according to at least these two modalities. Phonological coding identifies pro-nunciation and sound production as the essential moment. Orthographic coding, texts where cues from pronunciation are not given, enables readers to gain lexi-cal access through whole image disambiguation. Interestingly, some researchers have demonstrated that beginning alphabetic readers, relying upon a "sounding out" of words, do seem to gain lexical access through phonological productions, but highly-skilled readers are able to gain lexical access orthographically, espe-cially for familiar words and words for which they had been recently primed, and some even show the ability to read without full pronunciation, in fact being able to read faster than listeners can hear. Perhaps more significantly for present purposes, one of the accepted conclusions in this large area, one directly in line with Merleau-Ponty's ideas, is that the "two modalities" are not independent (either/or) cognitive processes, but interactive and co-developmental. In a word, recent cognitive study research evidence increasingly supports David Olson's (1994) claim that writing, rather than being a poor or weak representation of our speech, provides a model through which we interrogate and come to experience our speech. We train our ears to see the boundaries between and even within words.[14]

Finally, the stark differences between the spatial and temporal bearings of vision and hearing well illustrate how alphabetic literacy fosters the experience of the *transcendence* of meaning. This is, arguably, one of the main sources of symbol model commitment #1: the two-world hypothesis. The "other-worldliness" of signifieds, the way they appear to transcend the "real" empirical world, is exemplified and amplified because alphabetic literacy gives direct and immediate experience to content separable from form. Not only is the sensibility that the seen is separable from the act of seeing brought to the spoken word, but more significantly, the "decontextualization" between such different spatio-temporal bearings demonstrates concretely the separability of content and form.[15] The common-sense notion of using different forms for the "same" content (that is, the notion that the same idea can be conveyed in different ways, orally or in writing), belies prejudices formed through alphabetic literacy. As Steven A. Tyler suggests, "Writing is the means for a systematic separation of form and content more pervasive than that conditioned by pictorial representation ...Writing expresses the separation of form and content, produces it visually, and promotes our consciousness of it" (1987, pp. 192-193).[16] "The conduit metaphor," (Lakoff & Johnson, 1980; Reddy, 1979) and common-sense beliefs regarding ideational content passed along through word-containers are partly symptoms of this separation.

Modern Alphabetic Literacy

I have argued that early developments in Western writing and phenomenological differences between hearing and vision, together, bear directly upon the crisis of representation identified by John Stewart. I have tried to articulate relevant background for demonstrating that Stewart's attempt at a post-semiotic conception of language underestimates the subtle and pervasive influences of alphabetic literacy upon our sensory capacities and our experience of speech. I now return to Stewart to resume my critique, corrective, and advancement of his project.

Subtle Problems of Literacy in Post-Semiotic Philosophy

The claim that we do not use individual words in our speaking and listening fails to appreciate the literate (i.e. visually oriented) ways of "oral/aural" contact. Difficulties thus appear where Stewart argues for the "centrality of articulated sound" and draws upon the works of Eric Havelock and Walter Ong, among others. In that section, Stewart problematically quotes from their discussions of "*primary* orality" to clarify what he means by "oral/aural contact" (1995, p. 123). By paying too little attention to the differences between discussions of "primary orality" and "secondary orality," Stewart misconstrues the modern literate experience of speech. A similar difficulty appears earlier in his text, where Stewart addresses the development of the alphabet:

> The change from a primary aural medium to a primarily visual one was also consequential. As Ong emphasizes, "sound...exists only when it is going out of existence." In the lived experience of oral-aural communicating, one can seldom have all of even one word present at once. The written alphabet, [he again quotes Ong] "implies that matters are otherwise, that a word is a thing, not an event, that it is present all at once, and that it can be cut up into little pieces." (1995, p. 36)

Stewart then further interprets the above to mean, basically, that "the Greek alphabet...was a thin and partial abstraction which represented only some elements of the human communicative experience it was designed to capture" (1995, p. 36). Ong's point, on the contrary, is that literate people need to be reminded of the fact that on the purely oral and acoustical level, the whole of a word is not given simultaneously. It unfolds through time and so the whole is not present all at once.[17] Ong's example used at numerous places is the word, "evanescent." Although we can see the simultaneous whole of the written word, the spoken word is drastically distinct; by the time we get to pronouncing the "ent" in evanescent, the "evan" is already passed. But Ong's point was not, as Stewart suggests, that in "oral-aural communicating, one can seldom have all of even one word present at once." Quite the contrary, as literate speakers in secondary-orality, our experience of the spoken word is that it is "a thing, not an event, that it is present all at once, and that it can be cut up into little pieces" (cf. Ong, 1982, 91). Because we can see words right in front of us, self-standing and individuated in their simultaneous wholeness, we have transformed our experience of talk to accord with literacy. Thus, while Stewart wants to align himself with Ong's claim that the *real* word is the spoken word and the written word is no word at all (to which we perhaps can agree), he misses how Ong maintains that spoken words are no longer what they were once literacy sets in. "Once writing had established itself," Ong writes, "talk was no longer what it was...After writing, in other words, oral speech was never the same" (1977, pp. 86-87). Language, which cannot adequately be understood independent of its technological modifications, is neither merely natural nor merely historical; it is a "naturally historical" phenomenon (Anton, 2001, pp. 83-113).

Another difficulty arises where the alphabet offered a kind of paradigm for pursuing language as representational. In this instance, Stewart correctly identifies the alphabet as having a representational character but unfortunately mistakes the direction of that representation:

> It is worth underscoring the sense in which this very first achievement of language scholarship was *representational*...each character of the Greek alphabet was different in kind from and stood for a vowel or consonant sound...In this way the initial impetus of language scholarship led to efforts that were fundamentally repre-

sentational...a second important feature of alphabetization is that the process established a representational paradigm for thinking about language generally. As I noted, it seemed patently obvious--and still does--that writing represents speech. *But it did not necessarily follow that speech also represented something else--e.g. ideas or objects*. And yet early thinking moved in precisely this direction. (1995, p. 36)

Writing does not, as Stewart suggests, simply "represent speech." Speech for those in literate cultures--and because communication includes both speaking and listening--tacitly represents those visual objects (written words) for which the sounds, as now lexically delimited, stand. Literate spoken utterances represent themselves as they could be written down. Modern alphabetic scripts have taught people to listen to living speech as if it were comprised of discrete words and have trained ears to analyze sounds in term of visual boundaries and visual spatial organization. This position is articulated by literacy scholar David R. Olson, in his *The World on Paper:*

Contrary to writers from Aristotle to Saussure, I have argued that "writing is not a transcription of speech" but rather provides a model for speech; we introspect language in terms laid down by our scripts...writing was responsible for bringing aspects of spoken language into consciousness...in learning to write and read one comes to think of speech in terms of entities in the representational system. Writing provides a series of models for, and thereby brings into consciousness, the lexical, syntactic and logical properties of what is said. (Olson, 1994, pp. 258-259; also cf. Olson, 1996)

These issues can be explained by using the terms figure and background. The figures of "definite individual words," as they can be heard within the continuous flow of speech, appear only upon and against the background of "modern alphabetic script." Individual words heard within living acts of speech represent, at the very least and if only implicitly, their background: written words. This does not mean that all spoken words must appear in the O. E. D., though some literates may insist upon something like this [e.g. "That's not a *real* word; it doesn't appear in 'the' dictionary!"]. It means, more basically, that literate speech is guided by an underlying alphabetic principle: "anything said can be written."[18] Said otherwise, we come to introspect and experience our speech by conceptually shaping its appearance to the model that writing provides for it. This leads directly to my next point.

One of Stewart's early critiques is the challenge he brings to Kristeva's account of the representational nature of language. Stewart grants to Kristeva that some nouns, in some cases, seem to refer to things if only ostensibly. At least we can locate and identify "objects" or "facts" in the world that such nouns presumably signify. But he also contends that most words, most of the time, remain without a referent or have only a dubious one. Thus, language does not, primarily or mainly, symbolize, signify, or represent:

Kristeva asserts, "In fact, every speaker is more or less conscious of

the fact that language symbolizes or *represents* real facts by naming them. The elements of the spoken chain—for the moment let
us call them words—are associated with certain objects or facts
they *signify*"...But are they? In these sentences, the words, *speaker*,
words, and *objects* appear to support her contention....Moreover, it
is difficult to apply this analysis to almost any other words in these
two sentences. What objects or facts are signified by *in, every, is,
or, of, the, that, symbolizes, real, naming, let, call, are, with, certain,
they*... How does one think about the object or fact allegedly signified by *in* or *is*? Could it actually be the case that words other than
nouns represent by naming? (1995, p. 13)

The difficulties Stewart identifies are both subtle and profound. And the routes
of ostensible "representation" may be more dialectical than direct, and, maybe
all spoken words for literates do represent objects and facts, but not the immediate facts and objects that either Kristeva or Stewart had in mind. Isolated parts
of speech such as those identified by the above sentence represent that by which
their original delineation was made possible (i.e. modern alphabetic literacy).
Modern alphabetic nouns easily fool us into approaching the issue of reference by
looking for relations between single words and single objects, rather than attending to the living synthesis of *literate speech* within particular situations.[19] We too
quickly forget the background, the now permanently implied separation of form
and content. Many signifiers would not have been isolated out, made into discrete
signs that now stand with no referent, if writing had not analytically released them
into self-standing objects (cf. Olson, 1996).

Relevant here is the obscure and controversial section 20 of Aristotle's *Po-
etics*, where he summarizes what he takes as the natural parts of "language and
diction." [We already should note Aristotle's indiscriminate cross-applying of concepts for both writing and speech.]. He writes, "Language as a whole consists of
the following parts: the letter, the syllable, the connective, the noun, the verb, the
article, the case, and the statement" (Aristotle, 1958, p. 41). Of the letter, the syllable, the connective, and the article, Aristotle makes clear that such sounds are,
by themselves, *without meaning*. Only the noun and the verb are in themselves
meaningful combinations of sounds, and the statement holds only parts of which
are meaningful in themselves. Not only does Aristotle not identify adjectives,
adverbs, nor clauses, but he seems to have a significantly different understanding
of what is meant by a "word." Arguably, Aristotle has no concept directly synonymous with the modern word "word." By his description, what we call prepositions,
conjunctions, pronouns and articles, are meaningless sounds that accompany the
meaningful parts within statements. This suggests that many of the sounds we
recognize as "words"—especially those for which Stewart demonstrated highly
dubious reference—Aristotle would not. Unlike Aristotle, we assume that prepositions such as "with" and "in," and pronouns such as "it" as well articles such as
"the" and "a" have meaning in their own right. It could be that words such as
"the," "and," and "in," etc. can seem to be without referents, but these sounds
in speech have been identified and rendered meaningful (i.e., are assumed to be
words in the first place) only because of modern alphabetic literacy (cf. Olson,

1996, p. 95). Literate people know of words as individual words, discrete sounds that are meaningful in the abstract. They know that somewhere their meaning is written down; they believe in and operate by the dictionary. Interestingly, the word "dictionary" first appears in England in the 16th Century. We modern dictionary-using literates have inherited a speech tradition and an understanding of language much different from that of Aristotle. In summary, modern alphabetic writing, once internalized, becomes the ground upon which speech can be experienced as broken into definite words, and, the supposed "problem of reference" for these words is but a symptom of forgetting that they already represent the writing system which sponsored their now apparent independence.

Writing enables us to experience words as discrete possibilities consciously selected from and brought into combination with other words. This narrows the length-horizon of the paradigmatic axis in discourse. Whereas selection and substitution from schemata, tropes, and other such multilexical strings of clichéd sounds enables persons to stitch together comprehensible utterances, such stringing historically proceeds with increasingly finer selections: From multilexical oral formula, down to multilexical logographs to polysyllabic strings to discrete self-standing lexical units to that odd selection which is only seen but not heard: the "différance" of alphabetic spelling.[20] Although speech always retains much of this formulaic repetition and patch-work character, our conscious experience of selection seems narrower, more fine grade. For example, a person might say, "I was understanding what you were saying, but then you used a word that I didn't know, and, you lost me." How can the person be sure that it was only one word? What if, rather than an unknown word, it actually was a multilexical unit such as "Status quo" or even "such as"? This example holds two noteworthy features. First, we use the expression "multilexical unit" because literates can and do differentiate between a polysyllabic word and a multilexical unit (e.g. an expression). Second, *regardless* of whether it was one missed word or several, literate people have a sense of encountering and operating by individual words.

Future Direction for Literate Oral/Aural Contact

We may fail to recognize the ubiquitous influences of alphabetic writing because we too commonly assume that literacy is confined to visible acts of pen, text or written words.[21] In a related manner, we may think that literacy occasionally comes into play only when reading or writing tasks demand it. This too quickly reduces literacy to a discontinuous activity, something that happens in and at specific moments of time.[22] If only by implication, Stewart's project seems not to sufficiently reckon with our linguistic inheritance. The primarily oral nature of "constitutive articulate contact" must accommodate for how our speech continues to be shaped by alphabetic literacy. Ong well addresses these needs in three different places. First, he maintains that "Without the mental processes implemented by writing and print, it is impossible even to discover that there are such things as oral cultures…The word must die and be resurrected if it is to come into its own" (1977, p. 257). Second, he states, "Orality needs to produce and is destined to produce writing. Literacy, as will be seen, is absolutely necessary for the development not only of science but also of history, philosophy, explicative understanding of literature and of any art, and indeed for the explanation of language (including oral speech) itself" (1982, p. 15). And lastly, he writes that, "By contrast with natural, oral speech, writing is completely artificial. There is no way to write 'naturally.'...but--paradox again--artificiality is natural to human beings" (Ong, 1982, pp. 82-83). Ong's points could be summarized by noting how literacy shapes the concrete and specific ways that articulate contact accomplishes differentiation or categorization. Writing, alphabetic literacy in the particular case, has grown into oral/aural contact, radically modifying its earlier character. As literate speakers, we can and do speak literally, often too literally. And, the artificiality of writing, including the sense that written language is a semiotic system used by humans, is "natural" to our now current practices of literate speech. Literacy is not an alien addition to speech; there is not, for the alphabetically literate, both speech *and* literacy.

Because literacy is a condition rather than an activity, people in everyday face-to-face interactions are highly prone to literate ways of thinking. As Ong suggests, "Without writing, the literate mind would not and could not think as it does, not only when engaged in writing but normally even when it is composing its thoughts in oral form" (1982, p. 78). Some people can speak pedantically and at length, exercising powers of analytical speech unknown to primary oral cultures. Much of this talk will be nit-picky reflection over *particular* words and their meanings. Philology, even novice philology, is a product of the literate mind, even as it plays out in mostly face-to-face interactions. Everyday domestic squabbles can testify: we not only have words about words, we are capable of knowing the difference between a paraphrase and a verbatim recount. As people learn to use writing as a model for understanding their speech and learn to attend to it according to that model, they come to experience speech as comprised of words, even if only in reflection and after they have said them.

The idea that language should not be understood as the act of using individual words, or the claim that distortion results from accounts that "begin from or focus on discrete terms," subtly invites us to pretend that we are not alphabetically literate. Given that alphabetic literacy occurred and is occurring, might not Burke's analyses of individual words be more appropriate than Stewart had first led us to believe? Our ability to haggle over the meaning of individual word choices illustrates, if only symptomatically, how constitutive articulate contact grows literate. From this perspective, the use of individual words is a positive possibility that has come to fruition with literacy. Alfred North Whitehead has observed that we "so habitually intermingle writing and speech in our daily experience that, when we discuss language, we hardly know whether we refer to speech, or to writing, or to the mixture of both" (1938, p. 37). This reveals not an obstacle for our understanding of language, nor does it display something merely "reductive and derived." It is, on the contrary, an insight about the constitution of language in the fullest sense.

Endnotes to Chapter 9

1 Abstract from the original: This paper interrogates the so-called "crisis in representation" as a symptom of forgotten alphabetic literacy. My analysis launches its critique by attending to John Stewart's recent writings on "the symbol

model" and advances through two main sections. The first reviews historical developments in alphabetic technologies, identifying both basic differences and early impacts. The second section addresses phenomenological differences between hearing and vision and attempts to document how alphabetic writing enables speech to be heard as it could be seen if it were written. In summary, I try to demonstrate how literacy, the modern condition of logos, inseparably fuses with "oral/aural articulate contact."

2 An earlier version of this paper was presented to the Media Ecology Association at the 2003 National Communication Association conference in Miami. I wish to thank both Brett Lyszak and John Dowd for their helpful research assistance in this project, and I also need to thank Valerie V. Peterson for her many suggestions and criticisms.

3 This is not to imply that Stewart's work has gone unnoticed. In fact, Stewart published an edited collection called *Beyond the Symbol Model* (1996), which advanced his ideas and also included initial responses from thinkers in a wide array of disciplines. Recently, I (1999; 2002) brought two different critiques to Stewart's position, both of which argue for contemporary incorporation of phenomenological orientations toward "intentionality." Additionally, broad considerations of Stewart's work can be found in *Selfhood and Authenticity* (2001), pp. 85-87; 126.

4 Language should not be treated as a store-house of accumulated terms, and it makes little sense to ask questions such as, "How many words do you know?". Nevertheless, people often do ask about individual words and will seemingly acquire them one by one, sometimes from a dictionary.

5 David Olson (1996, 1995, 1993) has produced a wealth of research in this area.

6 I caution in advance against identifying these "developments" as evolutionary progressions. Peter D. Daniels, co-editor of *The World's Writing Systems* (1996) suggests that the first two shifts were addressed initially in Isaac Taylor's *The Alphabet* (1883), and that what Taylor first introduced, Gelb, whose *A Study of Writing* (1952) reigned authoritative for three decades, came to totalize and over-state. Daniels writes,

> It seems to be Taylor who first laid out (vol. I, p. 6) the tripart typology of writing systems-
> -logographic, syllabic, alphabetic--that has dominated grammatology for more than a
> century...Gelb claimed that syllabaries could only develop from logographies, and that
> alphabets could only be developed from syllabaries, and that these steps could be neither
> skipped nor reversed. He called this sequence the "principle of unidirectional develop-
> ment," and this principle has become the accepted view. (1996, pp. 6-7)

Also see the discussions of the "transformational thesis" within both Heim's *Electronic Language* and Baron's *Alphabet to Email*.

7 Examples of different functions include sacred symbols, the purposes of which include incantation, apotheosis, and divine evocation.

8 Consider the insightful discussion of "interpretation" in Josiah Royce's (1967) Chapter "Conception, Perception, and Interpretation," in *The Problem of Christianity*.

9 Jack Goody (1977) points out that 90% of the earliest writing holds lists, itemizations, and other bureaucratic records.

10 As Havelock (1971, p. 11) puts it: "What the Greeks did was to invent the idea that a sign could represent a mere consonant, a sound, so to speak, which does not exist in nature but only in 'thought.'" This is what Aristotle calls a "mute."

11 There may be a sense in which the development of spaces between words initiated a type of recovery of more logographical principles for the reading of alphabetic texts. Words as discrete lexical units can be learned piece-meal, as ideographs/logographs are learned one at a time.

12 Technical writing systems developed for communication research such as "Jeffersonian Transcription" and "conversation analysis" appear to be the lowest context writing so far. See also J . Peter Denny (1991, pp. 66-89) who argues that the claims advanced by many of the transformational theorists, claims regarding the origin of logical thinking and analytical reason, are misconstrued and exaggerated. In their place and as a corrective, he offers "decontextualization" as the distinctive characteristic of modern alphabetic literacy.

13 This is less surprising given that Stewart is heavily influenced by the everyday language philosophies spawned in the wake of Wittgenstein's *Philosophical Investigations*. Wittgenstein's astute investigations of everyday language and "language games" fail to address how kinds of games rely upon sensory differences and historical facts of writing. Unfortunately, Wittgenstein interchangeably discusses games of writing and speech, as if all games could be played in any way or simply according to the ways the play "goes on" from there. Radically different contributions of sense organs to the human sensorium are downplayed and taken as tangential, metaphysical, even irrelevant to the emergence and practice of specific language games (cf. Tyler, 1997, p. 160-165). I also should here note that Stewart explicitly identifies his early beginnings as informed by "ordinary language philosophers," including Wittgenstein, Ryle and Austin. This is significant not only because, as Stewart suggests, "although ordinary language philosophers provided a useful critical perspective, their work did not point clearly toward a credible alternative" (1995, p. ix), but more particularly because such philosophers have not adequately taken into account histories of literacy nor have they taken seriously phenomenological address to sensory differences, Stewart included. Granted that Wittgenstein's *The Blue and Brown Books* (1958) includes address to reading and speaking, Wittgenstein does not address different histories of particular writing systems (cf. pp. 78-79, 82-91, 118-125, 153, 167, 172-180). Granted also that Wittgenstein (1958, p. 79) suggests that we assume that the function and instrumentalities of language must be but one, for we take words as they appear in a dictionary. Such arrangements induce the prejudice toward homogenizing the multivaried functions of speech. And note too that he here opens with the question, "What is the meaning of a word?" To the degree that Wittgenstein correctly diagnosis the representational "problems" of contemporary philosophical analysis, he offers anything but the final word (cf. Rosen, 1969, pp. 1-27).

14 Interesting lines that explore how alphabetic writing both solidifies a notion of "word" as well as facilitates a tearing

asunder of syllables can be found in Kolinsky, Cary and Morais (1987) and Morais, Bertelson, Cary, Alegria (1996), respectively. For the latter also see Read, Yun-Fei, Hong-Yin, Bao-Qing (1986).

15 Although Denny (1991) grounds the origin of such capacities in population size and social organization, I support his claims regarding decontextualization on mainly phenomenological grounds.

16 Also consider Tyler's (1987) suggestion:

> Writing displaces the subject from the world and alienates it from him...It sets up the universal problematic of reconnecting signs and signifieds, words and things. In contrast, postmodern anthropology asks, 'how did signs and signifieds get pulled apart?' and identifying writing as the culprit, argues that sign and signified are mutually constituted in 'saying,' where the sign is immanent in the signified and the signified is immanent in the sign. (p. 194)

17 Consider the following contrast: Bolter writes that, "In reviving spoken language, the [phonetic] reader is turning discrete images into continuous sound" (1991, p. 49). Now consider that "we hear speech in our native tongue as a sequence of distinct words separated by tiny gaps of silence. That is, we have a clear sense of boundaries between words" (Dennett, 1991, 50-51). Here we find the dialectical relationship "between" speech and written words exemplified in both directions.

18 Stewart argues that,

> And no morpheme, word or phrase can coherently be said to stand for another morpheme, word or phrase. Even synonyms are mutually substitutable but not representationally related. As a result, it cannot make sense to claim that two related phenomena are of the same ontological status and that the relationship between them is representational. If the purported relationship is a signifying or symbolizing one, then the phenomenon needs to be different in kind. (1995, p. 22-23)

I think we can agree with Stewart that spoken words do not represent other spoken words yet we should note that writing does not simply represent pre-existing speech sounds; it is a set of instructions for making sounds. Speech, for the phonetically literate, represents itself as it could be written. As Jahandarie (1999, p. 154) observes, "evidence seems to indicate that, for literate individuals, these lexical entries also have a corresponding orthographic representation."

19 For direct and extended discussion of how utterances ("statements") make possible "referential moments in discourse" see Paul Ricoeur's *Interpretation Theory* and for more direct address to Stewart's project see Anton (1999).

20 Derrida suggests that différance, neither a word nor a concept, is the key for understanding relations between signifier and signified. Interestingly, he uses alphabetic differences in spelling (visual but inaudible) to bring out his issue. Tyler thought observes that,

> What Derrida does not make clear in his deconstruction of the signified is that speech is the other writing invents in order to give itself an origin...Our sense of the arbitrariness, of the possibility of a disjunction between signifier and signified is created by writing. It is writing that makes it possible for us to think of speech as if it were an object, or to think of the sounds that are other than the written objects before our eyes. Writing invents its own origin in the disjunction of signifier and signified and sets itself to the problem of overcoming the self-inflicted amputation which was its own parthenogenesis. (1987, p. 19-20)

21 In *The Unspeakable*, Tyler further writes,

> The chief advantage to eliminating the idea of representation is that representation emphasizes the differences between sign and signified at all levels. There is always a constant world of things and a separate world of signs, and this defines the essential problematic as one of words and things and leads us to overemphasize mimesis, description, and correspondence theories of truth, and tricks us into thinking of language as if it were a form of calculus where we can abstract signs away from their representational functions and treat them as "pure forms," focusing exclusively on their modes of collection. The "constitutive'" mode emphasizes not the separateness of the signs and signifieds, but their interpenetratability and mutuality. There is no problematic relationship between word and world, for both are mutually present. It is only where there is the possibility of the absence of the one or the other that problems arise, and it is, of course, just this possibility that writing enables. (1987, p. 196)

Using terms that stand in tight alignment with Stewart's ideas, Tyler correctly identifies writing as a contributor to the signifier/signified split, but we must question the idea that only writing per se sustains the possibility of the absence of one or the other; it is literacy which holds open this perennial possibility, for all spoken words also equally imply their written counterparts.

22 For an excellent address regarding the scope of the impact of alphabetic writing see Logan's *The Alphabet Effect* (1986).

Chapter 10: Clocks, Synchronization, and the Fate of Leisure: A Brief Media Ecological History of Digital Technologies[1]

> *"America:... 'I'll see you at 4:10, then' is a sentence that would have been comprehensible to no other civilization this earth has seen."*
> — *Sebastian de Grazia, 1964, p. 294*

> *"Prick me, and I bleed time."*
> — *Jules Henry, 1965, p. 11*

Prelude[2]

Every year more and more U.S. citizens spend more time in the digital world. We hear of digital recording systems, digital cell phones, digital cameras, and high-definition digital television sets. The digital environment also includes various computer-based social networking sites as well as upload and sharing technologies known collectively as Web 2.0. Given these many technological developments in the last decade or so, my goal in this chapter is to sketch a framework for understanding their emergence and to outline the larger and more subtle impetus to the digital age.

Sheer feasibility is a major contributor to the growth of digital technologies. But something else is going on as well. A key to understanding the recent developments in digital technologies can be found all the way back in the mid-1800s with the advent of the telegraph. The telegraph not only separated communication from transportation, it made possible a new kind of substance, one that was divorced from the confines of materiality: information. Without a doubt, telegraphy, and electricity writ large, paved the way for all kinds of digital electronic circuitry. Electricity and circuit boards made all of the newly emerging digital—and largely informational—technologies possible. But this point, important as it is, obfuscates something else that deserves our attention: the telegraph transformed clocks, and this transformation brought profound and thoroughgoing changes in people's temporal sensibilities. In fact, although the contemporary buzzword, "digital," now typically refers to the aforementioned communication technologies, its first mainstream use was in reference to digital wristwatches. In seeking to gain or display status (rationalizing their subservience?), many people even today, "like watches as a symbol of wealth and modernity" despite the fact that a watch is basically, "a despot to be obeyed" (de Grazia, 1964, p. 297). This seemingly trivial observation points to a deeper logic within digital technologies.

If we are to grasp part of the logic of the digital age, we need to understand how the synchronization of clocks introduced something genuinely novel, and arguably, something genuinely tyrannical, something from which people would soon seek relief. With the telegraph came unprecedented coordination and orchestration of action and interaction: electricity transformed not only the meaning of "machines," it radically altered the master machine of machines: the clock. Time itself was radically transformed by electricity and this transformation was nearly all encompassing. It included such now taken-for-granted aspects of our experiences as the standardization of time zones, increasingly accurate weather-prediction, the News, the creation of the distinction between work time and leisure-time, the massive scheduling of life into minute-by-minute forms of interaction, and the futures market (compare Carey, 1989; Citzstrom, 1983; McLuhan, 1964).

Within a span of under two centuries, the U.S. increasingly subjugated itself to a pervasive though mostly invisible despot. The despot initially seemed to rule only on the job or at the workplace. He blew his whistle and rang his bell at particular times to help workers synchronize their labors. As Sebastian de Grazia (1964), in *Of Time, Work, and Leisure*, writes,

> The clock, first placed in a tower and later hung up wherever work was to be done, provided the means whereby large-scale industry could coordinate the movements of men and materials to the regularity of machines…a new conception of time developed and spread over the industrial world. (p. 291)

Soon enough, the despot ruled over the entire land, not only inside the factory but also inside the home. The despot worked his way down into the micro-segments of private lives, and the synchronization of clocks gave birth to today's commonsense distinction between work time and free time. Prior to mass coordination by way of synchronized clocks, the expression "work time" referred to the time when workers showed up to work, whenever that was. Punctuality was calibrated to seasonal or diurnal needs, not as it mostly is today, according to what the clock says.

As mass orchestration through synchronization became more and more possible, workers were led to believe that acceptance of schedules and carefully disciplined economical movements eventually would lead to a world of less work and more leisure. What they ended up with was quite the contrary: an objective, neutralized time, one that became increasingly commercialized. Work time, moreover, became the defining metaphor of the culture, the very ground against which everything else was set in relief. It created a largely invisible yet pervasive tethering effect. As de Grazia (1964) writes, "Most men today may not be aware that they are geared to machines—even while they are being awakened by the ringing of a bell and gulping down their coffee in a race with the clock" (pp. 288-289). Part of the reason we fail to notice the ways we are geared to machines and their inhuman pace is because we are indoctrinated into them from birth.

> The synchronizing of activities by the clock begins early. The child sees the father rise by the clock, treat its facial expression with great respect, come home by it, eat and sleep by it, and catch or miss his entertainment—the movies, a TV show—by it. …there is thenceforth less a feeling of imposition that people have for the clock when introduced to it only at a later age. (ibid., p. 297)

Although modern life is scheduled down to hour-by-hour and minute-by-minute intervals, time has not always been dealt with this way. The highly modern notion of objective time, the three-armed despot, needs further exploration if we are to understand the emergence of the digital age. Said most directly, not even 200 years old, synchronized clock-time enabled the possibility of—and slowly created the warrant for—newly emerging digital technologies.

If media ecology explores how media become environments, then electric clocks are perhaps the supreme example of how a medium has become environmental (also see Strate, 1996). Such clocks are not inside an already existing time and merely registering it. On the contrary, they make possible the kinds of time to which we moderns subject ourselves; we, those who have submitted ourselves to them, are within the kinds of time that they create. To advance this discussion, I briefly review the history of timepieces and show how the modern notion of time marked a significant change from the past. Questions guiding my exploration are: How different is the modern, electric, notion of time? Why is modern synchronization so different? And how, exactly, does synchronization relate to today's digital environment?

Historical Varieties of Timekeeping

Some of the most well-known and often-cited lines regarding the experience of time come from St. Augustine's (1951) *Confessions*. He writes, "What then is time? If no one asks me, I know: If I wish to explain it to one that asketh, I know not" (p. 224). To this day, time remains more felt or experienced (incorporated and obeyed?) than thematically and analytically comprehended. It remains as one of the ambiguous mysteries of human experience: in a single instant, time can seem to be more objective than any object in the world, while at the next instant it can seem to be completely subjective. It can drag, stand nearly still, or pass quickly without notice. With a single glance, we can look back over a long journey and feel it as having taken no time at all. Such conditions are part of the reason why humans desire to get a handle on time, grasp it, measure it, or, at the very least, subdue it in some way (for more phenomenological considerations of time, temporality, and measured-time see Anton, 2001; Fraser, 1987).

Prior to the modern wholesale objectification and commercialization of time, time was measured, but in a mostly subjective way. This measuring is clearly articulated in Aristotle's definition of time: "something counted which shows itself in and for regard to the before and after in motion, or in short, something counted in connection with motion as encountered in the horizon of the earlier and later" (cited in Heidegger, 1982, p. 235). This definition, in rough form, is relevant even today, though the degrees of precision and the notions of objectivity have changed considerably.

The earliest and perhaps most natural form of timekeeping was simple attention to day and night, and then to shadows, even one's own, created by the daytime sun. The high point of the day's sun, what was called noon, was that time when shadows were at their shortest. Stationary clocks were used in Ancient Egypt, and the ancient Greeks created the first sundial. In ancient Rome, following the Greek use of sundials, hemicyclia and conical sundials were made for the courtyards of villas. By this period in history there was sophisticated time measurement, including not only attention to the daylight sun, but also measurement of seasons of the year. Other quite sophisticated means of timekeeping were the hourglass, the candle, and incense (McLuhan, 1964).

We might imagine that the ancients subjected themselves to an objective sense of time of the same sort that we do today. That would be an anachronism. By modern sensibilities, all of these time keeping devices were imperfect; all suffered from various kinds of imprecision. Hourglasses were rather imprecise within the hour and could get clogged. Candles and incense could be blown out and demanded considerable attention and care. Sundials only worked during the day and required a sunny sky. The rough hour was the smallest unit of time registered—and even here, its delineation depended upon ideal conditions. The water in early water clocks did not always flow at a constant rate. When a clock tower rings a bell every hour, all within hearing range could know the time by the ringing, but distances could vary between and among the hearers, and, therefore, the task of calling people together would take varying amounts of time. Across these cases, the most important point to note is that all of these forms of timekeeping were local (not portable, not lightweight, and not widely available to everyone). The devices told the time that it was then and there. They were for enabling synchronized coordination or measurement in the present within a mostly local sense of here and now.

The Mechanical Despot
Mechanical clocks, a significant breakthrough, date back to the mid 1300's but they, too, suffered from various kinds of imprecision. The escapement mechanisms within mechanical clocks, a significant innovation, were still subject to small variations in measurement and required regular resetting. Making an appearance in Italian cities, the earliest clocks had faces but no hands. They were built to be heard rather than to be watched, and they were mainly used for coordinating activities in the present. As late as the mid-1600s mechanical clocks were regularly "off" by about 15 minutes a day. Then, by 1673, Christiaan Huygens invented the pendulum clock, which used weights and a swinging pendulum (Fraser, 1987). These clocks brought more accuracy than any the world had seen; they were off by less than a minute a day.

The use of early clocks deserves consideration as well. For centuries the use of clocks was limited to churches and monasteries, where clergy intimately compartmentalized their lives according to measured units of time. After the clergy, the next to discipline time were the military and schools. In *Discipline and Punish* (1977), Michel Foucault explores how the application of power and the subjugation of bodies were made possible through highly disciplined uses of time and schedules. The very notion of the individual changed as bodies became sites for exercising power. With the clock, writes Foucault, "A sort of anatomo-chronological schema of behavior is defined. Time penetrates the body and with it all the meticulous controls of power" (p. 152). Rather than Taylorism in the workplace (still a century or two in the future), there was a meticulous regimentation of behavior, circumscriptions of bodily movements in an attempt to wean more life out of every moment. Describing the changeover from earlier monastic practices to disciplining the body in schools, the military, and the workplace, Foucault writes

> The principle that underlay the time-table in its traditional form was
> essentially negative; it was the principle of non-idleness: it was for-

bidden to waste time, which was counted by God and paid for by men; the time-table was to eliminate the danger of wasting time—a moral offence and economic dishonesty. Discipline, on the other hand, arranges a positive economy; it poses the principle of a theoretically ever-growing use of time: exhaustion rather than use; it is a question of extracting, from time, ever more available moments, and from each moment, ever more useful forces. This means that one must seek to intensify the use of the slightest moment, as if time, in its very fragmentation, were inexhaustible or as if, at least by an ever more detailed internal arrangement, one could tend toward an ideal point at which one maintained maximum speed and efficiency...By other means, the "mutual improvement" was also arranged as a machine to intensify the use of time. (p. 154)

The mechanical age, the literate age, was culminating into the bodily use of highly fragmented time units from the 1600s-1800s. Minuscule time units exercised their power rather locally, over immediate bodies, and the smallest motions of present persons became subject to control. Much of Foucault's insight, without explicitly focusing on the alphabet, gives support to McLuhan's general ideas that both clocks and phonetic literacy conspired together to issue new sensibilities of time and self.

With the increase in highly circumscribed behavior in accordance to temporal units (coupled with increasing pressures of literacy), the mechanical age might seem to be merely continuous with the modern era and its clock time. But telling the story this way too quickly passes over qualitative differences between today's sensibility of time and the notions of time from the ancient world all the way up until the invention of the telegraph. Time in its modern sense is not merely more accurately kept time, and here we need to be precise. Post-telegraphy time (modern time) is in some ways more objective, though it is less accurate. By this I mean that time zones, first invented in the 1840s for railway coordination and then widely adopted by the mid-1880s, somewhat arbitrarily broke the passage of time into units coordinated to clocks in distant lands and around the globe. Time zones help considerably for orchestrating the schedules of trains, planes, and automobiles, but they are not more accurate than carefully attending to shadows. Their arbitrary character is evident if we simply consider that two people can be in the same time zone despite the fact that both of them are nearer to other people who are in different time zones! Prior to the telegraph, "the distant" was synonymous with "other than now." Today, we can telephone someone half way around the globe, and, although it is equally "now" for both of us, we each can be at a different time, perhaps even on a different day. Modern sensibilities of time require a highly abstract management of space-time: we have learned to break apart time and distance. It is indeed one thing to wake from a church bell. It is quite another to know with confidence what time it is halfway around the world.

To understand the significant changes that arose in the mid-1800s, we need to examine the differences between mechanical clocks and the highly modern (post-telegraphy) clocks. "What we call time nowadays is but the movement of synchronized clocks...If two persons had moved together at the sight of a smoke signal or the sound of a pistol shot, the signal would have been considered personal because set off by a man, whereas we feel the clock as impersonal because it is automatic and tied in with other clocks" (de Grazia, 1964, pp. 302-303). For example, consider the significant difference between responding to a sound that then and only then announces what time it is and the visual act of continually looking at a watch to see what time it will be in ten or twenty minutes. The modern clock, depending upon clocks synchronized to each other, is mainly used for futural projection of synchronized interaction, for precise schedules and strict obeisance to them is the key issue to notice. De Grazia reminds us of the early meaning of the word, "watch." As a device worn on the wrists of individuals themselves, watches promoted a vigilant watchfulness over the time, and people's schedules grew synchronized into finer and finer exactitude. In the 1920s, the advent of the quartz watch was also significant as it enabled unprecedented precision, and today, people can have personal computers accurate within milliseconds by accessing atomic clock time online (Gleick, 1999). Note once again that it was synchronization that promoted and legitimated the proliferation of the watch. Timekeeping devices are ancient, but the widespread use of an accurately kept, objective time—an evenly divided and constantly visible time standing uniformly and shared by all, a time that is neutralized and commercialized, was ushered in not simply with mechanical clocks. The essential element was synchronization.

There always have been (and there always will be) seasonal time, rhythmic time (tempo and rhythm), or even kairos (humanly initiated and felt time), and yet, all of these are profoundly different from the time offered up by synchronized clocks. Synchronized clock time, especially to the uninitiated, seems to be utterly inhuman, rudely punctilious, and annoyingly insomniatic. And, with everyone's schedules so tightly interlocked, people live less and less according to diurnal time, or even time as measured by the hour. Today, people feel the drive to be calibrated to something more exacting and demanding than even the quarter-hour. Deals are made or not—careers are launched or broken—within a manner of minutes or even seconds, and human lives have never before been so scheduled, so bundled into constantly watched units, and so packaged into so many precisely measured moments (cf. Gleick, 1999). Consider, for one example, the amount of advertising dollars spent on thirty-second spots during "prime-time" viewing, and the way that these smaller-than-a-minute "mini-dramas" can make or break advertising executives; people try to "make every second count."

Resisting the Three-Armed Despot

Alan Watts (1966) comically illustrates how easily people create troubles for themselves when they take their own fictions as already given facts. He writes,

> Thus in 1752 the British government instituted a calendar reform which required that September 2 of that year be dated September 14, with the result that many people imagined that eleven days had been taken off their lives, and rushed to Westminster screaming, "Give us back our eleven days!" (p. 81)

We can laugh, but we are just as ruled by our own fictions: Today, we do not scream for missing days. We scream when someone is late for an appointment (see Henry, pp. 11-92). We moderns are hyper-scheduled, and the schedules we confine ourselves to are ultra-fine grade. Describing the modern scheduling that has become an accepted part of life in the U.S., de Grazia (1964) notes,

> Today...a dermatologist can schedule patients in his office at 10 minute intervals. Many people in business and government schedule 10 or 15 minute, sometimes 5 minute, appointments. Trains and planes go by a schedule in odd minutes—7:08, 10:43. All appointments must be kept by continual reference to the inexorable clock. (p. 295)

It is almost hard to believe that we have been affected so profoundly by little more than scheduling and synchronizing our lives around the minute. Who could have anticipated that something so small and invisible, the No-Thing that is the minute, could act back upon people and precipitate so many forms of dis-ease? Who could have imagined the inhuman pillory on conveyor-belts that could be made from these little units?

Early Marxists, to their credit, were among those who were quite concerned about the then emerging applications of automation and the newly emerging demands on workers. The clock and the machine coupled with automation made work something independent of the worker. A new notion of work time emerged, which now meant the precise time to be at work and doing work, and people came to feel a sharp contrast between work and non-work as they increasingly were paid for their time rather than their product. Payment by the hour came to be standard practice, and workers were reduced to "labor" and "human resources." The purpose here is not to rehearse this story but rather to stress that life more generally, including dominant communication media that were emerging during this time and subsequently, began to demand as much punctuality as did the workplace. And this arrangement grew more and more problematic because, at least since the early twentieth century, U.S. citizens had been promised a life of leisure. By punctually binding themselves to a machine-paced or automated workplace, people thought that eventually they would be more productive in less time and would have more time for leisure. In fact, people accepted the encroachment of demanded synchronicity in almost all aspects of non-work life, especially in dinner-time, mass media, and public entertainment.

The promise of more leisure time (after work and on weekends) eventually failed. In its place arose more and more forms of scheduling. Dinner-time, as one example, became a highly scheduled event, one tethered as if it were a satellite entering the visible horizon only around the end of work time. In his interesting studies of dysfunctional families, *Pathways to Madness*, Jules Henry documents how "waiting" and "being late" with regard to "dinner-time" can be some of the most pointed and emotionally-riling aspects of family life. Summarizing the subtle ways that emotional tensions and clock time interweave, Henry (1965) writes,

> The average man...is aware, for example, that if he is not home "on time," dinner will be "kept waiting," "the kids will be hungry and screaming" and his wife "worried and mad" because she "couldn't

imagine what had happened" to him, and because, since she has to go out, his getting home later has "spoiled everything." The expressions in quotes demonstrate the close connection between time and mood in our culture…a person's actions *in time* have this tight connection to other people's moods…Time…binds us to their emotional life. (p. 11)

Not only is all of this trying, but it is more and more difficult as the mechanical principle was extended down to the minute. And the stresses should not be surprising given the demand for a calibrated intersection of four horizons of minute-by-minute scheduling: dinner time, commute time, work time, and school time.

Consider, too, the early days of radio, movies, or television and how time-bound these media initially were and largely remain. When Roosevelt gave his fireside chats, people would gather in their living rooms around the radio and listen to the broadcast. Political uses aside, the relevant point is the synchronicity of the broadcast—everyone had to tune in at the same time. TV was just as bound: at first, programs came on early in the morning, and then, at night, the station went off. And even today, although most stations now stay on all the time, programs have remained largely unchanged in their punctuality: in the U.S., TV shows start exactly every hour or half-hour, and, if people do not want to miss any part of their favorite shows, they must be tuned in as punctually as any workman. Movie theaters, too, have changed very little in this regard. Moreover, movie theatres are known for having show times at rather specific times, for example, the 9:20 or 10:35 showing. In light of these highly scheduled and temporally synchronous media, it is easy to see the many drives toward asynchronicity as a palliative.

The resistance roughly began with the phonograph and tape recorder, which could record and then play back recorded material (live performances, lectures, or radio programs) any time the person wanted. Soon thereafter, video-recording technologies allowed people to record TV programs or movies and watch them "at their leisure." Next came movie rental stores and services, and the playing of movies on one's own time. As the computer made headway into U.S. popular culture, the digital file, along with digital recording and replaying technologies appeared. Digital video discs (DVD) and DVD-recorders soon appeared. Netflix, first as an at-home mail service and then as an online service, further broke movies free from the despot's demands of synchronicity. (And, Netflix is increasingly changing from the diurnal rhythm of the daily mail arrival to the 24/7 all online availability). Today, people have ample digital technologies for recording and selectively viewing media in an asynchronous and/or 24/7 fashion. With DVRs and with TiVo-like technologies, viewers can even pause live TV. There are MP3 players and websites like YouTube and MySpace where people can not only record and play back audio and video, but they can share digital files easily with anyone else who has computer access.

Email is perhaps the most obvious form of asynchronous interaction. By communicating through email, people make use of instantaneous transmission akin to the telephone, but they also retain the capacity to stall, wait, or otherwise make the exchange of information asynchronous. In many places, email has displaced the use of the telephone. For example, when college students wish to contact their professors, they typically send an email rather than call on the phone, and the reasons are perhaps obvious: they want the option of an asynchronous mode of communication. Moreover, email does display the time, but at this speed of interaction, time is used more as a record of the past than as a means for synchronizing with each other.

Cellular telephones might initially be offered as an example of increased synchronicity, as users are accessible anywhere at any time. However, the "message" of the cell phone has been felt most by the clock. First, it has considerably lessened the pressure of "dinner-time," as people can phone home for sudden schedule changes or updates. But more generally considered, time in the digital world seems less and less for futural projection into a schedule. It is used increasingly for present situations: young people resist scheduling in advance and instead exhibit a kind of "swarming behavior" in the present. Moreover, today's cell phones have message recording capacity and so are fully functional in an asynchronous mode. Many people "screen" their calls so that they can get back to individuals on their own time. Cell phones also commonly display the amount of time spent on a call made or received, and so, once again, time appears more as a past record than as a means of synchronization. As YouTube also records the amount of time logged in, might it be that recorded time will, soon enough, need to be paid for?

To discuss the fuller meaning and broader implications of social networking sites such as MySpace, Facebook and YouTube would surpass the scope of this chapter, but I will offer a few preliminary observations. First and perhaps most obviously, although these connectivity technologies allow users to act with awareness that others are also currently online, they equally display a kind of functionality for endless modes of asynchronous interaction. As Hassan's essay "Network Time," suggests,

> Connected asychronicity is a central feature of the network society and network time…Network time fundamentally changes our relationship with the clock—it doesn't negate or cancel it. Instead, the…asynchronous spaces of the networked society…*undermine* and *displace* the time of the clock. What we experience, albeit in very nascent form, is the recapture of the forms of temporality that were themselves displaced by the clock. (2007, p. 51)

With shards and fragments of spare time cropping up in overly scheduled lives, Myspace, FaceBook, and YouTube fill the void by providing a kind of momentary getaway. For people who are calibrated down to the minute and second, these interfaces offer some kind of relief from work, though the workers themselves often remain somewhere between amusement, lollygagging, and more work. Note that YouTube permits at most a ten-minute video for uploading or viewing, and most clips are significantly shorter, typically a few minutes long. Time is so precise on YouTube that the system displays the user's last login in seconds. Note too that video editing, an increasingly popular pastime, works with software packages that measure time down to the hundredth of the second (Gleick, 1999). Social networking sites and other Web 2.0 technologies traffic in a digital world where everything there is available all of the time. In addition, these technologies have enabled and facilitated interactivity in ways that earlier mass media have never been able to do.

In sum, early media technologies such as radio and TV began with the mechanical principle and were scheduled around the synchronization of the clock. Within the past decade or so, with the pervasive scheduling of life down to min-ute-by-minute intervals, people could not keep up. Cell phones, Email, YouTube, MySpace, and Facebook and the like, can be interpreted as a unified dialectical backlash against two centuries of tightening temporal strictures (also see Strate, 1996). We should not be surprised that in recent times we hear people describ-ing their activity as multitasking. Whether or not multitasking is increasing, and regardless of whether this is boon or bane, I would simply argue that the phenom-enon shows itself (makes more and more sense to us) mainly because our lives have been so precisely scheduled. Might multitasking be a symptom of changing sensibilities of time, or the product of clashing time frames?—a clash between the hours of the older media and the minutes and seconds of the newer ones?

The Future of Work, Leisure, and Time Spent

Do you remember when you couldn't tell the time? You'd say, "the big hand is on the three and the little hand is on the six." "Quarter after six," a par-ent or teacher would say. There began your early disciplining into a temporally scheduled world. Parents normally are eager to help their children learn to tell time. Knowing the time is taken as a virtue: punctuality equals industriousness and "God loves a workingman." But when digital watches hit the mass market, many parents expressed a fear that children would no longer know how to "read" a clock. They sensed that something was going wrong, but little did they seem to get the real message: Soon enough, digital clocks would be found absolutely everywhere: on automobile dashboards, shoes, hats, pencils, notebooks, ovens and microwaves, cameras, checkbooks, calculators, radios, televisions, computer screens, cell-phones, golf-bags and in countless public places, everywhere.

One of Marshall McLuhan's (1964) great insights was to grasp the kind of *reversal* implied by the electric revolution. The change-over to the electric age was not, he suggested in contrast to what seemed to be the dominant view, a mere continuation of the mechanical age. Delineating the progression of the mechanical age and then showing the reversal implied by the electronic revolu-tion, he writes,

> In the ancient world the only means of achieving power was getting a thousand slaves to act as one man. During the Middle Ages the communal clock extended by the bell permitted high coordination of the energies of small communities. In the Renaissance the clock combined with the uniform respectability of the new typography to extend the power of social organization almost to a national scale. By the nineteenth century it had provided a technology of cohesion that was inseparable from industry and transport, enabling an en-tire metropolis to act as an automaton. Now in the electric age of decentralized power and information we begin to chafe under the

uniformity of clock-time. In this age of space-time we seek multiplicity, rather than repeatability, of rhythms. This is the difference between marching soldiers and ballet. (p. 138)

The ends of electric time and connected asynchronicity are wholly different than the one-at-a-time serial organization characteristic of the clock and mechanical age. At first, modern objective time seemed uniform, progressively enabling more synchronization than had been possible in the past. But the more that people trafficked in that odd immateriality called information (perhaps financial information), the more they were freed up for asynchronous interaction. Whereas the mechanical age used the clock to synchronize bodies and group actions, today massive synchronization of information has inverted associations to allow for various forms of asynchronous interaction.

The more that people spend time in digital environments, the less that time is used for futural projection. Moreover, where everything is always already available, there is no longer a need for synchronization: at this speed, we are already there. Part of the meaning of the digital is that you are already synchronized or that synchronicity is no longer needed. To become digital is to live by the minute and the second, but such minutes and seconds are not felt as tyrannical, for they are geared not into the future as much as into the present or the past.

The clock is not disappearing, but there are places, digital spaces, where its uses are changing considerably. Early timekeeping was largely an issue of coordination in the present: it used the ear to gather and orchestrate in the local now. Then came the watch and visual modes of futural projection that enabled the scheduling of life into minute-by-minute intervals. With the emergence of contemporary dawdling and lollygagging online, the clock increasingly serves as a record of time-spent. Spare time in the digital age thus approximates a kind of time, the recorded passage of which proves that there was, in fact, a time that was one's own.

Telegraphy first separated communication from transportation so that information could travel faster than any messenger. What this made possible—and we can see it all around us—is the clash we now witness between two kinds of culture: the older material culture that requires various forms of synchronized bodies and the newer culture that handles mainly forms of information and is available anytime anywhere (see also Rifkin, 1987). As an illustration, consider the traditional workplace: people go away to work and need to be on time and to do work when they are at the work site. In this world, bodies must synchronize in space according to clocks; people need to tightly calibrate themselves, and this is accomplished by the futural projection that clocks and schedules make possible. In contrast, consider the online workplace, where all the materials for the job are completely available at any time. With a laptop in hand, some people no longer go into an office, and they face no machine nor co-workers waiting for them come 7 a.m. They may work through the night, or even do work ahead of time to gain a little spare time in the next week. While part of the culture is ultra-scheduled and moves like military soldiers, other parts are less and less scheduled and increasingly flexible regarding the where and when of work time. If the synchronization of time first helped people to work together, today it comes into its own by enabling flexi-time, working at home, distance education, movies-on-demand, and a world where work and entertainment can be had at anytime by anyone (also see Waite, 2003).

McLuhan, in 1964, wrote that global travelers "have the daily experience of being at one hour in a culture that is still 3000 B.C., and at the next hour in a culture that is 1900 A.D." (p. 141). Something similar to this is happening today within U.S. culture but we need not travel far to experience it. Simply walk around in parks and public places and notice the WiFi world, the cellular users and those who are text messaging. Many people are yearning for a kind of time and a kind a space that is not so tyrannical. They'd like one ruled by a kinder and more lenient despot.

Nevertheless, we are and will remain bodies whose health depends upon regularly ingesting perishables, and, the distribution of perishables, even regional perishables, depends upon tightly interlocked schedules. We must be honest about the distribution of produce and other forms of perishables as well as the demands of mass transportation: there will always be demands of synchronization. Bodies are not digital information. Someone may be a powerful avatar in Second Life, but that person is also someone sitting somewhere in front of a computer screen (Slouka, 1995). This basically means that times that are most exacting and peculiar, times like movie, bus, and plane schedules, are times when bodies must be synchronized in space. Unlike perishable objects, which remain where placed, people can wander around and lose sense of the passage of time. And so, until we are all led to the "Big Rock Candy Mountains", or unless robot slaves of the future do all of the work that demands tight synchronization, or unless the future brings cheap, reliable, and easily available food replicators and teleporters, we shall, as bodies, remain within various demands for synchronized interaction.

An important distinction for the arguments made in this chapter is the difference between leisure and free time. Leisure, it would seem, is antithetical to "objectively measured time" (de Grazia, 1964). If something has to be scheduled in, it is not leisure. Thus, we might be able to contrast free time with leisure, but we begin to make conceptual errors if we thoughtlessly use the expression "leisure time." As de Grazia writes,

> not being divided up by time, leisure does not suffer fragmentation as free time does...self-improvement, the always pursuing-something and bettering-oneself aspects of present free time are negative qualities as far as leisure is concerned. Life is not on a vertical incline, nor is truth. It comes not to him who is always on the run after something that tickles his senses...Free time is opposed to work, is temporary absence from work, but leisure has little to do with work as with time. (p. 331)

Activities engaged in as ends in their own right and without any reference to time may in fact be leisure, but in a world where the clock and schedules are all pervasive, leisure seems increasingly impossible.

I conclude this brief paper by cautioning against the ideas that the digital age is a return to earlier tribal life or the beginning of a global village, or less still, a new age of leisure. There may be various forms of return, but there is also something quite different afoot. We can get at this difference by fixing our attention on the expression that describes where we increasingly find ourselves: "24/7." The notion of 24/7 media, Wikipedia; Google, YouTube, MySpace, and so forth moves us out of seasonal and rhythmic time in a way that preceding media did not (Hassan and Purser, 2007).

One main weakness of the 24/7 digital environment is that it fails to deliver leisure and instead opens new horizons of spare time for the commercialization of identity and selfhood. This commercialization comes in two main forms. First is sheer hardware dependency (F.E.X. Dance, personal communication, November 2007). Today, as more and more people confine themselves to indoor and sedentary lifestyles, people are invited to change their scenery by keeping up with endless upgrades, newer versions, platforms, and newer products. We are bombarded with messages, announcements, unveilings, and various news flashes regarding anything that is faster, smaller, thinner, better, or cheaper. And all of these messages subliminally chant, "BUY! BUY! BUY!" These new media may well be the preferred means of communication of the commercializing insomniac.

The second commercialization occurs because would-be media presences need to break through anonymity and have their names, voices, and/or images gain public mind-share. In a global world where anyone can contact anyone, and where everyone is potentially available, not everyone can be seen, recognized, and listened to regularly. So, in becoming a blogger, MySpacer, or YouTuber, people basically need to turn themselves into a brand or product. They need to advertise themselves in order to create brand name recognition. If there is a concern, it is that the very notion of leisure has been covered over, and in its place we find little other than amusement, lollygagging, and various forms of self-commercialization or branding for consumption.

Some twenty years after de Grazia's (1964) *Of Time, Work, and Leisure*, Neil Postman (1985) published his most celebrated book, *Amusing Ourselves to Death*. Now, more than twenty years after Postman's book, one can't help but see the drive for amusement as a displaced and mostly distracted drive for leisure. So, is there, today, anytime left for leisure? E.M. Cioran offers thoughtful guidance where he writes, "Though we have conquered the universe and taken possession of it, so long as we have not triumphed over time, we remain slaves…All things considered, the century of the end will not be the most refined or even the most complicated, …but the most hurried" (1975, p. 95). Indeed, people who want to read and think—and by that I mean have the leisure for study and contemplative thought—need more than a few shards of spare time now and again throughout the day. They need good-sized stretches of time, spans that, if measured at all, are measured in hours and days or even weeks and months, certainly not minutes. Without the conditions for leisure—time off of all clocks, the time of no time when we lay still or walk around and contemplate—people will be rushed around in an endless mall, frantically amusing themselves to death, caught in the pillory where they have only enough time to distractedly purchase the next item that tickles their senses.

ThnkEndnotes to Chapter 10

1 Abstract from original: This manuscript contextualizes newly emerging digital technologies including the World Wide Web, cell phones, and, more recently, social networking sites such as Myspace, Facebook and YouTube. The bulk of the exploration is not to understand how these technologies became feasible or physically possible but to speculate upon how they are part of a grand dialectic, a counterbalance to the massive straightjacket imposed within the last 200 years or so: synchronized objective time. I first review how time became more and more objectified, neutralized, and commercialized and therein show how leisure dwindled in modern U.S. culture. Second, after exploring the social and psychological consequences of the increased synchronicity demands imposed by objective clock time measured down to the minute, I explore subsequent communication technologies as dialectical remediations to the demands of such synchronicity. The final part of the paper shows how newly emerging digital technologies promise yet fail to deliver a more leisured environment. If anything, the digital age may offer a world of increasingly flexible but more and more commercialized time.

2 I wish to thank Valerie V. Peterson, Janet Sternberg, Anthony Thompson, Anthony Nelson, Danielle Wiese, Brett Lyszak, Stephanie Bennett, and Sharon Kleinman for their helpful assistance.

Part IV:

Resources and Meditations

"Observe the herd as it grazes past you: it cannot distinguish yesterday from today, leaps about, eats, sleeps, digests, leaps some more, and carries on like this from morning to night and from day to day, tethered by the short leash of its pleasures and displeasures to the stake of the moment, and thus it is neither melancholy nor bored. It is hard on the human being to observe this, because he boasts about the superiority of his humanity over animals and yet looks enviously upon their happiness—for the one and only thing that he desires is to live like an animal, neither bored nor in pain, and yet he desires this in vain, because he does not desire it in the same way as does the animal. The human being might ask the animal: 'Why do you just look at me like that instead of telling me about your happiness?' The animal wanted to answer, 'Because I always immediately forget what I wanted to say'—but it had already forgotten this answer and hence said nothing, so that the human being was left to wonder." (Friedrich Nietzsche, *Unfashionable Observations*, p. 87)

Chapter 11: Words to Live By: Scholarly Quotations as Proverbial Theory

He who walks with me
shall walk from crest to crest:
You will need very long legs.
— Nietzsche

Theory and Practice

As bemoaned by some practitioners, "theory" is simply too impractical and too easily detached from real world relevance or application. The world of theory, such critics suggest, often becomes lofty and removed or perhaps too abstruse, erudite, and dense, and, as such, it remains considerably removed from the sticky, gummy interactions of everyday life. Even the word itself, "theory," in the mouth of its critics, can be said in an accusatory tone, e.g. "Probably just a theory," or "That might be fine in theory, but in the real world things are different." This also means that abstract and theoretical systems, even ones that well account for various types of order in and throughout human interaction, may fail to be applicable to our daily lives. If ideas cannot be removed from their original theoretical context, if they cannot live outside of their indigenous textual domain, then such insights seem to be extremely limited. Such "lame abstractions," as William James might say, "fail to be cashed-in-on."

But on the other hand, serious theoreticians and academicians often maintain that practice bereft of theoretical reflection remains mostly tacit habit and uncritical encumbrance of one's tradition. Uninformed and mismatched strategies built through "just doing it" too easily fail to appreciate and take advantage of the resources available via theoretical reflection. Without the service of theory, the theorist maintains, people in their quotidian practices can remain blind to and unaware of solutions to daily problems as well to alternative life possibilities.

The twin concerns addressed above, when taken together and then re-evaluated, seem to offer not so much a problem as an opportunity. Both scholars and practitioners alike might accordingly focus their attention on those abstract ideas that best lend themselves to quick and useful application within everyday life practices. Calvin O. Schrag, in his book *The Resources of Rationality* (1992), offers a provocative lead in this direction where he suggests that we consider "provisional and case-oriented maxims for assessing what is to be believed and what is to be done in particular situations" (p. 60). Recognition of recurrent situations, the ability to abstract "things-to-look-out-for," and cultivated skill at strategically summing-up a situation within a sentence or two, all of these capacities refer to insight, foresight, and commemoration. Taken together, they bear the stamp of a rationality that is already operative in everyday life. Such rationality offers critical and evaluative distance yet is not overly suspended within larger philosophical and theoretical contexts. It offers and traffics in something similar to cultural wisdom by proverbial advice. And, it is precisely these types of ideas, in their specific employability, which I wish to further consider here.

Some Exemplars

The dual demand for what John Dewey (1925/1988) has aptly called, "reflection efficacious in action" (p. 80) has already been addressed in communication scholarship where scholars have examined anecdotes and proverbs. Lee Thayer tells a marvelous story to illustrate the potential pitfalls of overly reflective and literal considerations, especially with regard to metaphorical anecdotes. His story both exemplifies the potential utility of anecdotes, and additionally, it criticizes overly theoretical reflection that loses sight of utility. He states: "Listen closely. You must tell me what is wrong with the following question": "Why is it that a bad apple put into a barrel of good apples turns them all bad, but a good apple put into a barrel of bad ones doesn't turn them all good?" After a good deal of critical thought and consideration, including many scientific explanations regarding the relations among fruit decay, methane production and fruit ripening, we remained unable to discover what he thought "was wrong" in the question. His point, it soon dawned upon us, is that such questioning suffers from *too much* rationality, and moreover, such literalism proves disadvantageous when we deal with the world of anecdotes and proverbs. As he suggested, such types of questioning gravely miss the point. We should simply, given the logic of anecdotes and this one in particular, 'stay away from the bad apples!' *And note, we were not, obviously, really talking about apples*. What is at issue, and must not be lost from view, is the usability of our proverbs, not their scientific verifiability. Proverbs and anecdotes employ metaphorical language to keep us in the realm of "as if." We need to learn to dance with the "as if."

Max van Manen's *Researching Lived Experience: Human Science for an Action Sensitive Pedagogy* (1990) usefully discusses how anecdotes as well as phenomenological writing both address and manage the dual demand for 'reflection efficacious in action.' van Manen writes:

> The paradoxical thing about anecdotal narrative is that it tells something particular while really expressing the general or the universal...Anecdote particularizes the abstracting tendency of theoretical discourse: it makes it possible to involve us pre-reflectively in the lived quality of concrete experience while paradoxically inviting us into a reflective stance vis-á-vis the meaning imbedded in the experience. The important feature of anecdotal as well as phenomenological discourse is that it simultaneously pulls us in but then prompts us to reflect. (p. 121)

Anecdotes, I am suggesting, well exemplify theoretical tools: they operate as types of case-oriented maxims and are to be employed in a person's everyday routine engagements. Equipped with anecdotes, persons are able to gain a critical and evaluative distance without becoming trapped or bogged down in theoretical and technical minutia. But, on the other hand, in wending their way through everyday life, persons can be outfitted with resources for reflection which remain available and employable.

Kenneth Burke greatly contributes to this discussion, most particularly in his celebrated essay, "Literature as Equipment for Living." He provocatively considers aphorisms and proverbs as "tools for everyday life" and argues that proverbs can be made available as accoutrements for organizing and framing "recurrent" events. "Proverbs," Burke states, "are *strategies* for dealing with *situations*. In so far as situations are typical and recurrent in a given social structure, people develop names for them and strategies for dealing with them" (1957, p. 256). Taking advantage of the resources provided by proverbs, people more effectively predict the outcomes of events, further reflect upon their goals, and further enable the goals reflected upon. What needs explicit recognition is that proverbs are not merely attempts to explain how things are. On the contrary, they are more loosely geared for application and prediction from the person's *current* situation, *current* perspective, and *current* goals. That is, "the names for typical, recurrent social situations," Burke tells us, "are not developed out of a 'disinterested curiosity,' but because the names imply a command, what to expect, what to look out for" (ibid., p. 254).

Veracity for this type of "discourse," (e.g. proverbs or anecdotes) is demonstrated, then, not by logical coherence within a larger web of theoretical statements. That is, proverbs and anecdotes, those tools for reflection efficacious in action, need not an internally consistent system, a system in which the elements, formulations, and prescriptions are non-contradictory—as in classical logic where axioms in a proof cannot imply the truth of their opposites without falling into contradiction. Sequential and/or holistic logics as found in standard syllogisms are inappropriate for assessing the kinds of order/applicability under consideration here. Burke underscores that we best understand the nature of proverbs and anecdotes only as we recognize "the fact that there are contrary proverbs...Consider, for instance, the apparently contradictory pair: 'Repentance comes to late' and 'Never too late to Mend'" (ibid., p. 256). Consider, for further illustration, the oppositional bits of proverbial advice: "Look before you leap" but "He who hesitates is lost." Are these statements contradictory? Maybe to each other, but they never were intended for interrelational agreement: they are for "agreeing with" certain situations. They are artistic strategies or ready-to-apply sizing-ups of situations, ones that afford useful readings of re-current situations regardless of "ultimate truth-value."

More and more people ought to understand these distinctions: Some systems of belief, some types of theories, hold that a contradiction necessarily appears when one's assertions claim their opposites to also be true; this mode of rationality upholds the law of non-contradiction. But this rule applies only to cases that might be described as textually or semantically logical rather than practically or functionally logical. Whereas textual coherence obtains between and among textual premises and conclusions, practical coherence obtains between a premise and a practical outcome in a "non- or extra-textual" context. One might even argue that any theory of human communication that is fully and wholly internally consistent will likely be of little use to anyone. It will remain inadequately rigorous to the phenomena of life, partly because participation in life, as proverbs demonstrate, requires a taste for the paradoxical.

Proverbs, in summary, are not to be tested for logical (i.e. textual) coherence nor are they to meet the demands of statistical significance. Rather, judgment of effectiveness must be made by the person using said proverb within the context of everyday life and everyday practices. Burke, acknowledges this point when he states,

> The point of issue is not to find categories that 'place' the proverbs once and for all. What I want is categories that suggest their active nature. Here is no 'realism for its own sake.' Here is realism for promise, admonition, solace, vengeance, foretelling, instruction, charting, all for the direct bearing that such acts have upon matters of welfare. (1957, p. 255)

Ultimately, the logic of anecdotes and proverbs is that there is no necessary (i.e. exhaustively true) relationship between the world and how we come to talk about it, and thus, a poetic statement is no less useful than a scientific one, depending of course, upon one's goals. For a proverb to work we must ask not, "Is this proverb true?" but, "Can I strategically, can I actively and fruitfully, live the 'truth' this proverb opens up within a given situation?"

Taking this discussion regarding anecdotes and proverbs as its point of departure, the following collection of quotations comprises a loose body of communication "theories." They suggest a set of radically reflective attitudes regarding communication processes. Like anecdotes and proverbs, they offer a reflective distance--a summing-up which takes advantage of theoretical consideration but one which can also be employed spontaneously by specific individuals in everyday contexts.

The Collection

Several thinkers already have compiled scholarly quotations on communication phenomena. Although one easily finds many more than listed here, I would point briefly to five sources, all with some ties to the field of General Semantics, as models of inspiration and further reference. First, in the delightful now classic introduction to pedagogy, *Teaching as a Subversive Activity* (1969), Postman and Weingartner present a collection of quotations that emphasize the ubiquitous influence words and symbols have in our lives. Second, an array of interesting scholarly quotations can be found in Kenneth Johnson's *General Semantics: An Outline Survey*. This slim volume offers a wealth of insight into language habits and their bearing upon human endeavors. Third, Susan Sontag presents a thoughtful "Anthology of Quotations" regarding the nature of representation--with special attention to visual communication--in her, *On Photography* (1977). Fourth, Richard Lederer's *The Miracle of Language* provides of wide-ranging and useful collection of quotations upon language, a few of which are included here. Finally, Lee Thayer's *On Communication* (1987) presents an outstandingly provocative collection of quotations regarding process of human communication. In fact, his opening chapter, "The Idea of Communication: Looking for a Place to Stand," inspired many ideas for the present collection.

As a final introductory note, the following quotations offer a wealth of valuable insight. In an attempt to conserve space, the quotations are listed way too close to one another. Although this saves on paper, it may lead to a rapid and thoughtless progression down these pages. Readers are encouraged to slowly appreciate each entry, to ruminate and consider each quotation. It may also help to discuss with each other the everyday situations that bring out the wisdom(s) of each quotation. For convenience, I also have left the citation information directly with the quotation wherever possible.

A

St. Thomas Aquinas said: "Each receives according to his capacity."

St. Augustine: "To understand, you must first believe."

B

Henri Bergson: "In fact, there is no perception which is not full of memories...In most cases the memories supplant our actual perception, of which we then retain only a few hints, thus using them merely as 'signs' that recall to us former images." (In *Memory and Matter.* New York: Zone Books, 1991, p. 33).

William Blake from *The Marriage of Heaven and Hell*: "Truth can never be told so as to be understood, and not be believ'd." (In Kenneth Burke's *Towards a Better Life*. Berkeley, CA: University of California Press, 1983, pp. 177-178).

Jacob Bohme: "Whatever the self describes, describes the self."

Kenneth Burke writes, "Many of the 'observations' are but implications of the particular terminology in terms of which the observations are made. In brief, much that we take as observations about reality may be but the spinning out of possibilities implicit in our particular choice of terms." (In *Language as Symbolic Action.* Berkeley, CA: University of California Press, 1966, p. 46).

"Spontaneous speech is not a naming at all, but a system of attitudes, of implicit exhortations. To call a man a friend or enemy is *per se* to suggest a program of action with regard to him." (In *Permanence and Change.* Second edition, Bobbs-Merrill Co, 1954, p. 177).

"Words communicate to things the spirit that the society imposes upon the words which have come to be the 'names' for them. The things are in effect the visible tangible material embodiments of the spirit that infuses them through the medium of words. And in this sense, things become the signs of the genius that resides in words." (In *Language as Symbolic Action.* Berkeley, CA: University of California Press, 1966, p. 362).

And through Burke The Lord spoke to Satan: "And in any case, you will agree that, even if their ideas of divine perfection were reducible to little more than a language-using animals' ultimate perception of its own linguistic forms, this could be a true inkling of the divine insofar as language itself happened to be made in the image of divinity." (In *The Rhetoric of Religion*. Berkeley, CA: University of California Press, 1970, pp. 289-299).

"One talks about a thing by talking about something else." (In *Counter-Statement*. Berkeley, CA: University of California Press, 1968, p. 141).

C

Ernst Cassirer: "Physical reality seems to recede in proportion as man's symbolic activity advances. Instead of dealing with things themselves man is in a sense of constantly conversing with himself. He has so enveloped himself in linguistic forms, in artistic images, in mythical symbols or religious rites that he cannot see or know anything except by the interposition of this artificial medium." (In *An Essay on Man*. New Haven, CN: Yale University Press, 1944, p. 25).

Cioran: "To exist is to plagiarize."

Collingwood: "Understanding what someone says to you is thus attributing to him the idea which his words arouse in yourself." (In *The Principles of Art*. Oxford: Clarendon Press, 1938, p. 250).

Condillac once said, "Though we should soar to the heavens, though we should sink into the abyss, we never go out of ourselves; it is always our own thought we perceive." (In Lee Thayer's *Communication and Communication Systems*. University Press of America, 1986, p. 112).

D

Baba Ram Dass, formerly Richard Alpert: "Only that in you which is me can hear what I am saying."

John Dewey writes: "The word symbolism however, is a product of reflection upon direct phenomena, not a description of what happens when so called symbols are potent. For the feature which characterizes symbolism is precisely that the thing which later reflection calls a symbol is not a symbol, but a direct vehicle, a concrete embodiment, a vital incarnation." (In *Experience and Nature*, Carbondale, IL: Southern Illinois University Press, 1988/1925, p. 72).

"When the introspectionist thinks he has withdrawn into a

wholly private realm of events disparate in kind from other events, made out of mental stuff, he is only turning his attention to his own soliloquy. And soliloquy is the product and reflex of converse with others; social communication not an effect of soliloquy." (ibid., pp. 134-35).

Isak Dinesen: "It was no wonder that God had ceased to love him, for he had from his own free will exchanged the things of the Lord: the moon, the sea, friendships, fights for the words that describe them." (In *Winter's Tales*. 1942, p. 11).

E

From T. S. Eliot's dissertation: "Our only way of showing that we are attending to an object is to show that it and ourselves are independent entities, and to do this we must have names...{thus} We have no objects without language." (In Kenneth Burke's *Language as Symbolic Action*. Berkeley, CA: University of California press, 1968, p. 61).

Ralph W. Emerson: "Your actions shout so loudly at me that I cannot hear what you are saying."

"Man is only half himself--the other half is his expression." (as cited in William H. Gass. *Habitations of the Word*. New York: Simon and Shuster, 1985, p. 206).

F

Paul Fussell: "Your social class is still most clearly visible when you say things...'One's speech is an unceasingly repeated public announcement about background and social standing,' says John Brooks, translating into modern American Ben Johnson's observation 'Language most shows a man. Speak, that I may see thee.'" (In *Class*. New York: Ballantine Books, 1983, p. 175).

G

Hans-Georg Gadamer: "Every understanding of the intelligible that helps others to understanding has the character of language. To that extent, the entire experience of the world is linguistically mediated." (In *Philosophical Hermeneutics*. Berkeley, CA: University of California Press, 1976, p. 99).

"A question is behind each statement that first gives it its meaning...For the 'meaning' of such a text is not motivated by an occasion, but on the contrary, claims to be understandable 'anytime,' that is, to be an answer always, and that means inevitably also to raise the question to which the text is an answer." (ibid., pp. 89-90).

William H. Gass: "We fall upon cliché as if it were a sofa and not a sword...it is true that prefab conversation frees the mind, yet rarely does the mind have a mind left after these interconnected clichés have conquered it." (In *Habitations of the Word*. New York: Simon and Shuster, 1985, p. 211).

"To an almost measureless degree, to know is to possess words, and all of us who live out in the world as well as within our own are aware that we inhabit a forest of symbols...Every photograph requires a thousand words." (ibid., pp, 207-209).

Theodor Geiger: "Being confirmed by others frees me from being responsible for the absurdity of my belief." (as cited in Lee Thayer, *On Communication*. Norwood, NJ: Ablex, 1987, p. 9).

Kahlil Gibran--*The Prophet*--tells us,

"And in much of your talking, thinking is half murdered.

For thought is a bird of space, that in a cage of words may indeed unfold its wings, but cannot fly." (New York: Alfred A. Knopf, 1923, p. 60).

Gibran again: "It takes only two to create a truth, one to utter it, and one to believe it."

Erving Goffman speaks of what he calls "prognosticative expression," and further clarifies: "An open and friendly address conveys that overtures will be welcomed; a wary and stiff mien, that importunement will result in open rejection. Anyone wending his way through his daily round is guided not only by self-interest but also by these expressions." (In *Relations in Public: Microstudies of the Public Order*, New York: Basic Books, 1971, p. 375).

According to Nelson Goodman, "We are tempted to say that the facts are determined when the framework is chosen; but then we must recognize that facts and frameworks differ only in scope, and that a mistake may be made in either. An astronomer miscalculating the position of a planet very likely has a wrong fact under a right framework, while a guard who shot prisoners ordered to stand still, explaining that they then moved rapidly around the sun, seems to have a right fact under a wrong framework." (In *Of Mind and Other Matters*. Cambridge, MA: Harvard University Press, 1984, p. 14).

"We are confined to ways of describing our descriptions of the world."

Georges Gusdorf: "In fact, the life of the mind ordinarily begins not with the acquisition of language, but with the revolt against language once it is acquired. The child discovers the world through the established language, which those around prescribe for him. The adolescent discovers values in the revolt against the language he had until then blindly trusted and which seems to him, in the light of the crisis, destitute of all authenticity." In *Speaking (La Parole)*, Trans. P. T. Brockelman. Evanston, IL: Northwestern University Press, 1965, p. 40).

H

Abraham Heschel: "The truth of a theory of man is either creative or irrelevant, but never merely descriptive." (In *Who is man?* Palo Alto, CA: Stanford University Press, 1965, p. 8).

"The image of man affects the nature of man. We become what we think of ourselves." (ibid., p. 10)

Martin Heiddegger: "Any interpretation which is to contribute understanding must already have understood what is to be interpreted." (In *Being and Time*. 1962, p. 194).

"Language is not a mere tool, one of the many which man possesses; on the contrary, it is only language that afford the very possibility of standing in the openness of the existent. Only where there is language, is there world..." *(Hölderlin and the Essence of Poetry*, trans. Douglas Scott, In *Language and the world: a methodological synthesis of the writings of Martin Heidegger and Ludwig Wittgenstein*, New Jersey, Humanities Press, 1974, p. 134).

"It is the custom to put speaking and listening in opposition: one man speaks, the other listens...Speaking is of itself a listening. Speaking is listening to the language we speak. Thus, it is a listening not *while* but *before* we are speaking...We do not merely speak *the* language--we speak *by way of* it. We can do so solely because we always have already listened to the language. What do we hear? We hear language speaking." (In *On the Way to Language*, Harper and Row, 1971, pp. 123-124).

Werner Heisenberg: "What we see in nature is not nature in itself, but nature exposed to our method of questioning." (In *The Physicists Conception of Nature*. Trans. A.J. Pomerans. New York: Harcourt, Brace, 1958).

Douglas Hofstadter puzzles with/on/over/from self-reflection: "If this sentence were in Chinese, it would say something else." (In *Metamagical Themas*, New York: Bantam Books, 1985, p. 13).

"What would this sentence be like if it were not self-referential?" (ibid., p. 14).

J

William James: "Properly speaking, a man has as many social selves as there are individuals who recognize him and carry an image of him in their mind." (In *Principles of Psychology*, Vol. I. New York: Henry Holt & Co. 1890, p. 179).

"Why may not thought's mission be to increase and elevate, rather than simply to imitate and reduplicate, existence?...The notion of a world complete in itself, to which thought comes as a passive mirror, adding nothing to fact, Lotze says, is irrational. Rather is thought itself a most momentous part of fact, and the whole mission of the pre-existing and insufficient world of matter may simply be to provoke thought to produce its far more precious supplement." (In *Pragmatism and other essays*. New York: Washington Square Press, 1963, p. 175).

K

Earl Kelly: "Now it comes about that whatever we tell the learner, he will make something that is all his out if it, and it will be different from what we held so dear and attempted to 'transmit.'...Thus he builds a world all his own, and what is really important is what he makes of what we tell him, not what we intended." (as cited in Neil Postman and Charles Weingartner's *Teaching as a Subversive Activity*, New York: Dell Publishing, 1969, p. 92).

Alfred Korzybski's Rule of Non-Identification: "Whatever I say a thing is, it is not." (In *Science and Sanity*, Lakeville, CN: The international Non-Aristotelian Library Publishing company, 1958).

Remy Kwant: "One who wants to exercise thought control must control its embodiment in speech." (In *Phenomenology of Language*. Pittsburg, PA: Duquesne University Press, 1965, p. 167).

L

R. D. Laing wrote, "By the time the sociologists study these projected-introjected reifications, they have taken on the appearance of things...we obey and defend beings that exist only insofar as we continue to invent and perpetuate them." (In *The Politics of Experience*. New York: Pantheon Books, 1967, p. 78).

Susanne K. Langer writes, "Peaches are too good to act as

words; we are too much interested in peaches themselves. But little noises are the ideal conveyers of concepts, for they give us nothing but their meaning...Vocables in themselves are so worthless that we can cease to be aware of their physical presence at all, and become conscious only of their connotations, denotations, or other meanings. Our conceptual activity seems to flow <u>through</u> them, rather than merely accompany them, as it accompanies other experiences that we endow with significance." (In *Philosophy in a New Key*. New York: Mentor Books, 1948, pp. 61-62).

"In a sense language is conception, and conception is the frame of perception...Without words our imagination cannot retain distinct objects and their relations, but out of sight is out of mind... The transformation of experience into concepts...is the motive of language." (ibid., pp.102-103).

Walter Lippman: "For the most part we do not first see, and then define, we define first and then see." (In *Public Opinion*. New York: Harcourt, Brace & Co., 1922, p. 81).

M

Malinowski, Bronislaw: "A word is used when it can produce an action and not to describe one, still less to translate thoughts. The word therefore has a power of its own, it is a means of bringing things about, it is a handle to acts and objects and not a definition of them." (as cited in Ogden & Richards' *The Meaning of Meaning*. Harcourt, Brace & World: New York. Eighth Edition. 1932, p. 322).

According to Abraham Maslow "...the world can communicate to a person only that which he is worthy, that which he deserves or is "up to"; that to a large extent, he can receive from the world and, give to the world, only that which he himself is." (In Eds. F. W. Matson & A. Montagu. *The Human Dialogue*. New York: The Free Press, 1967, p. 195).

George Herbert Mead: "A person who is saying something is saying to himself what he says to others; otherwise he does not know what he is talking about." (In *Mind, Self, and Society*. Chicago: The University of Chicago Press, 1934, p. 147).

Maurice Merleau-Ponty: "The word, far from being the mere sign of objects and meanings, inhabits things and is the vehicle of meanings. Thus, speech, in the speaker, does not translate ready-made thought, but accomplishes it." (In *Phenomenology of Perception*. Trans. Colin Smith Routledge and Kegan Paul Ltd. 1962, p. 178).

"Word and speech must somehow cease to be a way of designating things or thoughts, and become the presence of that thought in the phenomenal world, and, moreover, not its clothing but its token or its body...the process of expression brings the meaning into being or makes it effective, and does not merely translate it... Thought is no 'internal' thing, and does not exist independently of the world and of words. What misleads us in this connection, and causes us to believe in a thought which exists for itself prior to expression, is thought already constituted and expressed, which we can silently recall to ourselves, and through which we acquire the illusion of an inner life." (ibid., pp. 182-183).

"The wonderful thing about language is that it promotes its own oblivion: my eyes follow the lines on the paper, and from the moment I am caught up in their meaning, I lose sight of them." (ibid., p. 401).

"Expressive operations take place between thinking language and speaking thought; not, as we thoughtlessly say, between thought and language." (In *Signs*. Evanston, IL: Northwestern University Press, 1964, p. 18).

"Speaking to others (or to myself), I do not speak of my thoughts, I speak them." (Ibid., p. 19).

"One of the effects of language is to efface itself to the extent that its expression comes across...As I become engrossed in a book, I no longer see the letters on the page...all that remains is meaning. The perfection of language lies in its capacity to pass unnoticed...In the way it works, language hides itself from us." (In *The Prose of the World*, Trans. John O'Neil. Evanston, IL: Northwestern University Press, 1973, pp. 9-10).

"If we were to make completely explicit the architectonics of the human body, its ontological framework, and how it sees itself and hears itself, we would see that the structure of its mute world is such that all the possibilities of language are already given in it." (In *The Visible and the Invisible*, Trans. A. Lingis. Evanston, IL: Northwestern University Press, 1968. p. 155.)

Thomas Moore: "A symbol is the act of throwing together two incongruous things and living in the tension that exists between them, watching the images that emerge from that tension." (In *Care of the Soul*. Harper Collins Pub. 1992, p. 161).

Dennis Mumby: "The most successful theories are judged not on their ability to reflect an objective reality, but on the extent to which they challenge us to engage in self-reflection and hence emancipation from conditions of discursive closure." (In *Communication and Power in Organizations: discourse, ideology and domination*. 1988. Norwood, NJ: Ablex publishers., p. XV).

Lewis Mumford: "The physical universe is unable to behold itself, except through the eyes of man, unable to speak for itself, except through the human voice..." (In *The Myth of the Machine. Vol.1: Technics and Human Development*. New York: Harcourt Brace and Jovanich, publishers, 1967, p. 31).

N

Friedrich Nietzsche: "We always express our thoughts with the words that lie at hand... we have at any moment only the thought for which we have at hand the words." (In *Daybreak*, Book IV, Para. 257. Cambridge University Press, 1982).

"Every idea originates through equating the unequal." (In *The Complete Works of Friedrich Nietzsche: Early Greek Philosophy [VOL II]*. New York: Russell & Russell, Inc., 1964, p. 179).

"...truths are illusions of which one has forgotten that they *are* illusions. Worn-out metaphors which have become powerless to affect the senses; coins which have their obverse effaced and now are no longer of account as coins but merely as metal." (ibid., p. 180).

"A period which suffers from a so-called high general level of liberal education but which is devoid of culture in the sense of a unity of style which characterizes all its life, will not quite know what to do with philosophy and wouldn't, if the Genius of Truth himself were to proclaim it in the streets and the market places. During such times philosophy remains the learned monologue of the lonely stroller, the accidental loot of the individual, the secret skeleton in the closet, or the harmless chatter between senile academics and children." (In *Philosophy in the Tragic Age of the Greeks*. Chicago, IL: Henry Regnery Co. p. 37).

"Valuing is creating: hear it, ye creating ones! Valuation itself is the treasure and jewel of the valued things. Through valuation only is there value; and without valuation the nut of existence would be hollow. Hear it, ye creating ones!" (In *Thus Spake Zarathustra*. Modern Library. p. 60).

"He is a thinker; that means, he knows how to make things simpler than they are." (In *The Gay Science*. Trans. Kauffmann. Random House. Section 189, 1974, p. 205).

P

Octavio Paz tells us: "Man is a being who has created himself in creating a language. By means of the word, man is a metaphor of himself."

Walker Percy: "The collision of two galaxies and the salivation of Pavlov's dog, different as they are, are far more alike than either is like the simplest act of naming. Naming stands at a far greater distance from Pavlov's dog than the latter does from a galactic collision." (In *The Message in the Bottle: How queer man is, how queer language is, and what one has to do with the other*. New York: Farrar, Straus and Giroux, 1954, p. 154.)

Michael Polanyi said that "Truth is something that can be thought of only by believing it."

"We do not see things as they are; we see them as we are." (In *Teaching as a Subversive Activity*. Neil Postman and Charles Weingartner, Dell Publishing Co., 1969).

"Truth does not, and never has, come unadorned. It must appear in its proper clothing or it is not acknowledged, which is a way of saying that the "truth" is a kind of cultural prejudice..." (In Neil Postman, *Amusing Ourselves to Death*. New York: Penguin Books, 1985, p. 23).

Postman and Weingartner: "Scientists, particularly, are becoming increasingly aware that what anything 'is' depends on how who looks at what." (Postman and Charles Weingartner's *Teaching as a Subversive Activity*. Dell Publishing Co., 1969).

Plato: "When the mind is thinking; it is talking to itself." (as cited in Neil Postman and Charles Weingartner's *Teaching as a Subversive Activity*. Dell Publishing Co., 1969, p. 126).

R

Jurgen Reusch: "We are not interested in the way nature is constructed but in how the observer perceives it, and his method of perceiving." (In "The Observer and the Observed: Human Communication Theory." From R.R Grinker, Eds. *Toward a Unified Theory of Human Behavior*. New York: Basic Books, 1956, p. 36).

"...the science of communication deals with the representation of outside events inside and of inside events outside." (ibid., p. 41).

Bertrand Russell: "No matter how eloquently a dog may bark, he cannot tell you that his parents were poor but honest." (as cited in Richard Lederer's *The Miracle of Language*. New York: Simon & Schuster, 1991, p. 235).

S

George Santayana: "I would agree with Spinoza where he says that other people's idea of man is apt to be a better expression of their nature than of his." (In *Character and Opinion in the United States*. Garden City, NY: Doubleday & Company, 1956. p. v).

Antoine de Saint-Exupéry: "Whether you wish it or not, your meaning is made of others' meanings, and your taste of others' tastes...For you live not by the things, but by the meaning of the things." (In *The Wisdom of the Sands*. {Trans. S. Gilbert}   New York: Harcourt, Brace, 1948, p. 263).

"You give birth to that on which you fix your mind. For, by defining a thing, you cause it to be born, and then it seeks to nourish, perpetuate and augment itself." (Ibid., p. 269).

"If you were to understand men, begin by never listening to them" (ibid., p. 219).

Jean-Paul Sartre: "Whether our language is overt or 'internal' our thoughts become more and better defined by means of it than we ourselves were able to make them; it <u>teaches us</u> something." (In *The Psychology of Imagination*, New York: Citadel Press, 1991, p. 121).

Alfred Schutz: "the so-called 'Thomas theorem' well known to sociologists: 'If men define situations as real, they are real in their consequences.'" (In *Collected Papers, Vol. I The Problem of Social Reality*, Martinus Nijhoff publ. 1962, p. 348).

George Sefler: "Language and the world are two sides of one and the same reality. The world I know is known inseparably from the language I use." (In *Language and the world: a methodological synthesis of the writings of Martin Heidegger and Ludwig Wittgenstein*, New Jersey: Humanities Press, 1974, p. 188).

Liu Shao: "You cannot recognize in another a quality you do not have yourself."

George Steiner: "Language is the main instrument of man's refusal to accept the world as it is...Ours is the ability, the need, to gainsay or 'un-say' the world, to image and speak it otherwise... It is not, perhaps, 'a theory of information' that will serve us best in trying to clarify the nature of language, but a 'theory of misinformation.'" (In *After Babel*, New York: Oxford University Press, 1975, pp. 217-218).

"Language is not a description of 'reality,' but an answer to it, an evasion from it." (In *Psychology Today*, February, 1973, p. 66).

Laurence Sterne: "Writers of my stamp have one principle in common with painters. Where an exact copying makes our pictures less striking, we choose the less evil; deeming it ever more pardonable to trespass against truth, than beauty." (In *The Life and Opinions of Tristam Shandy, gentleman.* {Ed. Ian Watt}. Houghton Mifflin Co. 1965, pp. 69-70).

T

Lee Thayer: "In secularizing the process {communication} and conceiving of it as strategy and tactics to be deployed as means to secular and rational ends, the later Greeks also 'de-epistemologized' the idea of communication. It therefore became possible to think of 'knowledge' or 'information' as a meaningful entity, substance, or commodity *sui generis*, as having legitimate human pertinence regardless of the 'knower.' Thus 'knowledge' became transcendent, and people became substitutable in the process." (In *On Communication*. Norwood, NJ: Ablex, 1987, p. 224).

"And what shall we say of that which doesn't exist until we say it?" (ibid., p.12).

"Is a theory of communication to be a theory of ideas, or of living?
Or a theory of the difference?
Or the difference itself?" (ibid., p. 15).

V

Thorstein Veblen: "Except where it is adopted as a necessary means of secret communication, the use of a special slang in any employment is probably to be accepted as evidence that the occupation in question is substantially make-believe." (In *The Theory of the Leisure Class*. {1899-Macmillan}, Dover publications, 1994, p. 157).

Eric Voegelin: "Human society is not merely a fact, or an event, in the external world to be studied by an observer like a natural phenomenon. Though it has externality as one of its important components, it is as a whole little world, a cosmion, illuminated with meaning from within by the human beings who continuously create and bear it as the mode and condition of their self-realization." (In *The New Science of Politics, An Introduction*. Chicago, IL: University of Chicago Press, 1952, p. 27).

W

Alan Watts: "The notion of a separate thinker, of an 'I' distinct from the experience, comes from memory and from the rapidity with which thought changes...There is not something or someone experiencing experience! You do not feel your feelings, think your thoughts, or sense your sensations any more than you hear hearing, see sight, or smell smelling." (In *The Wisdom of Insecurity*. Vintage Books, 1951, p. 85).

"To say that certain events are causally connected is only a clumsy way of saying that they are features of the same event, like the head and tail of a cat." (In *The Book: On the Taboo Against Knowing Who You Are*, New York:Vantage Books, 1966, p. 82).

Paul Watzlawick: "If as he {Vico} says, the world that we experience and get to know is necessarily constructed by ourselves, it should not surprise us that it keeps relatively stable." (In *The Invented Reality*, New York: Norton & Company, 1984, p. 29).

Allen Wheelis tells us: "We have to be something before we can know anything. And when we have become something...the something we can know is less than the something we have become." (In *The Moralist*. Baltimore, MD: Penguin, 1974, p. 109).

"Man's consciousness is as man standing before a mirror, asking the man he sees in the mirror what the man in the mirror is asking."

Ludwig Wittgenstein: "To speak is to philosophize."

"Many words in this sense then don't have a strict meaning. But this is not a defect. To think it is would be like saying that the light of my reading lamp is no real light at all because it has no sharp boundary." (In *The Blue Book, the Blue and Brown Books: preliminary studies for the "Philosophical Investigations."* New York, Harper and Row Publishers, 1958, p. 27).

Benjamin Whorf: "The world is presented to us in a kaleidoscopic flux of impressions which has to be organized by our minds... We cut nature up, organize it in concepts, ascribe significance to it, largely because we are parties to an agreement to do it in that way." ("Science and Linguistics," *The Technology Review*, 1940, 42, p. 231).

Chapter 12: Aphorisms, Insights, and Other Comic Resources for Modern Intellectuals[1]

Media

Sofa Indents: We leave no footprints in the T.V. world. We were never there.

Deluded Heroics: T.V. offers entrance to a world where we are the only people who are not actors and yet we cannot act.

Irrelevant by Remote: To idly surf by remote control is to confess that we have no clue what we want to be when we grow up. It is the medium preferred not so much by the lazy as by the comfortably irrelevant. Would a stranger please tell me who I am?

Gravitational Perspectives: You cannot know lots of stuff about celebrities, have them know nothing about you, and then still retain your own sense of relevance. If you are in any way relevant, you are a satellite in orbit, never a star.

The Golden Age: In the ancient world, the Golden Age was behind people but retrievable. Moderns imagine the Golden Age as ahead of them, a future that will arrive one day. In the "postmodern" world, the Golden Age is always elsewhere, at a distance, some place other than this one.[2]

How to Shoot Your Own Feet: The more information that people access that they either do not or cannot act upon, the more impotent they will be. Clearest case: college students who don't vote and yet who watch world news while they ought to be doing their homework.

Defining Pornography: Some pornographic magazines have pictures of faceless, near bodiless, sex organs. Such porn is not hard to define: Despite the world's rich diversity, its infinite complexity of relations, pornographic images are overly reductive; they are forced synecdoche.[3]

One and Only One: Can any one photograph raise a highly specific and context-dependent question? If so, then I'd like to see a photograph convey that question.[4]

The "I'm not Alone" Parade: Cell phones allow people to persuade others (and themselves) that they don't feel alone. Seen publicly on the phone, we dance around and gesticulate the fact that we are "with someone."[5]

Not You, Not Here: Cell phones are a ritual medium for the displaced happily-ever-after. There is, quite evidently, more fun to be had elsewhere with another than there is right here, with you.

Look Purposefully Ahead: Cell phones have replaced wristwatches as means for declining interpersonal encounters. Simply have your cell phone out and ready. Start to walk forward, pull out your phone and pretend to take a call, preferably the call you've been waiting for. Keep walking.

The Question Advertisers Want Us to Keep Asking: Am I who others think I am?

Capitalist Anonymity: The more that people do not know who they are, the more time, energy, and money they spend on performing themselves.

Relationships

Interpersonal Dialectics: If you cannot be a different person with different people, then all of those people will be the same person. What makes people who they are is who you are when you're with them.[6]

Being Larger than Yourself: No one says, "I don't like what you say, eat, wear, buy or own, don't like your family, friends, co-workers or neighbors, don't like your past, your beliefs, or even your aspirations, but I really like you!" Even children on the playground need to share in favorite colors and ice-cream flavors.

Memories of Umbilical Cords: Navel gazing is highly underestimated. We should celebrate meditations on the incontrovertible proof of our sociality. Look down. You bear the mark; you are caught in the web where beings emerge out from others of their kind.

The 12:00 Unmasking: Imagine the release of energy and social impact if people completely gave up all belief in an afterlife and simultaneously realized our common plight.[7]

Many Ages: Because everyone ages, you can experience others' experience of you as younger, older, or about the same age. As transactive beings, we are never just one age.

Dialogue: If the bulk of everyday conversation is disguised persuasion or simply self-confirmation, then genuine dialogue is when two people risk not knowing who they'll be at the end of their encounter.

Pecuniary Respect: As if on parade with a famous and well-respected celebrity, many people strut about when they are out on the town with Money.[8]

Enviable Justice: Often the cry for justice is merely the howl of a green-eyed pain. If it were pruned of all envy, what would justice look like?[9]

Love and Freedom: Imagine a love potion where anyone who drinks it falls forever in love with the next person they see. Who would use such a concoction? Would love be love if it could not be withdrawn?[10]

What Evidence Do You Want?: Without a sense of freedom, you could never know love. That also means: if you've ever felt love, you can be certain that you experience free will.

Small Town Mentalities: A new neighbor was insulted when I tried to make him feel welcome. He retorted: "I grew up around here, lived just up the road my whole life." The subtext was clear: "I'm not one of those people, you know, 'strangers.'"

Self-Relation

Gatherings: What must the nature of humanity be if, despite the fact that we had 'forgotten all about it,' we can unexpectedly feel remorse over a deed done long ago?

The Taste of Soul Groves: Humans are the only kind of tree that can weep in the anguish of having failed to ripen its fruit. We are the only fruit that, ripe or not, must taste what it has become.[11]

Fall from Grace: Other animals seem wholly spared the possibility of not liking themselves. To be human is to suffer the possibility of self-despisal.

The Root of Plastic Surgery: In class, Lee Thayer once said that the mirror pulled God out of the center of the universe and put humans into it. Today, many people wake up and worship themselves at the morning altar.

How to Have No Friends: A friend is someone who likes you more than you like yourself. This means that some people have no friends not because nobody likes them but because they like themselves more than anyone else possibly could.

Not Having an Alibi: The most important words that you need to hear, only you can say. Too many things are left unsaid by those who forget that they themselves need to say them.[12]

Having to Live with Yourself: Language is an otherization that leaves each speaker utterly alone and yet simultaneously makes any aloneness now impossible.

The Community of the Silently Speaking Self: Solitude is refuge for those who already contain multitudes.[13]

The Hypocrisy of Aspirations: We commonly think of people as either genuine or not. We thus forget the truth of moral history. We are the animal who can be a hypocrite, that is, the animal who can aspire.[14]

Time and Memory

Trust Your Becoming: The question is not can we relearn what we know we forgot but can we discover what we never knew we know? Can we become who we never knew we are?

Final Causes: As what we're moving toward, the past is actually ahead of us, meaning that what we call the future is just as much a species of the past. It is the "certain but indeterminate past, the past that will-have-been."[15]

Useless Recycling: Contemporary psychology has infected people with personal pasts in unprecedented ways. We learn from Nietzsche that most people today do not need any more self-understanding; they need to learn the arts of forgetting.

Time for Distinctions: Memory never feels much like thought until you can't remember something. But the thought that we can't remember we forgot is not even a thought temporarily forgotten. Who could say what it is?

Memory is Resistance: Is it possible to have a theory of rhetoric that does not boil down to persuasion? *Who,* exactly, would be able to know if persuasion had not happened?

The Pre-Reflective

Remembering Forgotten Preoccupations: How many gray moods dawn by suddenly finding ourselves unable to remember some knot of concern that we left partly untied?

From the Other Shore: I wake up in the morning and start singing a song to myself, then I think, "I hate that song; why is it stuck in my head?" The next thought to follow: "Well, someone must like it."[16]

A Call for Thought: Martin Heidegger has a book titled, *What is Called Thinking?* His title points not only to what we call "thinking," but also to what could be called "called thinking," that thinking which is done when what is to be thought about "calls" the thought.[17]

Distractions and Impositions: Sitting down to write, I've now twice checked the clock. Anticipating the later arrival of some dinner guests, I try to hurry up, but it is here, precisely, that I should stop, for the guests rather than the substance of the writing are calling the thought.

Kinds of Vegetables: You start the car, put it in drive, and suddenly realize, as if waking from a spell, that you just arrived and parked the car. So preoccupied by some thought or concern, you now don't remember the driving. But how about this one: you are doing some handiwork, washing dishes or some other absorbing activity, when all the while you've been talking to yourself without fully realizing it.[18]

What Breathes Who?: Right now take a moment and try to stop thinking. Isn't the first impulse to hold your breath? Speech--especially that inner speech we call 'thought'--seems as semi-autonomous as breathing.[19]

Culture As Auto-Pilot: Without direct effort or conscious guidance, self-talk moves by its momentum, eddies swirling wherever they may: a continuing current of culture and background, this is thought without conscious direction.[20]

Where to Attend: Initially vexed by the difficulty of ceasing inner dialogue, I prematurely concluded that it was impossible. But then I realized that one way to stop talking to oneself is to actually listen to other people.

Rhythms of Shrouded Self-Awareness: Could it be that people like to surround themselves with music, not to drown thought out, but so that they may think thoughts without having to think about the fact of thinking them?

For the Beautiful, Talented, Brilliant or Well Dressed: The works of Erving Goffman advise against openly claiming for yourself attributes that others would willingly grant. You only need to state what can't be taken for granted.[21]

Mind

Home of the Unthought Thought: Without questions you can't recall all that you know. For example, what color are the walls in your kitchen? How, if not by words, would you have gained conscious access to that piece of knowledge? But you can believe you know something yet be unable to remember it when asked. So, how do you know what you know if you aren't always knowing it?[22]

Who Knows?: Where is a thought before you think it? Which one?

Language as Order: Mental life is more than the occurrence of inner talk; we can find cognition, computation, inner images, sensations, and feelings. Still, if not by words, how could we identify, catalog, and maintain the boundaries between and among different aspects of mental life?[23]

Thought's Registrar: If we admit the occurrence of some kinds of thought that are independent of language, we must quickly add that the thought that cannot be talked about is the thought that no one ever can remember. [24]

No Thinker Outside of Thought: Thinkers do not think thought so much as thinking thinks thoughts of thinkers thinking thought.[25]

Re-cognizing Non-sense: A mind is never solely one's own. If you can make sense of what no other person can understand, you'd better watch out: you may have a broken one. For example, try to say something that is perfectly intelligible to you but utterly unintelligible to every other person. Fortunately, "Eggplant lenses shoe participle without" doesn't make sense to me either.

Missing the Obvious: Because native tongues are learned from others, we thoughtlessly can conclude that language is not natural. Truth is, we are naturally social.[26]

Words Don't Die: The you who can be thought about when you think about you, Alan Watts tells us, is the you who need not fear death; it is that you who never was born.[27]

Speech & Language

More Than any Named: Language is thoroughly misunderstood when it is cast as discontinuous, as in: "I ran for a while, ate dinner and then I spoke with some friends, and finally, I went to bed." A horizon that is present all along, language is the continued condition of trying to tell what is going on.[28]

No Pity in Stupidity: When we learn a new word we often notice it used around us. This also means that we never hear all of the different words that we don't know; all unknown words can seem the same, and so we easily pretend they are only a few.

Ed Lorenz's "Deterministic Non-Periodic Flow": Leonard Bloomfield suggests that no two individuals have the exact same lexicon nor use language in precisely the same way. Each and every person speaks 'the language' uniquely.[29]

Sustainability: The great advantages of everyday speech are its economy of production, ease of use, and zero cost for post-production clean-up. At low low expenditure of resources, speech can be produced and made relevant for a one-time occurrence.[30]

Speaking of Possibilities: What could be more precarious than an animal that has learned to talk. Such strange and fanciful beings come mostly to concern themselves with what is not the case.[31]

What Was That?: Creativity is often the mishearing, that is, a mess earing or an I-play that can be eared.

Ugly Clarity: We imagine that communication would be improved if we could more clearly transmit ideas. We forget that we are living breathing organisms, creatures capable of aesthetic in-building through the slow and partly staggering grope toward meaning; conversational structure takes its aesthetic appeal not by any information transferred, but through the moment by moment forms of disambiguation.[32]

Unsaid Truth Beside Itself: The truthfulness of an unsolicited statement is never a warrant for its assertion. No one is comforted by a departing guest who suddenly and quite truthfully announces, "Just to let you know, I didn't steal anything."

Always a Little Late: Words are often most apt for worlds that no longer exist. Language speakers are antique dealers.

Utterance as Revelatory Echo: Photos, like written texts or things already said, are expressions. Speaking, on the other hand, is an expressing where we commonly remain unable to examine our utterances until others already have them.[33]

Singing an Advance: Speech is never merely regarding the things immediately surrounding us. We spend the bulk of our time in a kind of echolocation, with words navigating us to distant and unseen futures.

Where and When: A dog never barks about the stranger who didn't stop by yesterday.

Mirrors and Windows: Speech is no mere mirror of reality: it opens the window through which we may escape.

Mimesis (Or Repeat After Me): A toddler points to an object and says, "What is that?" The parent says, "It's a fire hydrant." The child's question used the words "what," "is," and "that" despite the fact that none of these were learned as names for tangible things.[34]

Experiencing Our Interpretations: It makes sense to say that we interpret our experiences, but what we experience is always already an interpretation.[35]

Interpreting Interpretations: Because we interpret messages, we easily forget that all messages already are interpretations.

Ode to Epictetus: There is one and only one freedom: the freedom to interpret.

Freedom Actualized: I cannot make any interpretation that I desire; I can make only those interpretations that I actually make.

Forgotten Beginning: If at birth we spoke rather than bawled, we in all likelihood would talk often about the trauma.[36]

On Sound Living: When asked which sense she would choose if she could have her sight or hearing back, Helen Keller chose hearing. Her reasoning? Sound is inherently vibrant while vision, if utterly silent, often epitomizes a distant and dream-like detachment from the world. The eye, unlike the ear, opens to the the motionless and the dead.[37]

Literacy

Reading Drifts: Several pages into an interesting book, I suddenly realize that I had drifted off from the reading. Now, when that happens why do I always seem to catch myself only *after* slipping off the reading?[38]

Ruminate: To read is to be unable to break down and absorb all we have swallowed. Later, after an event or perhaps talking with a friend, we cough up and give another go at what was previously indigestible.

Inspiration: Much writing writes itself yet provides itself with an alibi. It makes us the laborer, supervisor, and curious onlooker.

How a Writer Becomes a Language: Authors sometimes coin new words or bring new meaning to old ones. Their writings eventually become a language that others can learn to speak. With time and practice, you too could speak Thorstein Veblen, Marshall McLuhan, or perhaps Kenneth Burke.

Who Needs Not Remember?: Too many students have failed to learn that the critical issue is who we become by way of study, not merely what we remember afterward.

The Difference Between Books and Doorstops: At first pass, a book can seem to be little more than a physical object present in a room. From that vantage, it's easy to pretend that books and minds are basically separate. But, the "inside" of a book is more like the drunken stupor that can be found in a bottle of alcohol. As books make their way inside us, we fall under their influence.[39]

Questionable English Majors: I have heard some young would-be writers say, "Ya know, it's funny. I hate to read but I love writing." Have they ever thought who would want to read their stuff? Maybe they're aspiring to be bloggers.

Philosophy

Old Saws with New Teeth: If a tree falls in a forest but nobody is there to hear it, does it make a sound?

--I don't know, did that one?

--The question isn't, "does it make a sound?," but rather, "what sound does it make?"

--If a rainbow is in the sky but nobody is there to see it, is there a rainbow in the sky? [40]

--If tree falls in a forest but no one is there, was there both the forest "and" the tree?

--If a tree falls in a forest, but you don't believe in the natural occurrence of hypotheticals...?

Toe-Holds and Reductions: If we should be reluctant to essentialize, we should be just as reluctant to deny the essential. [41]

Locating the Substance of Adjectives: Philosophers say that adjectives are used to predicate substances. This means that we can specify a quality of something by using an adjective. For example, "That was a hairy bear," or "the cup is heavy." How odd that the supposed quality, a predicate, is a comparison. To what does an adjective refer?

Figures and Backgrounds: For Nietzsche the basic issue is how humans are able to equate the unequal. For Bateson the issue is the human ability to recognize differences. Which comes first, difference or sameness?

Non-Sense is No Constraint: Which option makes less sense: the universe arose out of nothing or it always was? Neither makes much sense and yet this does not preclude either option. Being is not limited by our ability to make sense.

A Pedantic Philosophical Argument: Which is more purple, purplish blue or bluish purple? Imagine two fools debating the question solely upon semantics. *That* answer is obvious: it is the sound of one hand clapping, a full bowl of snow, and three pounds of flax. [42]

Religion

The Bane of Modernity: In the ancient world, many people believed in the gods but not in a personal afterlife. Today, the Western world is populated with countless people who believe in some kind of personal experience post-mortem but do not believe in the divine.

The Twofold Attitude: The proper attitude toward our parents is the same as to the Gods. We should thank them and forgive them in the same gesture.[43]

Look Both Ways: Prayers should be offered as if others could hear and conversations with others should be had as if the Gods were listening.

Grow Up: The resentment toward life that many people feel comes from the fact that they never asked for all of the suffering and injustice in life and then they have to die in the end regardless. Still, what is more wretched than an animal unable to forgive life for its many imperfections?

The Lazy God: Maybe in the proverbial beginning, God was basically lazy and tried to get someone else to carry the burden of dealing with the created cosmos, and so, births and deaths and the whole lot of it are an old trickster's way of having "others" perennially bear the weight of keeping the show on the road.

Life Strategies: Get a group together and ask each person to write in good detail what they would do if they knew for certain that they had only 1 month left to live. Collect the responses. Now, repeat the exercise but this time on the condition that in one month, the world itself would cease to be. Why are the two sets of responses so different?[44]

Popular Christianity

Gratitude Requires Forgiveness: Imagine there is no afterlife, just this world with all of its suffering and injustice. In light of this fact how many people would be able to forgive God?

No Egress: Christian doctrine prohibiting suicide partly makes people resent the fact of living. Isn't that a central part of the trouble with being born? None of us asked for it.

You Must Be Kidding!: So much of Christianity today is pure individualism. It is hard to think of anything more presumptuous and self-aggrandizing than a cemetery plot.

Properties of the Soul: A self is a substance defined by its properties: Animals do not long for the afterlife because they have never known ownership.

Pretending We Haven't Changed: Christmas is the grand capitalist guilt-expiation and ceremony of atonement. After spending the year hoarding and taking for ourselves, we spend a couple of days as primitives lived for centuries: *givers*.[45]

On Becoming a Person: Jesus is the perfect symbol of transcending both body and culture. Erich Kahler tells us that the life journey of the historically existing individual was destined to take on a spiritual significance. "My god, My god, why have you forsaken me?"[46]

Well Then There is No Hope: When asked if he was basically optimistic or pessimistic, devout Catholic Marshall McLuhan responded by saying, "I have never been an optimist or a pessimist. Apocalypse is our only hope."[47]

Death and Dying

Look Them in the Eyes: When you are dead you will never see your friends and family again. Always remember this when you talk with them.[48]

Knowing Someone Personally: We say that things can be understood only by assuming many different perspectives. Remember this when a loved-one dies; be sure to consider the reaction of all the people who never knew the deceased.

Wake Up: Death is not simply a future event that will one day come to pass, as if our only possible relation to it is anticipation. Death is right here right now, life's picture frame. Not knowing that you are going to die would be like being in a dream but remaining unable to realize that you're dreaming. All living things die, but awareness of death is the pre-condition for life's meaningfulness.[49]

Kiarostami's Fruit: Three kinds of people refrain from suicide: those who are too cowardly, those who are too obedient, and those who find the little joys of life to be enough.

Never Enough Time for Some: Some people so misunderstand time that they actually think it would be desirable to live on indefinitely.

Nietzsche on Heavenly Observations: Gods were invented so that human actions and deeds, down to the finest detail, could take on cosmic significance. When divinities are imagined for whom suffering matters, even the lonely whimpers of the deserted and dying take on a spiritual light.

What's on the Menu?: If we must be food for worms, then let us hope to taste best to the bookworms.

The World

How is Distance Possible?: I am not the world, but I am not not it either. I am of it, indigenous to it and my body has always already made room for itself. Even with all of this, the world is at a distance.[50]

Everyone's Face But My Own: We don't see our own heads for a reason; a face is a 'room-making absence.' Without our own headlessness, other people wouldn't have a face.[51]

The Whole of Reality: Want to talk about the real world? It can't just be nature untrammeled by humanity, for the real world already includes humans. If, as Alan Watts suggests, "Just as a tree flowers, so the earth peoples," then we must add: people world.

Truth by Perspective: Perspective is not the obstacle to truth; it constitutes truth as a possibility. Only where there is perspective can truth be found.[52]

Allies at Great Lengths: Distance is the friend of desire.

You Were There!: We think back over our lives and say, "When I chose to do X, I just as well could have chosen to do Y or Z." Could there be a clearer case of pretending that we weren't there? It is only your imagination that makes it possible for you to think you could have not been. Make no mistake, the only world that you could have not been in is the fictional one.[53]

Problems

What a Waste of Understanding: It is best to avoid people who need to understand every one of their problems. As Thayer suggests, it's often easier to solve a problem than it is to figure out what it is.

Worry About it After You've Started: So many people want to fix their lives but don't know where to start, so they don't. [54]

Ideas Don't Pick Potatoes: Intelligence is not how many things you can think about, nor the complexity of the things you can think about. It is a measure of how much good you can do for yourself and others without having to think about it. Some students will write that down so that they can later think about it while others, without a second thought, leave the room as vegetarians.

Bass-ack-Words: When things in life start to slide downward, don't try to understand how this happened. Simply set things straight, now.

Therapeutic Incantations: Magic lore holds that one cannot dispel demons without knowing their proper names. As William Gass suggests, the struggle to articulate our thoughts is the only way of being truly possessed by them. But don't forget Burke's insight that we can dispel most of our demons by comic misnomer.[55]

Our Dreams and Longings: The problem is not that many people want something for nothing. It is that most people, thinking that nothing is something, don't know what is worth wanting.[56]

The Two Kinds of Error: We can say that something is different than something else when in fact it is not. But we also can say that something is no different than something else when in fact it is. How many problems come from ambiguities between these two kinds of error? How many thoughts owe their existence to these?[57]

Being More Than You Achieve: The ancient Stoics openly scorned personal ambition. Today we see how social mobility--its ups and downs--is the greatest source of stress in most people's lives.[58]

A Primer for Stoicism: Not everything that happens is good but it is always good to begin by accepting what already happened.[59]

Decisions

The Wherein of Decisions: Many decisions are made only in reference to our habits. Some people can decide to have a drink while others must decide to not have one.

Recipe for Power: Access only that information that you can and do act upon.[60]

Wandering Around: If you don't know who you are nor what you want to be when you grow up, you are dangerous, both to yourself and to others.

All Implementation: The great enemy of decision-making is the illusion of it.

Contemporary Dostoevsky Agonizer: Unable to talk their parents out of sending them off, some college students have their revenge by dragging their feet, doing just enough to barely graduate, and then, as they move back home, jobless, they can have the last laugh: "I told you 'it' wouldn't work."

Endnotes to Chapter 12

1 In gratitude and recognition, I dedicate this chapter to Lee Thayer: scholar, teacher, and friend. So much of its form and substance is taken from him and inspired by the many things that he said in class and that we have talked about over many years.

2 Cf. Georg Simmel's *The Philosophy of Money*.

3 Cf. Kenneth Burke's "Four Master Tropes" at the end of *A Grammar of Motives*.

4 Cf. Walter Ong on the differences between the senses, also cf. Jonas and Straus.

5 Cf. Erving Goffman's discussion of "Gloss" in *Frame Analysis*.

6 From class notes in Thayer's course *Communication and Human Condition*

7 Cf. Jean-Paul Sartre's *Being and Nothingness*, and my *Selfhood and Authenticity*.

8 Cf. Georg Simmel's *The Philosophy of Money*.

9 Cf. Friedrich Nietzsche's *Beyond Good and Evil*.

10 Cf. Julian Barnes's "Parenthesis" from his *A History of the World in 10$^1/_2$ Chapters*.

11 Cf. Walter Ong's work on Gerard Manley Hopkins; also *The Wisdom of the Sands* by Antoine de Saint-Exupery

12 Cf. Mikhail Bakhtin's *Toward a Philosophy of the Act*, and Michel Foucault later work, "About the Beginning of the Hermeneutics of the Self."

13 Cf. William Gass's *Habitations of the Word*.

14 Cf. Friedrich Nietzsche's *Genealogy of Morals*, also Kenneth Burke's various writings on the "comic corrective."

15 Cf. Martin Heidegger, *The Concept of Time*.

16 Cf. Octavio Paz, *The Bow and Lyre*.

17 Cf. Martin Heidegger's book, *What is Called Thinking?*, also see, Eugen Herrigel's *Zen and the Art of Archery*.

18 Cf. Michael Polanyi's *The Tacit Dimension*, and the phenomenological tradition's distinction between thetic and pre-thetic intentionalities.

19 Cf. Alan Watts's *The Way of Zen*.

20 Cf. Jean-Paul Sartre's *Critique of Dialectical Reason*.

21 Cf. Erving Goffman's "On-Face Work" from his book *Interaction Ritual*.

22 Cf. Lee Thayer's essays, "How Does Information Inform" and "Deconstructing Information," from *Pieces*.

23 Cf. Ludwig Wittgenstein's *Blue and Brown Books*.

24 Cf. William Gass *Habitations of the Word*, and Richard Mitchell's *Less Than Words Can Say*. Both maintain we don't have memories from infancy because we had not yet the language.

25 Cf. Jiddu Krishnamurti in *Freedom From the Known*.

26 Cf. my *Selfhood and Authenticity*.

27 Cf. Alan Watts, particularly his poem "Om: Creative Mediations" from the book titled *OM*.

28 Cf. Hubert Dreyfus, *Being-in-the-world*.

29 Cf. Edward Lorenz's work in *The Essence of Chaos*, and consider the work on linguistic variety by Leonard Bloomfield, in *Language*.

30 From personal conversation with Frank E. X. Dance.

31 Cf. George Steiner, *After Babel*.

32 Cf. John Dewey's *Art as Experience* and Kenneth Burke's *Psychology and Form*.

33 Cf. David Bohm's *On Dialogue*.

34 Cf. Walker Percy's "Delta Factor," in *The Message in the Bottle*.

35 Class notes from Thayer's course Communication The Human Condition.

36 Cf. Otto Rank's *The Trauma of Birth*.

37 Cf. Walter Ong's *The Presence of the Word* and his *Orality and Literacy*.

38 Cf. Jean-Paul Sartre's *Transcendence of the Ego* and Aron Gurwitsch *Studies in Phenomenology and Psychology*.

39 Cf. Richard Rorty's essay in the Umberto Eco collection *Interpretation and Overinterpretation*, & Heidegger's account of "in-being," *The History of the Concept of Time*.

40 Cf. Alan Watts's "The World is Your Body," from *The Book*.

41 Cf. Diana Fuss's *Essentially Speaking*.

42 Cf. Robert Sohl's *Games Zen Masters Play*.

43 Cf. David K. Reynolds *The Handbook for Constructive Living*.

44 Cf. Zygmut Bauman's *Mortality, Immortality and Other Life-Strategies*.

45 Cf. Hugh D. Duncan on Christmas and guilt expiation, *Commmuncation and Social Order*.

46 Cf. Erich Kahler's *Man the Measure*.

47 Cf. Marshall McLuhan's *The Medium and the Light*.

48 Cf. Martha Nussbaum's *The Therapy of Desire*.

49 Cf. Gregory Bateson's, "A Theory of Play and Fantasy," from *Steps to an Ecology of Mind*.

50 Cf. Maurice Merleau-Ponty's *The Visible and Invisible*.

51 Cf. Douglas E. Harding's "On Having No Head," and also Drew Leder's *The Absent Body*.

52 Cf. Mikhail Bakhtin's *Toward a Philosophy of the Act*, and Søren Kierkegaard's *Concluding Unscientific Postscripts to Philosophical Fragments*.

53 Cf. Mikhail Bakhtin's *Toward a Philosophy of the Act*.

54 Class notes from Thayer's course "Language, Thought and Communication."

55 Cf. William Gass's *Habitations of the Word* and Kenneth Burke's *Counter-Statement*.

56 Class notes from Thayer's course "Knowledge and Decision-Systems"

57 Cf. William K. Rawlins's *The Compass of Friendship*.

58 Cf. Seneca's *Epistles*, & *The Enchridion* of Epictetus.

59 Cf. *The Discourse of Epictetus*.

60 Cf. Lee Thayer's *Pieces*.

References

Anton, C. (1998). "About Talk: The Category of Talk-Reflexive Words," *Semiotica*, 121, 193-212.

Anton, C. (1999). "Beyond the Constitutive/Representational Dichotomy: The Phenomenological Notion of Intentionality," *Communication Theory*, 9, 26-57.

Anton, C. (2001). *Selfhood and Authenticity*. Albany, NY: SUNY Press.

Anton, C. (2002). "Discourse as Care: A Phenomenological Consideration of Spatiality and Temporality," *Human Studies*, 25, 185-205.

Anton, C. (2003). "Playing With Bateson: Denotation, Logical Types, and Analog and Digital Communication," *The American Journal of Semiotics*, 19, (1-4), 129-154.

Anton, C. (2005). "Early Western Writing, Sensory Modalities, and Modern Alphabetic Literacy: On the Origins of Representational Theorizing," *Explorations in Media Ecology: The Journal of the Media Ecology Association*, 4, (2), 99-122.

Aristotle. (1958). *On Poetry and Style*, (G. M. A. Grube, Trans.). New York: The Library of Liberal Arts.

Augustine, A. (1951). *The Confessions of Saint Augustine*. (E. B. Pusey, Trans.). New York: Pocket Books.

Bakhtin, M. M. (1993). *Toward a Philosophy of the Act*. (V. Liapuno, Trans.). Austin, TX: University of Texas Press.

Barnes, S. (2001). *Online Connections: Internet interpersonal relationships*. Cresskill NJ: Hampton Press.

Barnes, S. (2003). *Computer-Mediated Communication: Human-to-human communication across the internet*. Boston, MA: Allyn and Bacon

Baron, N. S. (2000). *Alphabet to Email: How written English evolved and where it's heading*. New York: Routledge.

Barzun, J. (1991). *Begin Here: The forgotten conditions of teaching and learning*. Chicago, IL: University of Chicago Press.

Bateson, G. (1955). "A Theory of Play and Fantasy: A Report on the Theoretical Aspects of the Project for Study of the Role of Paradoxes of Abstraction in Communication." *Approaches to the Study of Human Personality*. American Psychiatric Association. Psychiatric Research Reports, no 2. Reprinted in 1972 as "A Theory of Play and Fantasy," In *Steps to an Ecology of Mind*. New York, NY: Ballantine Books.

Bateson, G. (1956). "The Message, 'This is Play'" In *Group Processes*. (Ed., B. Schaffner). New York: Josiah Macy, Jr. Foundation.

Bateson, G. (1966). "Problems in Cetacean and Other Mammalian Communication" in *Whales, Dolphins, and Porpoises*. (Ed. K.S. Norris.) Berkeley, CA: University of California Press. Reprinted in *Steps to an Ecology of Mind* New York: Ballantine Books, 1972.

Bateson, G. (1967). "Cybernetic Explanation," *American Behavioral Scientist*, Vol. 10, No. 8, April. Reprinted in *Steps to an Ecology of Mind*. New York: Ballantine Books, 1972.

Bateson, G. (1968). "Information and Codification: A Philosophical Approach," In Gregory Bateson and Jurgen Ruesch *Communication: The social matrix of psychiatry*. New York, NY: W.W. Norton & Company.

Bateson, G. (1968a). "Information and Codification: A Philosophical Approach," In Gregory Bateson and Jurgen Ruesch Communication: The social matrix of psychiatry. New York: W.W. Norton & Company.

Bateson, G. (1968b). "Redundancy and Coding," in *Animal Comminication: Techniques of Study and Results of Research*. (Ed.). T. A. Sebeok. Bloomington, IN: Indiana University Press. Reprinted in *Steps to an Ecology of Mind* New York: Ballantine Books.

Bateson, G. (1972). "A Theory of Play and Fantasy," In *Steps to an Ecology of Mind*. New York, NY: Ballantine Books. Originally presented in 1955 as "A Theory of Play and Fantasy: A Report on the Theoretical Aspects of the Project for Study of the Role of Paradoxes of Abstraction in Communication." *Approaches to the Study of Human Personality*. American Psychiatric Association. Psychiatric Research Reports, no 2.

Bateson, G. (1972). *Steps to an Ecology of Mind*. New York: Ballantine Books.

Bateson, G. (1977). "Afterword," In *About Bateson*. (Ed.). J. Brockman. New York, NY: E. P. Dutton.

Bateson, G. (1979). *Mind and Nature: A necessary unity*. New York: Bantam Books.

Bateson, G. and Jackson, D. D. (1964). "Some Varieties of Pathogentic Organization," in *Disorders of Communication*. (Eds.). D. M. Rioch and E. A. Weinstein. (Baltimore: Williams and Wilkins Co.) Reprinted (without the discussion) in *Communication Family and Marriage* (Ed.). D. D. Jackson, Palo Alto, CA: Science and Behavior Books, 1968.

Bergson, H. (1991). *Memory and Matter*. New York: Zone Books.

Berman, M. (1989). *Coming to Our Senses: Body and spirit in the hidden history of the west*. New York: Bantam Books.

Berman, M. (2000). *Wandering God: A study in nomadic spirituality*. New York: SUNY press.

Birkerts, S. (1994). *The Gutenberg Elegies: The fate of reading in the electronic age*. New York: Fawcett.

Bolter, J. D. (1991). *Writing Space: The computer, hypertext, and the history of writing*. Hillsdale, NJ: Lawrence Erlbaum Associates, Publishers.

Boorstin, D. J. (1978). *The Image: A guide to pseudo-events in America*. New York: Atheneum.

Burke, K. (1952). *A Grammar of Motives*. New York: Prentice-Hall.

Burke, K. (1954). *Permanence and Change*. Second edition, Bobbs-Merrill Co.

Burke, K. (1957). *The Philosophy of Literary Form*. (2nd Ed.). New York: Vintage Books.

Burke, K. (1961). *The Rhetoric of Religion: Studies in logology*. Berkeley, CA: University of California Press.

Burke, K. (1966). *Language as Symbolic Action: Essays on life, literature and method*. Berkeley, CA: University of California Press.

Burke, K. (1968). *Counter-Statement*. Berkeley, CA: University of California Press.

Burke, K. (1970). *The Rhetoric of Religion Studies in logology*. Berkeley, CA: University of California Press.

Burke, K. (1983). *Towards a Better Life*. Berkeley, CA: University of California Press.

Carey, J. W. (1989). *Communication as Culture: Essays on media and society*. Boston: Unwin Hyman.

Carothers, J. C. (1959). "Culture, Psychiatry, and the Written Word," *Psychiatry*, Nov. 18-20, 22, 26-28, 32-34.

Carpenter, E. (1973). *Oh, What a Blow that Phantom Gave Me!* New York: Holt, Rinehart & Winston.

Carpenter, E. & Heyman, K. (1970). *The Became What They Beheld*. New York: Outerbridge and Dienstfrey.

Cassirer, E. (1944). *An Essay on Man*. New Haven, CN: Yale University Press.

Cioran, E. M. (1975). "Civilized Man, A Portrait," In *Psychological Theory*. (Ed.). R. Boyers. New York, NY: Harper and Row Publishers.

Collingwood, R. G. (1938). *The Principles of Art*. Oxford: Clarendon Press.

Crowley, D. J. & Heyer, P. (2003). *Communication in History: Technology, culture and Society*. (Eds). Boston: Allyn & Bacon.

Czitrom, D. J. (1983). *Media and the American Mind: From Morse to McLuhan*. University of North Carolina Press.

Dance, F. E. X. (1989). "Ong's Voice: 'I,' the Oral Intellect, You, and We," *Text and Performance Quarterly*, 9, 185-198.

Daniels, P. D. (1996). *The World's Writing Systems*. (Ed.). New York: Oxford University Press.

de Grazia, S. (1964). *Of Time, Work, and Leisure*. Garden City, New York: Doubleday.

de Saint-Exupéry, A. (1948). *The Wisdom of the Sands*. (S. Gilbert, Trans.). New York: Harcourt, Brace.

de Saint-Exupéry, A. (1950). *The Wisdom of the Sands*. (S. Gilbert, Trans.). Chicago: University of Chicago Press.

DeFrancis, J. (1989). *Visible Speech: The diverse oneness of writing systems*. Honolulu, HI: University of Hawaii Press.

Dennett, D. C. (1991). *Consciousness Explained*. Boston, MA: Little, Brown and Company.

Denny, J. P. (1991). "Rational Thought in Oral Culture and Literate Decontextualization," *Literacy and Orality*, (Eds.). D. R. Olson and N. Torrance. Cambridge, MA: Cambridge University Press.

Diringer, D. (1953). *The Alphabet: A key to the history of mankind*. 2nd ed. New York: Philosophical Library.

Eco, U. (1995). "A Medieval Library," *Communication in History: Technology, culture, society*, (Eds.). D. Crowley & P. Heyer. New York: Longman Press.

Eisenstein, E. (1979). *The Printing Press as an Agent of Change: Communication and cultural reformations in early modern Europe*. 2 vols. New York: Cambridge University Press.

Ellul, J. (1964). *The Technological Society*. (J. Wilkinson, Trans.). New York: Knopf.

Elson, L. (2010). *Paradox Lost: A cross-contextual definition of levels of abstraction*. Cresskill, NJ: Hampton Press.

Farrell, T. J. (2000). *Walter Ong's Contribution to Cultural Studies: Phenom-*

enology and I-thou communication. Cresskill, NJ: Hampton Press.

Foucault, M. (1977). *Discipline and Punish.* (A. Sheridan, Trans.). New York: Random House.

Fraser, J. T. (1987). *Time: the familiar stranger.* Amherst: University of Massachusetts Press.

Fussell, P. (1983). *Class.* New York: Ballantine Books.

Gabor, D. (1972). *The Mature Society.* New York: Praeger Publishers.

Gadamer, H-G. (1976). *Philosophical Hermeneutics.* Berkeley, CA: University of California Press.

Gass, W. H. (1985). *Habitations of the Word.* New York: Simon and Shuster, 1985.

Gelb, I. J. (1952). *A Study of Writing.* Chicago, IL: University of Chicago Press.

Gencarelli, T. F. (2000). "The intellectual roots of media ecology in the thought and work of Neil Postman," *The New Jersey Journal of Communication.* (8) 1, 91-103.

Gergen, K. J. (1991). *The Saturated Self: Dilemmas of identity in contemporary society.* New York: Basic Books.

Gibran, K. (1923). *The Prophet.* New York: Alfred A. Knopf.

Gleick, J. (1999). *Faster.* New York: NY: Pantheon Books.

Goffman, E. (1967). *Strategic Interaction.* Philadelphia, PA: University of Philadelphia Press.

Goffman, E. (1969). *Strategic Interaction.* Philadelphia, PA: University of Pennsylvania Press.

Goffman, E. (1971). *Relations in Public: Microstudies of the public order.* New York: Basic Books.

Goffman, E. (1974). *Frame Analysis: An essay on the organization of experience.* Boston: Northeastern University Press.

Goodman, N. (1984). *Of Mind and Other Matters.* Cambridge, MA: Harvard University Press.

Goody, J. (1977). *The Domestication of the Savage Mind.* Cambridge, MA: Cambridge University Press.

Goody, J. (1986). *The Logic of Writing and the Organization of Society.* Cambridge, UK: Cambridge University Press.

Goody, J. (1987). *The Interface Between the Written and Oral.* Cambridge, MA: Cambridge University Press.

Greenburg, D. (1966). *How to Make Yourself Miserable.* New York: Random House.

Gronbeck, B. E., Farrell, T. J., & Soukup, P. A. (1991). *Media, Consciousness, and Culture: Explorations of Walter Ong's thought.* (Eds.). Newbury Park: Sage.

Gumpert, G., & Cathcart, R. (1979). *Inter/Media: Interpersonal communication in a media world.* New York: Oxford University Press.

Gusdorf, G. (1965). *Speaking (La Parole),* (P. T. Brockelman, Trans.). Evanston, IL: Northwestern University Press.

Hall, E. T. (1966). *The Hidden Dimension.* Garden City NY: Doubleday.

Hall, E. T. (1976). *Beyond Culture.* New York: Anchor Books.

Hall, E. T. (1983). *The Dance of Life: The other dimensions of time.* New York: Anchor Books.

Hall. E. T. (1959). *The Silent Language*. Garden City NY: Doubleday.

Hassan, R. (2007). "Network Time," In *24/7: time and temporality in the network society*. (Eds.). R. Hassan & R. E. Purser. Stanford, CA: Stanford University Press.

Hassan, R. & Purser, R.E. (2007). *24/7: time and temporality in the network society*. Stanford, CA: Stanford University Press.

Havelock, E. A. (1963). *Preface to Plato*. Cambridge, MA: Harvard University Press.

Havelock, E. A. (1971). *Prologue to Greek Literacy*. Cincinnati, OH: University of Cincinnati Press.

Havelock, E. A. (1986). *The Muse Learns to Write: Reflections on orality and literacy from antiquity to the present*. New Haven, CN: Yale University Press.

Heiddegger, M. (1971). *On the Way to Language*. Harper and Row.

Heidegger, M. (1982). *The Basic Problems of Phenomenology*. (A. Hofstadter, Trans.). Bloomington, IN: Indiana University Press.

Heim, M. (1987). *Electronic Language: A philosophical study of word processing*. New Haven, CN: Yale University Press.

Heim, M. (1993). *The Metaphysics of Virtual Reality*. New York: Oxford University Press.

Heisenberg. W. (1958). *The Physicists Conception of Nature*. (A.J. Pomerans, Trans.). New York: Harcourt, Brace.

Henry, J. (1965). *Pathways to Madness*. New York, NY: Vintage Books.

Heschel, A. (1965). *Who is Man?* Palo Alto, CA: Stanford University Press.

Hofstadter, D. (1985). *Metamagical Themas*, New York: Bantam Books.

Holenstein, E. (1976). *Roman Jakobson's Approach to Language: Phenomenological structuralism*. (C. Schelbert & T. Schelbert, Trans.). Bloomington, IN: Indiana University Press.

Hutchins, R.M. (1968). *The Learning Society*. New York: Mentor Books.

Ihde, D. (1982). "A Phenomenology of Voice," *Consequences of Phenomenology*. Albany, NY: SUNY Press, 1982.

Illich, I. (1991). "A plea for research on lay literacy," *Literacy and Orality*, (Eds.). D. Olson & N. Torrance. Cambridge, Mass: Cambridge University Press.

Innis, H. A. (1951). *The Bias of Communication*. Toronto: University of Toronto Press.

Innis, H. A. (1952). *Changing Concepts of Time*. Toronto: Toronto University Press.

Innis, H. A. (1972). *Empire and Communications*. (Rev. Ed). Toronto: Toronto University Press.

Innis, H. A. (2004). *Changing Concepts of Time*. Lanham, MD: Rowman & Littlefield.

Ivins, W. M. (1953). *Prints and Visual Communication*. Cambridge, MA: MIT Press.

Jahandarie, K. (1999). *Spoken and Written Discourse: A multidisciplinary perspective*. Norwood, NJ: Ablex Press.

James, W. (1890). *Principles of Psychology*, Vol. I. New York: Henry Holt & Co.

James, W. (1958). *Talks to Teachers on Psychology: And to students on some of life's ideals*. New York: W. W. Norton & Company.

James, W. (1963). *Pragmatism and Other Essays*. New York: Washington Square Press.

Johnson, W. (1946). *People in Quandaries: The semantics of personal adjust-ment*. New York: Harper & Brothers.

Johnson, K. G. (2004). *General Semantics: An outline survey*. (3rd Ed.). Insti-tute of General Semantics.

Jonas, H. (1966). "Image-making and the Freedom of Man," in *The Phe-nomenon of Life: Toward a philosophical biology*. Chicago, IL: The University of Chicago Press.

Jonas, H. (1966). *The Phenomenon of Life: Toward a philosophical biology*. Chicago, IL: The University of Chicago Press.

Kierkegaard, S. (1967). *Søren Kierkegaard's Journals and Papers*. Vol. 1, A-E. (H. V. Hong & E. H. Hong, Trans.). Bloomington, IN: Indiana University Press.

Kierkegaard, S. (1992). *Concluding Unscientific Postscript to Philosophical Fragments*. (H. V. Hong and E.H. Hong, Trans.). Princeton, NJ: Princeton Univer-sity Press.

Kolinsky, R., Cary, L., & Morais, J. (1987). "Awareness of Words as Phonologi-cal Entities: The Role of Literacy," *Applied Psycholinguistics*, 8, 223-232.

Korzybski A. (1933). *Science and Sanity: An introduction to non-Aristotelian systems and general semantics*. Lakeville, CONN: The International Non-Aristote-lian Library Publishing Company.

Korzybski, A. (1949). "Fate and Freedom" in *The Language of Wisdom and Folly: Background readings in semantics*. (Ed. I. Lee). New York: Harper and Row Publishers.

Kwant, R. (1965). *Phenomenology of Language*. Pittsburg, PA: Duquesne University Press.

Laertius, D. (1991). *Lives of Eminent Philosophers*. 2 vols. (R. D. Hicks, Trans.). Cambridge, MA: Harvard University Press.

Laing, R. D. (1976). *The Politics of Experience*. New York: Pantheon Books.

Lakoff, G., & Johnson, M. (1980). *Metaphors We Live By*. Chicago, IL: Univer-sity of Chicago Press.

Landow, G. P. (1997). *Hypertext 2.0: The convergence of contemporary criti-cal theory and technology*. Baltimore: Johns Hopkins University Press.

Langer, S. K. (1942). *Philosophy in a New Key: A study in the symbolism of reason, rite and art*. New York: Mentor Books.

Lanigan, R. (1992). *The Human Science of Communicology: A phenomenol-ogy of discourse in Foucault and Merleau-Ponty*. Pittsburgh, PA: Duquesne Uni-versity Press.

Leder, D. (1990). *The Absent Body*. Chicago, IL: The University of Chicago Press.

Lederer, R. (1991). *The Miracle of Language*. New York: Simon & Schuster.

Lee, D. (1959). *Freedom and Culture*. Englewood Cliffs, NJ: Prentice Hall.

Lee, D. (1976). *Valuing the Self: What we can learn from other cultures*. En-glewood Cliffs, NJ: Prentice Hall.

Lee, I. J. (1941). *Language Habits in Human Affairs: An introduction to gen-*

eral semantics. New York: Harper & Brothers.

Levinson, P. (1999). *Digital McLuhan: A guide to the information millennium*. New York: Routledge.

Levinson, P. (2000). "McLuhan and Media Ecology," *Proceedings of the Media Ecology Association*. 1, 17-22.

Levinson, P. (2004). *Cellphone: The story of the world's most mobile medium, and how it has transformed everything*. New York: Palgrave Macmillan.

Lingis, A. (1994). "The Murmur of the World," in *The Community of Those Who Have Nothing in Common*. Bloomington, IN: Indiana University Press.

Lippman, W. (1922). *Public Opinion*. New York: Harcourt, Brace & Co.

Logan, R. K. (1986). *The Alphabet Effect: The impact of the phonetic alphabet on the development of Western civilization*. New York: William Morrow and Company, Inc.

Logan, R. K. (1997). *The Fifth Language: Learning a living in the computer age*. Toronto: Stoddard.

Logan, R. K. (2000). *The Sixth Language: Learning a living in the Internet age*. Toronto: Stoddard.

Logan, R. K. (2011). *Understanding New Media: Extending Marshall McLuhan*. New York, NY: Peter Lang Publishin

Lum, C. M. K. (2005). *Perspectives on Culture, Technology, and Communication: The media ecology tradition*. (Ed.). Cresskill, NJ: Hampton Press.

Malinowski, B. (1932). *The Meaning of Meaning*. Harcourt, Brace & World: New York. Eighth Edition.

Manguel, A. (1996). *A History of Reading*. New York: Penguin Books.

Maslow, A. (1967). "Isomorphic Interrelationship between Knower and Known," in *The Human Dialogue*. (Eds. F. W. Matson & A. Montagu.). New York: The Free Press.

Matson, F. W. & Montagu, A. (1967). *The Human Dialogue*. New York: The Free Press.

McCloud, S. (1993). *Understanding Comics: The invisible art*. New York: Paradox Press.

McCloud, S. (2000). *Reinventing Comics*. New York: Paradox Press.

McLuhan, E. (2005). "Concerning Media Ecology," Address delivered to the Media Ecology Association at the 2005 annual convention.

McLuhan, M. (1963). *The Gutenberg Galaxy: The making of typographic man*. Toronto: University of Toronto.

McLuhan, M. (1964). *Understanding Media: Extensions of man*. Cambridge, MA: The MIT Press.

McLuhan, M. (1969). *Counterblast*. New York: Harcourt, Brace & World, Inc.

McLuhan, M., & Fiore, Q. (1967). *The Medium is the Massage: An inventory of effects*. Corte Madera, CA: Ginko Press.

McLuhan, M., & McLuhan, E. (1988). *Laws of Media: The new science*. Toronto: University of Toronto Press.

McLuhan, M., & McLuhan, E. (2011). *Media and Formal Cause*. Houston, TX: NeoPoiesis Press.

McLuhan, M., & Nevitt, B. (1972). *Take Today: The executive as dropout*. New York: Harcourt Brace Jovanovich.

Mead, G. H. (1934). *Mind, Self, and Society*. Chicago: The University of Chicago Press.

Merleau-Ponty, M. (1962). *Phenomenology of Perception*. (C. Smith, Trans.). New Jersey: The Humanities Press.

Merleau-Ponty, M. (1973). *The Prose of the World*. (J. ONeill, Trans.). Evanston, IL: Northwestern University Press.

Meyrowitz, J. (1985). *No Sense of Place: The impact of electronic media on social behavior*. New York: Oxford University Press.

Moore, T. (1992). *Care of the Soul*. Harper Collins Pub.

Morais, J., Bertelson, P., Cary, L., & Alegria, J. (1986). "Literacy Training and Speech Segmentation," *Cognition, 24*, 45-64.

Moran, J. (1979). "Metacommunication, Logical Types, and Paradox: A critical examination and reformulation." (Unpublished Dissertation, Department of Speech, Temple University).

Mumby, D. (1988). *Communication and Power in Organizations: discourse, ideology and domination*. Norwood, NJ: Ablex publishers.

Mumford, L. (1934). *Technics and Civilization*. New York; Harcourt, Brace.

Mumford, L. (1967). *The Myth of the Machine. Vol.1: Technics and Human Development*. New York: Harcourt Brace and Jovanovich, publishers.

Nietzsche, F. (1964). *The Complete Works of Friedrich Nietzsche: Early Greek Philosophy [VOL II]*. New York: Russell & Russell, Inc.

Nietzsche, F. (1974). *The Gay Science*. (W. Kauffmann, Trans.). Random House.

Nietzsche, F. (1981). *Thus Spake Zarathustra*. Modern Library.

Nietzsche, F. (1982). *Daybreak*, Book IV, Para. 257. Cambridge University Press.

Nietzsche, F. (1995). *Philosophy in the Tragic Age of the Greeks*, Chicago, IL: Henry Regnery Co.

Nystrom, C. (1987). "Literacy as Deviance," *ETC: A Review of General Semantics, 44, (2)*, 111-115.

Olson, D. (1993). "How Writing Represents Speech," *Language and Communication, 13*, 1-17.

Olson, D. (1994). *The World on Paper: The conceptual and cognitive implications of writing and reading*. Great Britain: Oxford University.

Olson, D. (1995). "Writing and The Mind," *Sociocultural Studies of Mind*, (Eds.). J. V. Wertsch, P. Del Rio, A. Alverez. Cambridge, MA: Cambridge University Press.

Olson, D. (1996). "Towards a Psychology of Literacy: On the Relations Between Speech and Writing," *Cognition, 60*, 83-104.

Ong, W. J. (1958). *Ramus, Method and the Decay of Dialogue: From the art of discourse to the art of reason*. Cambridge, MA: Harvard University Press.

Ong, W. J. (1962). *The Barbarian Within*. New York: Macmillan.

Ong, W. J. (1967). *The Presence of the Word: Some prolegomena for cultural and religious history*. Binghamton, NY: Global

Ong, W. J. (1971). *Rhetoric, Romance, and Technology*. Ithaca: Cornell University Press.

Ong, W. J. (1977). *Interfaces of the Word: Studies in the evolution of consciousness and culture.* Ithaca: Cornell University Press.

Ong, W. J. (1982). *Orality and Literacy: The technologizing of the word.* London and New York: Methuen.

Ong, W. J. (1984). "Orality, Literacy, and Medieval Textualization," *New Literary History, 16*, pp. 1-12.

Ortega y Gasset, J. (1958). *Man and Crisis.* New York: W. W. Norton & Co.

Percy, W. (1954). *The Message in the Bottle: How queer man is, how queer language is, and what one has to do with the other.* New York: Farrar, Straus, and Giroux.

Postman, N. (1961). *Television and the Teaching of English.* New York: Appleton-Century-Crofts.

Postman, N. (1976). *Crazy Talk, Stupid Talk.* New York: Delacorte.

Postman, N. (1979). *Teaching as a Conserving Activity.* New York: Delacorte.

Postman, N. (1985). *Amusing Ourselves to Death: Public discourse in the age of show business.* New York: Viking.

Postman, N. (1992). *Technopoly: The surrender of culture to technology.* New York: Alfred A. Knopf.

Postman, N. (1995). *The End of Education: Redefining the value of school.* New York: Alfred A. Knopf.

Postman, N. & Weingartner, C. (1969). *Teaching as a Subversive Activity.* New York Delta.

Postman, N. & Weingartner, C. (1971). *The Soft Revolution: A student handbook for turning schools around.* New York: Delacorte.

Putnam, H. (1990). *Realism with a Human Face.* Cambridge, MA: Harvard University Press.

Rawlins, W. K. (1987). "Gregory Bateson and the Composition of Human Communication," *Research on Language and Social Interaction, 20*, 53-77.

Read, C., Yun-Fei, Z., Hong-Yin, N., Bao-Qing, D. (1986). "The Ability to Manipulate Speech Sounds Depends on Knowing Alphabetic Writing," *Cognition, 24*, 31-44.

Reddy, M. (1979). "The Conduit Metaphor," in *Metaphor and Thought*, (Ed.). A. Ortony. Cambridge: Cambridge University Press.

Reusch, J. (1956). "The Observer and the Observed: Human Communication Theory." In R.R. Grinker. (Ed.). *Toward a Unified Theory of Human Behavior,* New York: Basic Books.

Rheingold, H. (2003). *Smart Mobs: The next social revolution.* Cambridge, MA: Perseus.

Ricoeur, P. (1976). *Interpretation Theory: Discourse and the surplus of meaning.* Forth Worth, TX: The Texas Christian University Press.

Rifkin, J. (1987). *Time Wars.* New York: NY: Henry Holt and Co.

Rosen, S. (1969). *Nihilism: A philosophical essay.* New Haven, CN: Yale University Press.

Royce, J. (1967). "Perception, Conception, and Interpretation," *The Problem of Christianity.* Hamden, Conn,: Archon Books.

Saenger, P. (1991). "The separation of words and the physiology of reading,"

Literacy and Orality, (Eds.). D. Olson & N. Torrance. Cambridge, MA: Cambridge University Press.

Saenger, P. (1997). *Spaces Between Words: The origin of silent reading*. Stanford, CA: Stanford University Press.

Santayana, G. (1956). *Character and Opinion in the United States*. Garden City, NY: Doubleday & Company.

Sartre, J-P. (1956). *Being and Nothingness*. (H. E. Barnes, Trans.). New Jersey: Gramercy Books.

Sartre, J-P. (1991). *The Psychology of Imagination*. New York: Citadel Press.

Scheffler, I. (1967). *Science and Subjectivity*. New York: The Bobbs-Merrill Company.

Schmandt-Besserat, D. (1996). *How Writing Came About*. Austin: University of Texas Press.

Schmandt-Besserat, D. (1992). *Before Writing: From counting to cuneiform*. (2 vols.). Austin: University of Texas Press.

Schrag, C. O. (1992). *The Resources of Rationality,* Bloomington, IN: Indiana University Press.

Schutz, A. (1962). *Collected Papers, Vol. I The problem of social reality*. Martinus Nijhoff publ.

Schwartz, T. (1974). *The Responsive Chord*. Garden City, NY: Anchor Books.

Sefler, G. (1974). *Language and the world: a methodological synthesis of the writings of Martin Heidegger and Ludwig Wittgenstein,* New Jersey: Humanities Press.

Shenk, D. (1991). *The End of Patience: Cautionary notes on the information revolution*. Bloomington, IN: Indiana University Press.

Slouka, M. (1995). *War of the Worlds*. New York, NY: Basic Books.

Sontag, S. (1977). *On Photography*. New York: Farrar, Straus & Giroux.

Steiner, G. (1975). *After Babel*. New York: Oxford University Press.

Sterne, L. (1965). *The Life and Opinions of Tristram Shandy, gentleman*. {Ed. Ian Watt}. Houghton Mifflin Co.

Stewart, J. (1995). *Language as Articulate Contact: Toward a post-semiotic philosophy of communication*. New York: SUNY Press.

Stewart, J. (1996). *Beyond the Symbol Model: Reflections on the representational nature of language*. New York: SUNY Press.

Strate, L. (2005). "A Media Ecology Review," *Communication Research Trends*. Vol. 23, 1-48.

Strate, L. (1996). "Cybertime," In *Communication and Cyberspace*. (Eds.). L. Strate, R. Jackson, & S. Gibson. Cresskill, NJ: Hampton Press. pp. 351-377.

Strate, L. (2004). "Taking Issue," *afterimage: the journal of media arts and cultural criticism*. Vol 35, 55-56.

Strate, L., Jacobson, R. L,. & Gibson, S. B. (Eds.). (2003). *Communication and cyberspace: Social interaction in an electronic environment*. (2nd ed.). Cresskill, NJ: Hampton Press.

Straus, E. (1963). *The Primary World of Senses: A vindication of sensory experience,* trans J. Needleman. New York: Free Press of Glencoe.

Straus, E. (1966). *Phenomenological Psychology: The selected papers of Er-*

win W. Straus. New York: Basic Books.

Thayer, L. (1968). *Communication and Communication Systems*. University Press of America.

Thayer, L. (1987). *On Communication: Essays in understanding*. Norwood, NJ: Ablex.

Thayer, L. (1997). *Pieces: Toward a revisioning of communication/life*. Norwood, NJ: Ablex Publishing.

Tyler, S. A. (1987). *The Unspeakable: Discourse, dialogue and rhetoric in the postmodern world*. Madison, WI: University of Wisconsin Press.

van Manen, M. (1990). *Researching Lived Experience: Human science for an action sensitive pedagogy*. Albany: SUNY Press.

Veblen, T. (1994). *The Theory of the Leisure Class*. Dover publications.

Voegelin, E. (1952). *The New Science of Politics, An Introduction*. Chicago, IL: University of Chicago Press.

von Foerster, H. (1980). "Epistemology of Communication," In *The Myth of Information*. (Ed. K. Woodward). Madison, WI: Coda Press.

Waite, C. K. (2003). *Mediation and the Communication Matrix*. New York, NY: Peter Lang Publishing.

Watts, A. (1951). *The Wisdom of Insecurity*. Vintage Books.

Watts, A. (1957). *The Way of Zen*. New York: Vantage Books.

Watts, A. (1966). *The Book*. New York, NY: Vintage Books.

Watts, A. (1974). *The Essence of Alan Watts*. Millbrae California: Celestial Arts.

Watzlawick, P. (1984). *The Invented Reality*, New York: Norton & Company.

Watzlawick, P., Beavin, J. H., and Jackson, D. D. (1967). *Pragmatics of Human Communication*. New York: W. W. Norton & Company.

Wheelis, A. (1974). *The Moralist*. Baltimore, MD: Penguin.

Whitehead, A. N. (1938). *Modes of Thought*. New York: The Free Press.

Whorf, B. (1940). "Science and Linguistics," *The Technology Review, 42*, 229-231; 247-248.

Wilden, A. (1968). "Lacan and the Discourse of the Other," in *Speech and Language in Psychoanalysis*. Baltimore, MA: The John Hopkins University Press.

Wilden, A. (1972). *System and Structure: Essays in communication and exchange* London: Tavistock Publications.

Wilden, A. (1987). *The Rules Are No Game*. New York: Routledge & Kegan Paul.

Wilden, A. & Wilson, T. (1976). "The Double Bind: Logic, Magic, and Economics" in *Double Bind: The foundation of the communicational approach to the family*. (Eds. C. E. Sluzki & D.C. Ransom). New York: Brace, Jovanovich Publishers.

Wittgenstein, L. (1958). *The Blue Book, the Blue and Brown Books: preliminary studies for the "Philosophical Investigations."* New York, Harper and Row Publishers.

Xenophon. (1997). *Memorabilia, Eoconomicus, Symposium, Apology*. (E.C. Marchant and O.J. Todd, Trans.). Cambridge, MA: Harvard University Press.

About the Author

Corey Anton (PhD., Purdue University) is Professor of Communication Studies at Grand Valley State University and a Fellow of the International Communicology Institute. His publications can be found in journals such as: *Philosophy and Rhetoric, Communication Theory, Semiotica, afterimage, Communication Studies,* and *Human Studies*. He is author of *Selfhood and Authenticity, Sources of Significance: Worldly Rejuvenation and Neo-Stoic Heroism,* and is the editor of *Valuation and Media Ecology: Ethics, Morals, and Laws*. Past Editor of the journal *Explorations in Media Ecology*, and Past-Chair of the Semiotics and Communication Division of the National Communication Association, Anton currently serves on the Board of Trustees for the Institute of General Semantics, and on the editorial boards of both *The Atlantic Journal of Communication* and *Explorations in Media Ecology*.

CPSIA information can be obtained at www.ICGtesting.com
Printed in the USA
LVOW04s1929150115

423024LV00005B/15/P